PN   Berry, Herbert.
2596
.L7   The Boar's Head
B593   Playhouse
1986

$30.00   Cop. 1

PN   Berry, Herbert.
2596
.L7   The Boar's Head
B593   Playhouse
1986

$30.00   Cop. 1

DATE	BORROWER'S NAME	
NOV 1987		

© THE BAKER & TAYLOR CO.

The Boar's Head
Playhouse

The Boar's Head Playhouse

Herbert Berry

Illustrated by C. Walter Hodges

Folger Books
Washington: Folger Shakespeare Library
London and Toronto: Associated University Presses

Associated University Presses
440 Forsgate Drive
Cranbury, NJ 08512

Associated University Presses
25 Sicilian Avenue
London WC1A 2QH, England

Associated University Presses
2133 Royal Windsor Drive
Unit 1
Mississauga, Ontario
Canada L5J 1K5

Library of Congress Cataloging-in-Publication Data

Berry, Herbert.
  The Boar's Head playhouse.

  "Folger books."
  Bibliography: p.
  Includes index.
  1. Boar's Head Playhouse (Whitechapel, London,
England) 2. Theater—England—History. I. Title.
PN2596.L7B593   1986   792'.09421   84-48448
ISBN 0-918016-81-9 (alk. paper)

W.A.

Contents

Preface   7

CHAPTER 1, To 1561   11
CHAPTER 2, 1561–1597   21
CHAPTER 3, 1597–Autumn 1599   29
CHAPTER 4, Autumn 1599–1600   37
CHAPTER 5, 1601   47
CHAPTER 6, 1602   55
CHAPTER 7, 1603   63
CHAPTER 8, 1604–1615   72
CHAPTER 9, 1616–1676   76
CHAPTER 10, 1676–Present   84
CHAPTER 11, The Yard in Which the Playhouse Was Built   94
CHAPTER 12, The Playhouse Proper   106
CHAPTER 13, The Theatrical Enterprise   120

Maps   132
Illustrations   139

APPENDIX 1, The Study of the Boar's Head   156
APPENDIX 2, The Building of the Playhouse, 1598 and 1599   159
APPENDIX 3, Positions of the Galleries, Tiring House, and Stage   163
APPENDIX 4, Arrangements among Owners and Players for
     Managing the Playhouse   171
APPENDIX 5, The Dates of the Building of the Playhouse   175
APPENDIX 6, The Date of Robert Browne's Acquiring Part of the
     Boar's Head   177
APPENDIX 7, The Accuracy of Ogilby and Morgan's Map   179

APPENDIX 8, Deeds   186
APPENDIX 9, Robert Browne   191

Notes   198
A List of Documents, Maps, Books, and Articles   220
Index   231

Preface

I must explain some matters of form:

1. In referring to documents, I have begun with the place where one may find the document, except for those at the Public Record Office, for which I have given only the citation. By "G.L.C.," I have meant the record office and map room of the Greater London Council in Northampton Road, Clerkenwell; by "Middlesex R.O.," the record office of the County of Middlesex formerly in Dartmouth St., now combined with the record office of the Greater London Council in Clerkenwell; by "Guildhall," Guildhall Library at Guildhall; and by "Corporation of London," the record office of the Corporation, also at Guildhall.

2. In my first reference to most books, I have given the full title, place of publication, and date, and thereafter used abbreviations. I have, however, abbreviated all references to such familiar volumes as the calendars of documents at the Public Record Office, those issued by the Historical Manuscripts Commission ("H.M.C."), and the Victoria County Histories ("V.C.H.").

3. In quoting manuscripts, I have tried to follow the original except for "I" and "J," which I have modernized, and abbreviations, which I have expanded in italics.

4. Where I have referred to several documents from the same place and of the same class, I have cited the first fully and given only those parts of the other citations which are different, preceded by a slash. In referring to C.33/103/f.346 and C.33/104/f.359, for example, I have written C.33/103/f.346; /104/f.359.

5. I have modernized dates from 1 January to 24 March.

6. In referring to Henslowe's Diary, I have meant the edition of R. A. Foakes and R. T. Rickert unless I have specified that of W. W. Greg. In referring to C. J. Sisson's Book *The Boar's Head Theatre*, I have given only "Sisson" and the pages; for other works by Professor Sisson, I have given the

title. By "registers" I mean those of St. Mary Matfellon, which are at Clerkenwell (G.L.C., P.93/MRY 1).

I have tried to mention at the appropriate places hereafter those people who have helped me with particular problems. I am much in their debt. I am no less indebted to many other, unnamed people who have helped me less formally. I owe special thanks to Mr. C. W. Hodges, not only for the illustrations but for searching questions and useful ideas. I owe special thanks to the late Miss Mildred Wretts-Smith, who was sometimes my record agent and more often my adviser about abstruse matters of many kinds, especially Elizabethan legal Latin. I also owe special thanks to the Canada Council and the Principal's and publication funds of the University of Saskatchewan for financing much of this work.

Transcriptions of documents at the Public Record Office appear by permission of the Controller of Her Majesty's Stationery Office.

The Boar's Head
Playhouse

CHAPTER 1
To 1561

In 1581 an inn called the Boar's Head stood in what was and is usually called merely Whitechapel, and it had probably been there in the 1530s if not long before. "Whitechapel" refers as well to the parish of St. Mary Matfellon as to its main street, Whitechapel High Street, which are in Ossulston Hundred, County of Middlesex. The inn comprised several buildings and an entrance standing along the northern side of Whitechapel High Street, together with a group of yards and buildings behind. That high street is part of the main road leading eastward from the City of London, leaving the City walls at Aldgate, continuing for three hundred yards or so as Aldgate Street in the City ward of Portsoken, and then at the "bars" (posts once in the street to mark the end of the city jurisdiction) becoming Whitechapel High Street in the County of Middlesex and running toward Essex. At the bars a street led (and leads) north, called Hog Lane for centuries, then Petticoat Lane, and now Middlesex Street. The City boundary ran (and runs) north from the bars along this street, so that the western side of the street is in the City and the eastern was in Middlesex. The Boar's Head buildings standing along Whitechapel High Street began only a few yards from the corner of Hog Lane, and the buildings and yards to which the Boar's Head entrance led occupied, more or less, the ground behind the buildings around that corner. On a bright morning, the Boar's Head literally cast its shadow across the City boundary. This inn was inexpensively adapted to house plays in 1598, and expensively converted into a regular public playhouse a year later. Of all the playhouses built outside the City to escape the day-to-day control of the Lord Mayor and his aldermen, that in the Boar's Head was by far the closest to the City. It was also in several ways the third theatrical enterprise in the brightest day of English theatre.

A gunner, an artilleryman, seems to have owned the Boar's Head from the early 1530s until 1561. He was John Transfeild, as he spelled his name in his will, and it was he who introduced the lady to the Boar's Head who eventually decided that it should become a playhouse. He was a good gunner, it seems, certainly a successful one. He must have been born no later than 1500 or so. He gave "true and faithful service . . . in wars abroad" during the early years of the reign of Henry VIII, and from about 1520 he steadily amassed a great deal of capital.

In 1522, he joined two other Johns, Sandford and Robinson, in a combination of gunnerships at the Tower of London. He and Sandford acquired a gunnership that paid 6d. a day, £4 11s. 3d. paid at Easter and as much at Michaelmas. Sandford and Robinson already shared such a gunnership. Sandford must have been the principal financier in these acquisitions, for he received three-fourths of what they yielded. He collected, that is, one payment a year by himself for each gunnership and shared the second payment with Robinson in the one case and Transfeild in the other. Moreover, the gunnership that Sandford shared with Transfeild was to continue only until Sandford, not Transfeild, died. A year later, in 1523, Transfeild was probably the main financier in the acquisition of another gunnership at the Tower. It yielded the same amount and Robinson was the partner. It was to continue until both men were dead. The patent was not issued until September or November 1525, and payments did not begin until a half-year later still, but the first payment was for five half-years, £22 16s. 3d., all of which Transfeild collected. He then began with Robinson the same method of collecting payments that Sandford had with partners. Between his two arrangements, Transfeild had, in effect, a full gunnership.[1]

At the same time, Transfeild became a substantial resident of the parish of St. Mary Matfellon, and now or soon he had a wife. His acquisitions of gunnerships, a residence in Whitechapel, and a wife could well have had something to do with one another. She could have financed them, for example, or they her. He does not appear among those taxed in Whitechapel for the first subsidy of 1525, nor among those taxed there for earlier subsidies. For the second subsidy of 1525, however, he gave his goods as worth £6.[2] The parish was a populous one. Many men had goods worth more, and many worth less, but most, no doubt, were not worthy to pay toward the subsidy at all. Transfeild was on his way. One of his possessions was a lease on a house in Aldgate Street, just inside the City and a few yards along the street from the Boar's Head. He rented the house to a John Reynolds, clothworker (who may have been a relative), for three nobles (i.e., 20s) a year. In 1529, Transfeild's wife joined Sandford's wife in collecting one of the payments for the gunnership he shared with Sandford. In 1531, Transfeild must have bought out his partner Robinson, for Robinson ceased to collect payments.

If he was not already, he soon became an innholder in Whitechapel as well as a gunner in the Tower. The inn he held was probably the Boar's Head, which was near (and roughly halfway along the most direct route between) the Tower and another haunt of gunners, the Old Artillery Garden. He also made himself known in lofty circles. After collecting one of his payments at Michaelmas 1534, he joined the fifty-odd gunners serving in Ireland under an old gunner, the master of the ordnance who was now lord lieutenant of Ireland, Sir William Skeffington. Transfeild had collected the pay for Skeffington's son, Leonard, a ranking gunner at the Tower, two years before. In November, a man who signed himself H. Halgrave mentioned news that Transfeild had recently brought to Ireland from Whitechapel. Halgrave was writing from Ireland to Thomas Alen, brother of the recently slain Archbishop of Dublin, John Alen. Thomas Alen lived at Rayleigh in Essex, the road to which from London lies past the Boar's Head. "Yt was shewed me here," Halgrave wrote, "by yor olde [h]oste Master transfilde that ye wer sore syke throught the fall of a horse."[3] Evidently Thomas Alen sometimes stayed at Transfeild's inn on trips to London.

In the subsidy of 1535, Transfeild (or rather, probably, his wife) gave himself as worth £20, more than three times what he had given eleven years before. Only five people in the parish confessed to owning more, and only eleven to owning as much.[4] Transfeild remained in Ireland, apparently, until the winter of 1536–37 or the spring following, for his wife and a fellow gunner at the Tower, William Parker, collected his payments until those due at Lady Day 1537, which he collected himself.

Perhaps it was our Transfeild who was needed back in Ireland in 1538. A commission of Thomas Cromwell's to look into the Irish operations (including a John Alen) wrote Cromwell from Dublin urging that "necessaries" for the guns be sent "hither w^t spede by Transfelde who hath good experience boath of this lande and for the conveying of souche things. / We haue no souche choise of men now here as we may spare any to sende thither for souche *purpose*."[5] At about the same time, perhaps while he was again in Ireland, his wife was dealing with his tenant, Reynolds, and, it seems, raising his rent to five nobles. Transfeild was not gone so long, however, that he could not collect his own payments for the gunnerships.

Transfeild was a reliable as well as prosperous parishioner in the summer of 1539. Two years before, an illiterate bricklayer, John Harrydaunce, had preached "out of the Windowe of his owen mansion house in Whytchapell *parysshe* . . . openly the gospell w^{t}out licence or sufficient aucthoritie." Because the echoes of that massive uprising of 1536 called the Pilgrimage of Grace were still very much in the air, the Lord Mayor arrested the man at once, examined him and the parish priest, and notified Cromwell, who promptly had Harrydaunce and examinations sent over to Westminster. Now in July 1539, Harrydaunce preached again. The parish priest (William Longford, a new man who admitted spending most of his time at Oxford) questioned his parishioners about his rival. Transfeild told him darkly "that certen off the citie reparyd to his howsse att that tyme / but for what causse he ys oncerten." His house must have been his inn. The Lord Mayor and some of his aldermen examined Harrydaunce and the parish priest again, as well as one of Harrydaunce's hearers, but this time more than three weeks after the offense. The papers went off to Westminster and the Privy Council again, but there is no evidence that Harrydaunce did too.[6]

In 1540 when he was taxed again, Transfeild gave his goods as worth £30, five times his worth fifteen years before and half again his worth only five years before. Now he was collector of taxes for the whole parish and listed first on the subsidy roll—a detail that may have to do with his living at Boar's Head, near where the parish begins, rather than his being collector.[7] John Sandford died in the winter of 1540–41, so that Transfeild perforce gave up the gunnership he had shared with him, recommending a James Swygar *alias* Reynolds for it, who like Transfeild's tenant, Reynolds, may have been a relative. Transfeild now made some final settlement with his old partner, John Robinson. The two shared one final payment, and Robinson then began a gunnership of his own at 8d. a day, so that for the rest of his life Transfeild had a full gunnership entirely in his own name.[8] At about the same time, Transfeild threatened to evict his tenant, Reynolds, who had recently spent £4 on the place. Reynolds, of course, promptly sued him.[9]

Transfeild's wife may have died about 1540, for she last collected a payment of his in 1537 and did not collect payments when he next left London for a long time. That was in the summer of 1541, when he probably joined the English army on the northern borders and in Scotland. Nobody collected his payment at Michaelmas of that year, and his fellow gunner, William Parker, collected two the following Easter.[10] So prosperous was Transfeild that he contributed most of one of these payments, £4, to the royal loan sought in the spring and summer of 1542. About 104 people in London and Middlesex contributed.[11]

The master of the ordnance, Sir Christopher Morris (who had succeeded Skeffington), collected Transfeild's payment at Michaelmas 1542 and, probably, shipped it north along with the armaments he was also collecting.[12] Transfeild was back in London by the spring of 1543, but he was gone again a year or two later. Possibly he rejoined the army in the North in time for Morris's bombardment of Edinburgh in May 1544 and, gunners eventually needed no longer in the North, joined the army stationed in Boulogne during the spring and summer of 1546. Wherever he went, he left a wife, perhaps his second, to collect his payments in London. He was back in London in the fall of 1546, but his wife had to collect his payment again the following Easter. These years were Transfeild's rosiest period. In each of the six subsidies collected from 1545 to 1549, he gave his goods as worth £40. He was worth almost seven times what he had been twenty years earlier and had again increased his wealth half again in just five years. A second wife, like the first, could have had much to do with his success, but so might his campaigning abroad with the king's guns. Each of this three great jumps in wealth is recorded after a military excursion in another country. He was now, in any event, one of the five or so wealthiest men in his parish.

Almost immediately after, however, Transfeild's luck seems to have deserted him. He soon gave his goods as worth £34 (in a roll dated only "Edw. VI") and £20 in 1551.[13] Nobody collected his payments for his gunnership in the usual way at Michaelmas 1551 or at the Easter following (presumably he was not in London).[14] Then, at Michaelmas 1552, an Edmund Poley collected two payments, those, no doubt, for Easter and Michaelmas 1552 but not that for Michaelmas 1551, which Transfeild must have collected in advance in 1551, a very unusual event requiring the lord treasurer's authority.[15] Edmund Poley then collected all but one of Transfeild's payments until Michaelmas 1556 (eight in all), and Richard Poley collected the three payments from then until Easter 1558. The odd payment was collected by Thomas Skeffington, a gunner at the Tower who received twice Transfeild's pay, possibly Sir William's grandson. Transfeild could have assigned his payments to the Poleys for ready cash.[16] Transfeild's current wife died presently, too, leaving him (like the wife of the 1520s and 1530s) no children whom he would mention in his will. In 1555, finally, John Assheton, owner of the Three Nuns, an inn just along Aldgate Street in the City, bequeathed him "my gowne furred with conye and I clerelie forgive hym the xx[s] that he owethe me."[17]

Most property in Whitechapel, including the Boar's Head, was held by copyhold of the manor of Stepney. That manor had belonged to the bishops of London for centuries. In 1550, Bishop Nicholas Ridley passed it to the crown, and a few weeks later the crown passed it to Thomas Lord Wentworth, whom Henry VIII had ennobled in 1529.[18] The Wentworths had in their entourage the family of Poleys who now appeared in Transfeild's affairs. They were of Badley in Suffolk, and the head of the family was squire there. From 1549 that was John, who before 1548 had married Anne, one of the sixteen children of Lord Wentworth. The Edmund and Richard Poley who collected Transfeild's payments were very likely younger brothers of John, the squire of Badley, hence brothers in law to Lord Wentworth's daughter.[19]

One of Transfeild's responses to these symptoms of ill luck, if that is what they are, was to marry for perhaps the third time. Or maybe his latest marriage was part of the cause. For he was approaching old age, and the lady must have been at least thirty years younger. Transfeild could have had to pay, therefore, a very large jointure, including ownership of the Boar's Head, and those who collected the jointure and held it for the lady could have been the Poleys. The lady, in any event, was Jane Grove of White Walton in Berkshire. She had a sister who married John Squire, an innholder in

High Holborn, and a brother, John, who was an attorney of the Court of Common Pleas. A Thomas Grovys (or Greves) had been one of Transfeild's fellows at the Tower during the 1520s and 1530s.[20] Did the young lady "with a greedy ear / Devour up" an old soldier's discourse of "the battles, sieges, fortunes / That" he had passed? In any event, she set about bearing Transfeild two daughters, Frances, who was a young child in 1561, and Anne, who was born in July 1561.

Another of Transfeild's responses was early in September 1557, if not before, to allow the players to use the Boar's Head as a playhouse. The times, however, were not propitious. In June, the Privy Council had ordered the lord mayor "that Where there were yesterday certaine noughtie plaies plaied in London, as the Lordes [of the Council] were here enformed / he is willed bothe to make s^{r}che for the said plaiers, and having founde them to sende them to the com$m$issioners for religion to be by them furder ordered, and also to take order that no play be made hencefurth wthin the Cittie except the same be firste sene & allowed, & the plaiers aucthorized." A month later, the Privy Council had ordered the justices of the peace in Essex "to suffer no plaiers to play any enterlude wthin that Countye but to se them poonished that shall attempt the same, wherein they were admonished this laste terme in the Starre chamber and therfore it is thought strange that they haue not accordingly accomplisshed the same." At the beginning of August, moreover, the City had issued a proclamation to expel from the City and suburbs "all vagabondes maisterles men and other ydle per$s$ones whatsoeuer havinge no handy crafte or lawfull occupacionne to lyve by." Such language meant (among others) players who were not the retainers of noblemen, as the act for the punishment of vagabonds in 1572 specifies. All freemen of the City and suburbs who owned lodging places were to eject such persons from them.[21]

Although they do not seem to have belonged to a nobleman, Transfeild's players may have been authorized (in view of what happened to them) and so thought themselves secure. Someone, in any event, told the Privy Council at a meeting on 5 September 1557, at St. James's Palace, that players meant to perform a play with a threatening title later that day at the Boar's Head. Alarmed at the government's increasing lack of popularity in this last year of the reign of Mary Tudor, the Council acted at once. It ordered the lord mayor of London "to gyve ordre fourthewth that sum of his Officers do fourth^{wt} repayre to the Bores hed w^{t}out Algate Where the Lords [of the Council] are enformed a Lewde playe called a Sacke full of Newes shalbe plaied this daye / The players whereof he is willed to app^{r}hende and to com$m$itt to salfe warde vntill he shall here further from hense / and to take thiere playe booke from them and to send the same hither." The lord mayor, too, acted at once. He arrested the players that day, sent them to prison, and presumably sent their play book over to Westminster. The next day, having rifled, perhaps, the sack full of news and found it innocuous, the Council wrote the lord mayor again, "willing him to set at libertie the players by him apprehended by ordre fromhence yesterdaie and to giue them and all other plaiers thorough out the Cittie in Commaundement and charge not to playe any plaies but betwene the feast of All S^{ts} [1 November] and Shrofetide [the three days before Lent] and than only suche as are seen and allowed by thordynarye."[22] If the players were handled gently, Transfeild apparently was not molested at all, for the Exchequer continued to pay his money for the gunnership.

Late in 1561, Transfeild was mortally ill. He made his will on 5 November, describing himself as innholder, leaving his affairs to his wife, and leaving £20 to each of his daughters on their marriages. He mentioned his brother-in-law, John Grove (whom he made one of his overseers), and a godson, John Borne, son of another John Borne who may have been the licensed keeper of a tippling house in Whitechapel. He signed his will with his mark—one supposes he was illiterate—and it was witnessed by, among others, Edmund Poley, who had collected so many of the payments for his gunnership.[23] Transfeild died a few days later. He was buried on 11 November at the parish church of Whitechapel, St. Mary Matfellon, where his daughter had been baptized only the summer before, and his widow proved the will and took possession of his goods on the 14th. The Exchequer paid his annuity no more.[24] Exactly two months later, she went to the same church to marry Edmund Poley.[25] It was as Poley's widow in 1594 that she made the lease that ordained the building of a new public playhouse in the Boar's Head.

I have made several leaps in this relation. I have made the gunner and the innholder the same man when nothing necessarily combines the two. The numerous ways in which the two coincide, however, especially the ending of the gunner's annuity after the innholder's death, can leave only a little doubt that the two were the same. I have also made the innholder own the Boar's Head in Whitechapel when he could have owned some other inn there. Again no document necessarily connects the two. My reasons for thinking that his inn must have been the Boar's Head are first, of course, that from at least 1581 the Poleys owned it; next, that after 1535 Transfeild's name appears always near the top or bottom of the lists of residents of Whitechapel in the subsidy rolls—the Boar's Head was at the western extremity of the main road in the parish; and that when the place was leased in 1594 and then sold in 1621, Jane Poley's name was more prominent than those of wives and mothers usually were, as though the place were hers rather than her second husband's. In 1594 her name appeared first, her eldest son's second, yet that son was 24 years old when his father died (in 1587) and nearly 32 when the lease was made. In 1621 the heir repeatedly gave his title as descending from his father and mother, not just from his father. Doubt must remain, but it is very likely that Transfeild passed the Boar's Head to his latest wife either as a jointure or as part of his will.[26]

I have assumed, finally, that the inn called the Boar's Head where the lord mayor suppressed the *Sacke full of Newes* in 1557 was the same as that where Transfeild was evidently master and where a playhouse was built forty-one years later. Yet if the lord mayor suppressed a play there, must not the place have been in his city and not in Middlesex as Transfeild's inn and the later playhouse clearly were? Could the lord mayor, that is, act outside his apparent jurisdiction? If not, there must have been two Boar's Heads at the eastern edge of the City, one just inside the other just outside. The Privy Council probably thought that it was ordering the lord mayor to suppress a play inside the City. For it described the inn as "w^{t}out Algate," and in alluding to the players there it added, "and all other plaiers thorough out the Cittie."

Confronted by this problem, historians of the playhouses have generally taken one of two courses. Thinking, presumably, that there could not have been two inns with the same name a stone's throw from one another, they have (like Sisson, pp. 20–24) simply ignored the problem and declared that the Privy Council's inn and the place of the later playhouse were the same. Or, sometimes after much deliberation, they have concluded that there were two Boar's Heads thereabouts. Chambers even toyed with the idea that the late Elizabethan Boar's Head was not an inn at all, but a proper public playhouse built in Middlesex near the inn in the City and named for it.[27]

One does not have to look very far, however, to find that Tudor lord mayors could indeed act outside the City, especially if the Privy Council directed them to do so or if they thought the Privy Council would support them. The nicety about jurisdiction seems to belong more to Elizabethan times than Marian or earlier ones, but even in Elizabethan times lord mayors acted outside the City. In 1557 neither the Privy Council nor the lord mayor would have cared much whether the Boar's Head of the *Sacke full of Newes* was in the City or not.

The Marian and earlier Privy Councils often used the lord mayor and his brethren in cases of treason and sedition, though committed outside the City by people who lived outside the City. Harrydaunce is a spectacular case. The lord mayor twice arrested a resident of Middlesex for apparent sedition committed in Middlesex, and twice took depositions from him and from his parish priest, whose parish lay wholly in Middlesex. The lord mayor often sat on juries for cases of treason, wherever committed: he actually presided over the trial (held in Guildhall) of the poet the Earl of Surrey in 1547 for an offense committed in Norfolk by a resident of that county. The lord mayor and one of his sheriffs examined a man in May 1556 who had spoken treason near Finsbury Fields in Middlesex.[28] A year later, the Privy Council was evidently so urgently interested in the players who wanted to use the Boar's Head mainly because their play seemed seditious.

The Privy Council could also ask the lord mayor to deal with other matters outside his usual jurisdiction. He probably arrested the Earl of Bath's players in 1546 for playing "lewde playes in the suburbes in London." He certainly released them from the Counter at the Privy Council's order and bound them not to play without the Council's special license. In November 1556, the Privy Council ordered him "to cause secret and diligent s^rche to be made for oone *Christ*ofer Rawson being vehemently suspect of coyneng Who is supposed to be haunting at the Cocke in Shordiche [in Middlesex], and to apprehende him and to comitte him to safe warde, and to s^rche in his lodging for suche coyneng yrons or other matter as he [the lord mayor] supposeth may s^rue to the practiseng of his lewde Doings, and to signify what he shall do herein wth speade." In July 1557, the Privy Council ordered one of the sheriffs of London and the Recorder to question a man about robberies in London "and thereaboutes."[29]

At least one Elizabethan lord mayor acted exactly as his Marian predecessors had done. He investigated a disturbance at the Theatre in Shoreditch in the spring of 1580 so that, as he wrote, he "might have caused such redresse to be had as in dutie and discretion I might." He even sent for the players, because they "make assembles of cittizens and their familes of whome I have charge." Learning, however, that the Privy Council was already looking into the matter, he wrote the Council on 12 April to explain what he had done and to withdraw; and three years later, in a letter of 3 May 1583 to one of the two secretaries of state, Sir Francis Walsingham, the lord mayor described crowds at the Theatre, Curtain (also in Shoreditch), and other places as "being out of our jurisdiction."[30] In March 1602, however, the Privy Council actually addressed to the lord mayor the letter that licensed the Boar's Head, though that playhouse was manifestly outside the City. "We doe pray and require you," the Council wrote him, "that that said howse Namely the Bores head may be assigned vnto them [the Oxford-Worcester company] and that they be verey straightlie Charged to vse and exersise there plaies in noe other but that howse."[31]

Whitechapel, Finsbury Fields, and Shoreditch all bore exactly the same relation to the City. They were "suburbs" as Stow used the word—in Middlesex but adjacent to the City wards. One reason that the lord mayor was able to act in these parts of Middlesex must have been that the City appointed the sheriff of Middlesex. The City had bought that right from the crown early in the twelfth century. In practice, the two sheriffs of London served jointly "for the time being" for 600 years also as sheriff of Middlesex.[32] An impatient Privy Council must have found the lord mayor a handy way to use the police of Middlesex.

There is no reason, then, to suppose that the Boar's Head was in the City in 1557 because the lord mayor arrested persons there at the order of the Privy Council. From the 1530s, probably, if not before, and in one sense or another until 1964, there was but one Boar's Head without Aldagte, and that one was just outside the City bars in Whitechapel.

CHAPTER 2

1561–1597

Like nearly everybody else who invested in theatrical enterprises at the time, Transfeild and his successors at the Boar's Head were energetic, sometimes impatient, bourgeois who had no other visible connection with literature. He was an illiterate gunner, but he became a magnate of Whitechapel, known favorably in the upper reaches of government, connected better than he knew with the family of Lord Wentworth, and married to a woman a great many years younger than he whose brother was a lawyer. Transfeild left his two children £20 each on their marriages. He left his widow an inn, a "greate garden plott," and perhaps another garden plot of some eight acres called Woodlands, near or adjoining the great one, north of the Boar's Head on the east side of Hog Lane.[1] Transfeild's assets were probably less than those of the squire of Badley (Edmund Poley's two sisters had £26 13s 4d. on their marriages), but more than a younger brother like Poley could expect in the squirearchy. Whatever horizons Transfeild contemplated from his inn in Whitechapel, however, they were probably different from those of the Poleys in Whitechapel, who never lost sight of estates in Suffolk.

At least three Poleys went to Whitechapel, Edmund and Richard as we have seen, and one of Anne Wentworth's children, another Edmund. In his prime this Edmund was a lawyer at Gray's Inn, a kind of secretary to the second and third lords Wentworth, and from 1573 steward of the manor. In his old age he returned to Suffolk as squire of Badley, where he died in 1613.[2] The Edmund Poley of the Boar's Head was uncle to this Edmund Poley.

When Edmund Poley of the Boar's Head married Jane Transfeild, he must have been in his thirties.[3] Whitechapel was then changing from a partly rural suburb to a thickly residential, commercial, and manufacturing one. Stow described the process twice in his *Survey* (1603, pp. 128–29, 425–26). The Poleys used this setting to improve the assets Transfeild had left them and to

raise a large family. Their first child, Henry, was baptized at St. Mary Matfellon on 20 December 1562. A daughter, Isabel, may have followed in June
1564. A second son, John, was baptized there on 28 October 1565 (his god-
father was probably the squire of Badley), and a daughter, Elizabeth, on 13
December 1566. They may have had another son, Raphe, and, less likely, yet
another, Edward. Isabel and Raphe died within sixteen days of each other in
September 1577. Transfeild's daughter, Frances, married a man named Wybard and by 1601 had four children (Henry, Fabian, Edmund, Jane). His
daughter, Anne, married Henry Gibbes in August 1586 and had at least one
child by 1601, Mary. Elizabeth Poley married a man named Miller and died
in May 1602.[4]

In the 1560s, as a septuagenarian who had lived near the place for forty-
seven years told the Court of Chancery in 1591, much of Transfeild's great
garden plot was "a ver[i]e marrushe or wett grounde," and the rest "served
(savinge reverence to this ho[norable] Courte) to no better vse then to make a
lay stall for the butchers inhabetinge thereabouts." It had only one building,
an old "Shedd or Hovell." Yet the Poleys leased it in 1572 for £20 a year for
twenty-one years to a gardener, John Myllian, with the provision that if he
did not maintain all buildings, walls, hedges, ditches, and fences then or to
be on the property, the Poleys could forfeit the lease. Myllian began a process of enriching the Poleys there. Presumably he drained the wet parts. He
then planted root crops and built a house for himself at "greate cost." He
sold his lease after five years, and others took up the work. Even though the
lease had only sixteen years to run, presumably shrewd men built six more
dwellings on the plot and divided the rest into at least thirty gardens, all well
fenced, planted, and trimmed, most with a garden house and some with
tenters for use in the cloth trade. Myllian and the rest spent upward of £500.
Before long the lease was sublet for £36 a year, and by the time it was ready
to fall in on Lady Day 1593, it was worth something like £67 a year.

Edmund Poley of the Boar's Head was evidently a reliable and even
charitable businessman. In the late 1570s, his brother-in-law, the lawyer
John Grove, borrowed £20 from a man who worked in the Mint in the
Tower, George Tyson. Grove could not repay the money, so Tyson sued
him, presumably in one of the common-law courts at Westminster. Grove
repaired to the Tower Liberty, if he did not already live there, where the
bailiffs from Westminster could not arrest him. Tyson, therefore, sued him
again in the newly devised Tower Court in about 1578. There the steward of
the court entered the name of Poley's cousin, William Bedingfield, a clerk of
the ordnance in the Tower, as Grove's security, but without Bedingfield's
permission. Tyson got Bedingfield confined to the Tower Liberty, and after
five or six weeks, Grove (now a "sometyme" attorney) got his two brothers-
in-law, the innholders Poley and Squire, to relieve Bedingfield. In effect,
Poley agreed to pay Bedingfield over a period of years, Bedingfield to pay

Tyson over the same period, and Tyson to release Bedingfield at once. By 1582, Bedingfield and his widow had satisfied Tyson, but the widow insisted that Poley had not satisfied her. A lawsuit followed in which Poley produced two witnesses who swore that he had finished paying Bedingfield before Bedingfield had died and well before Bedingfield's widow had finished paying Tyson. Poley had dealt "honestlie" and left "not one pennye . . . vnpayd."[5]

The Boar's Head may have been the primitive group of buildings in the 1560s that the map attributed to Ralph Agas suggests, but Transfeild's wealth and the presence there eventually of Jane Grove and then Edmund Poley would argue otherwise. In any event, the Boar's Head is first connected absolutely, and not merely circumstantially, with Transfeild and his successors in about 1581, when Edmund Poley was clearly the landlord. Alice Saunders testified in 1601 that she had rented a part of the inn "twentie yeares & aboue," paying her rent first to Poley, then to his widow, and then to the people to whom his widow had leased the place. Mrs. Saunders should have known, too, because she and her husband, Roger, knew the Poleys well. He was one of those who witnessed Poley's widow's will, also in 1601.[6]

Edmund Poley died in August 1587, leaving no will. His widow buried him on 11 August at St. Mary Matfellon (she had buried Transfeild there on an 11 November), and she took possession of his goods on the fourteenth (she had taken possession of Transfeild's on the 14 November), but not without trouble, for in December she had to make some representation about them.[7] Poley left two children of Transfeild's and three of his own, all of age and at least one of them, Transfeild's daughter, Anne, married. His eldest son, Henry, was twenty-four years old, and, it seems, at the Boar's Head.[8] His other son, John , was twenty-one, and like Transfeild before him, he was seeking a military career, eventually in the service of the Earl of Essex. Poley left his widow the properties that Transfeild had probably left her: the inn, the great garden plot, and the other garden plot. When the lease on the great garden plot fell so richly in on Lady Day 1593, Jane Poley's properties were worth at least £109 a year to rent out, not counting a residence for herself and Henry at the Boar's Head.[9]

First, however, she set about making those entrepreneurs at the great garden plot get the buildings, fences, and the rest into repair so that she could rent it at full value in 1593. She warned them sternly, threatening to take over the property before the end of the lease, as she could do if the place were not in repair. The lease, however, had been sold and sublet many times, so that the present tenants were a long way from the tenant of 1577, William Meggs, who happened still to be responsible for repairs. They refused to let him disturb them to carry out the work. If Jane Poley should seize the property, perhaps they could sue him more profitably than they could hold their subleases. Meggs, therefore, sued her in July 1590 to get Chancery to force the subtenants to let him carry out the work or to deny her the right to seize the property. The subtenants gave way, and Meggs within a month or two carried out all the repairs Jane Poley had demanded, spending some £13 6s. 8d. Meggs continued his suit against her in the winter of 1591–92, however, probably to get her or Chancery to agree tht he had met her demands.[10] In the spring of 1593, therefore, probably with some self-congratulation, she was able to rent the property for, no doubt, a great deal more money than Transfeild could have thought possible.

She soon decided to deal with the Boar's Head as she had been doing with the great garden plot. Rather than give the inn to her son, Henry, to manage, or manage it herself, she would rent it out with a view to its substantial improvement by her tenants. She negotiated a lease with Oliver Woodliffe that they sealed on 28 November 1594. He would have the inn from Lady Day 1595 (giving her four months to wind up her affairs there) for twenty-one years at £40 a year. She would have rent-free residences there for herself and her son in the upper portions of two buildings on the west side of the yard. Woodliffe wanted to use the Boar's Head for a playhouse, at the very moment when another adventurer, Francis Langley, was organizing a playhouse on the south bank, the Swan. Remembering her success with the great garden plot, she saw to it that the lease contained an apt provision: Woodliffe would spend £100 within seven years on various projects on the west side of the yard or forfeit his lease and pay the Poleys £300 besides. In 1603, after he had done all the work, Woodliffe described these projects as "building of the Larder the Larder parler the well parler the Cole house the oate loaft the Tireing house & stage."[11] Jane Poley must have meant that her heir's old age woud be warmed as hers was, by the falling in of a nicely appreciated lease.

This lease, as Woodliffe must have known, was like that by which his theatrical neighbors in Holywell, the Burbages, held the site of their playhouse, the Theatre. By 1594, that lease and the financial arrangements derived from it had been before the law courts for some twelve years and would remain there for eight more; they had, moreover, provoked violent confrontations so that for a time the players "for sooke the said Theater to his [James Burbage's] great losse."[12] Woodliffe probably thought that he could avoid the snares into which the Burbages had fallen because his lease was simpler, the property conveyed was more profitable as it stood, and the implied theatrical schemes were less pretentious.

Both leases required the tenant to develop the property rather than merely use and maintain it, and, presumably, the rents were fixed accordingly. In order to carry out their theatrical schemes, the Burbages reckoned that they needed thirty-one years and should be allowed to dismantle and take away their playhouse at the end of that time. Woodliffe needed only twenty-one years and meant that his playhouse should consist partly of the buildings of the inn, so that it could not be dismantled and taken away and would be less expensive to build. The Burbages paid only £14 a year in rent plus a fine of £20 at the beginning. Woodliffe paid nearly three times as much, £40 a year, in rent, but he had paid no fine and got a functioning inn in good enough repair and repute that his landlady herself lived there and meant to go on doing so. The Burbages got a group of decrepit buildings in much need of repair and development. They agreed to spend £200 on these buildings in addition to what they would spend putting up their playhouse. Woodliffe agreed to spend only £100 on his buildings, and some of that was for part of the playhouse (the tiring house and stage). In the event, the Burbages and their partner spent nearly £900 on their playhouse and other buildings. It was this vast sum that caused many of their troubles. Woodliffe and his partner might have spent only some £200 had they been content with their playhouse as originally planned. It was after they decided to rebuild it into a much grander affair that they spent a vast sum, and then only about £600 altogether.

Probably because their landlord's title was shaky, the Burbages got a bond of £200 from him to guarantee his performance of the terms of the lease. He did not exact a bond from them to guarantee their performance, but he drew the lease for only twenty-one years and promised to renew it for ten more if they carried out their parts of it. This cumbersome device also caused the Burbages much trouble, and in the end they did not get their renewal. In effect, Woodliffe simply gave the widow Poley a bond of £300 to guarantee his performance. The Poleys' title to the Boar's Head was secure. The widow and her two husbands had held the place probably for more than sixty years, and, besides, one relative of hers was lord and another steward of the manor of which it was a copyhold. When troubles overtook the Boar's Head, they had little to do with either the lease or the property it described.

If Jane Poley hoped that her heir, Henry, would inherit a playhouse in 1615, she was soon disappointed. For he died in March 1596 and was buried at St. Mary Matfellon on the twenty-seventh,[13] well before the playhouse was even begun. The heir to the Boar's Head was now her other son, John, who by 1596 was one of two John Poleys well along in military careers under the earl of Essex. One was his ancient in the effort to relieve Calais in April 1596 and on the expedition to Cadiz in the summer following; the other was a captain on the same expedition. He took both with him to Ireland in 1599, and he knighted both in Dublin in that year.[14]

Jane Poley's son had followed her first husband's trade to a social eminence that none of the squires of Badley had reached. His social rank would be important to the Boar's Head later in its history. The still unmarried Sir John Poley, however, gave his goods in Whitechapel in 1603 or before as worth £20, only half the value of Transfeild's goods in his palmiest days. In 1598 and 1600, his mother gave her goods as worth £6, the figure with which Transfeild had begun in 1525, but she would by that time have given much of her substance to her three daughters as portions and to her sons. She followed both her husbands, her eldest son, and probably several other children into the burial registers of St. Mary Matfellon on 20 June 1601.[15]

Woodliffe was a different matter. He was made free of the Haberdashers' Company in May 1572, but he did not proceed to the livery as the princes of the London companies did. He remained a yeoman of his company, a freeman but not one of the merchants who ruled the company.[16] Like many others, including Francis Langley, he preferred to make his way in the money market, especially by lending money to hard cases at the going rates of 8% or 10% or better and then vigorously achieving repayment. In 1579 he had a fair sum of money to lend to William Huntley of Boxwell in Gloucester, who offered a piece of land in Norfolk and a bond of £100 as security. What followed was something to remember. Huntley could not repay, so Woodliffe seized the land and had Huntley imprisoned for the amount of the bond. He had him released in exchange for guarantees of payment from Huntley's relative, Henry Daunte, a Gloucestershire man, and Thomas Wood, a yeoman of London, but no payment was forthcoming. During the winter of 1581–82, therefore, and the spring following, Woodliffe got a conviction for debt against Huntley in the King's Bench and an "execution" for £100 plus £6 0s. 1d. damages against Daunte.

Woodliffe then set about propelling the law at a speedier pace than it was likely to go on its own. With his execution and a servant, William Chatwell, he set out for Gloucestershire, arriving at Dursley by 24 May 1582. He found that Daunte, some of his family, Barnaby Samborne, and others were feuding violently with Richard Gonne, Sr., and some of his family, originally, perhaps, because Samborne owed Gonne money and would not repay it. The Dauntes were also feuding separately with Giles Sparks. Gonne and his friends were from Dursley, the Dauntes from the countryside round about, and Sparks probably from Uley nearby. A small riot had taken place on 18 March, a much bigger one on 18 April (in which the bailiff and constables of Dursley along with upward of eighty citizens had pursued Daunte and his friends out of the town), and another on 25 April, the Fair Day in Dursley. On this occasion, Gonne said, his wife was constrained to cry, "Mr Samborne ys this the good will you beare to my husband for lending you his money to come to his howse to kill him[?] I praye you . . . paie my husband his money before you kill him." Samborne said some words that Gonne would not repeat, then "toke hir wth his hand by the belly very disorderly to be vsed vnto amans weyf." The lady struck Samborne in the face with her fist.

Giles Sparks's widowed mother, who was nearly eighty, was not so fortunate. A year before, Daunte called her "owlde wyche" and then "rane violently vppon hir," threw her to the ground, pulled her clothes over her head, and whipped her, tearing her skin in a hundred places at least, Sparks said, "from the knee vnto hir middell [,] some of the wounds all moste ane ynche depe."

Woodliffe must have paused to reflect when he heard these things in Dursley. He found, however, that Daunte's enemies had not been idle in the courts. Gonne had been to the Star Chamber and now had a subpoena to serve on Daunte. Sparks had been to the Court of the Council of the Marches and, because Daunte had refused to answer, now had a "placard" against Daunte—a document instructing the sheriff, his deputy, and Sparks, or his friend Walter Mericke (a cobbler in Dursley), to take Daunte and produce him in court. On 24 May, Woodliffe made common cause with these people, offering them £4 or £5 if Daunte were taken. The next day Woodliffe armed himself with "a dag wthout any Case," as he said, and his man with a sword and buckler. The locals were less dramatic. Sparks was unarmed, Gonne had a paddle staff, his man, Richard Smythe, a "baringe" bill, and Mericke a small staff. This company went to Daunte's house on Symondshall Down and camped outside. Daunte said he was impressed. He described the company as consisting of Woodliffe, "A man of smale conscyence & of harde dealinge who . . . Rydethe & goethe about the countrey wth a case of Pystolles" and about thirty others armed with bills, staves, guns, cases of pistols, and the like.

Nothing happened. The day went by, Sparks and Gonne left early, Woodliffe sent his man to see to the horses occasionally and to fetch food and drink from an inn—"two peny loves, Certayne butter & a bottell of Drincke"—on which the men dined under a tree on the down, and in the evening the company went back to Gonne's house in Dursley. They may have reappeared on Symondshall Down on the next day with similar luck. Daunte then decided to try law. He charged all his antagonists in the Star Chamber on 30 June with violence against him and his family and friends, and a few days later he sued Woodliffe in the Court of Requests, vainly trying to stop the case in King's Bench. After another affray near Dursley at midsummer, a commission of the Star Chamber took evidence at Wotton-under-Edge on 24 September, where Woodliffe appeared with the others, probably having returned to Gloucestershire to get something done about his execution against Daunte. For what his dag would not do the King's Bench eventually did, at least partly. The sheriff of Gloucester seized and sold 489 of Daunte's livestock and delivered the proceeds, £60, to Woodliffe. In 1584, Woodliffe was still trying to get the remaining £46 0s. 1d.[17]

Ten years later, Woodliffe embarked on a different route to substance. He married a lady of means, Susan Chaplyn, in January 1594. She was the widow of a citizen of London, John Chaplyn, who had died in July 1592, leaving no will but a considerable estate of which she had promptly got the administration.[18] Chaplyn was of St. Katherine Cree, London, not far from the Boar's Head. Woodliffe's marriage soon led him back to the law courts so that he could collect some debts still owed to his wife's former husband.[19] More importantly here, it also led him to the Boar's Head.

Ten months after marrying Susan Chaplyn, Woodliffe took his lease on the Boar's Head with a view to erecting a theatrical enterprise there. He had the lease drawn up in his wife's name as well as his,[20] no doubt because the enterprise was likely to involve a good deal of her money. He moved his family into the Boar's Head, where they joined Jane Poley and her son, Henry. Inevitably, Woodliffes began to appear in the registers of St. Mary Matfellon. A son, Oliver, was baptized in the parish on 19 April 1595, and one Philip Pound married a Susan Chaplyn there on 8 May 1597 who might well have been a daughter of Woodliffe's wife. If so, Susan Sr. had been married to John Chaplyn more than a summer or two.[21]

Woodliffe delayed building his theatrical enterprise partly, at least, because he lacked ready capital. In 1596, he borrowed £66 13s. 4d. from Bernard Southworth and foolishly got his nearly bankrupt brother, John Woodliffe, to guarantee the loan. John was also a haberdasher, but unlike Oliver he was trying to earn a living by owning a shop. He had apparently already lost, or was about to lose, his lease on a shop in the Royal Exchange (going briefly to jail in the process), and he had borrowed most of his wares from George Gaywood, whom he owned some £67 for them. Oliver repaid much of Southworth's money by the due date, but not all. Southworth took him smartly to court in the fall of 1596, and before Oliver thought proper, the sheriff had seized what remained of John's borrowed wares. Oliver repaid the amount still due Southworth, £14 5s. 8d., and the sheriff was to return John's goods, but by now John was bankrupt and his shop closed, so Gaywood bribed the sheriff's officers to turn the remaining wares over to him, even though the money for all the wares was not due until February 1597. Gaywood sold the wares for £40 12s. 0d., and when the money for them all was due, sued John for the rest, sending him to jail for thirteen weeks. In September, Gaywood let John out of jail in return for an agreement that John would repay the money over eight years at the rate of £3 6s. 8d. per year. In 1599 even that much was not being paid, so Gaywood sued once more and John countersued at equity, hoping to repudiate the agreement of September 1597.[22]

CHAPTER 3

1597–Autumn 1599

Could plays have taken place at the Boar's Head during the forty-one years between the *Sacke full of Newes* in 1557 and the appearance in 1598 of the playhouse that Woodliffe had contracted to build? One is tempted to think so because other inns on the edges of the City housed plays in those years. None of the evidence, however, even hints that plays did take place at the Boar's Head then, and some of it suggests that they did not.

The remark of 1557 is unique. The four inns often mentioned as housing plays from the 1570s until the 1590s did not include the Boar's Head.[1] Of the many things contemporaries said about the playhouse in the Boar's Head, none suggests that it was anything but new in 1598.[2] When the lord mayor and aldermen complained to the Privy Council on 28 July 1597 about "the great inconvenience wch wee fynd to grow by the Comon exercise of Stage Playes," and asked that orders be issued "for the p^{r}sent staie & fynall suppressing of the saide Stage Playes," they specifically mentioned the Theatre and Curtain on the north bank but not the Boar's Head or Whitechapel there. On 12 April 1607, however, when because of the plague the lord mayor asked the Privy Council to restrain "such comon Stage Plaies as are daylie shewed and exercised and doe occasion the great Assembleis of all sortes of people in the suburbes and partes adioyninge to this Cittie," he mentioned Whitechapel first and then Shoreditch (the Curtain) and Clerkenwell (the Red Bull).[3] Players, therefore, probably did not use the Boar's Head in any regular way before 1598, and if they used it occasionally as they wanted to do in 1557, they did so, as far as the evidence goes, silently.

Woodliffe organized a scheme to build his playhouse in the final weeks of 1597. A timid businessman could well have forborne just then, for on the previous 28 July the Privy Council had issued an order strenuously inhibiting playhouses and playing. According to his lease, Woodlifee still had more than four years in which to build his tiring house and stage. Yet there was also just then a conspicuous shortage of places in and around London from which people could watch plays. So Woodliffe decided to take the risks of the time, but very carefully.

Apparently responding to the letter of the lord mayor and aldermen also dated 28 July, the Privy Council had ordered the justices of the peace in Middlesex and Surrey to stop the acting of plays in public places within three miles of the City and to keep it stopped until November. Threatening enough, perhaps, to the man who had contracted to build a playhouse, but the Council had also ordered that the justices "injoyne" the owners of the "common" playhouses on both sides of the Thames to "plucke downe quite" their theatrical premises so that no one could use them for theatrical purposes again.[4] By December, however, not only had playing resumed, but the playhouses still stood and only the Swan had not been relicensed. All, or nearly all, seemed back to normal, and Woodliffe must have decided that it was worth a modest gamble that the Privy Council's bark was much worse than its bite.

Coincidentally, the number of active playhouses had dwindled in recent years. The Burbages had ceased, or were ceasing, to use one of Woodliffe's two neighboring rivals, the Theatre in Holywell, because they could not renew their lease on favorable terms (it had run out in April 1597), and their landlord seemed determined to "Converte the same to some other better vse," like flats or materials with which to repair other buildings. The old playhouse across the river at Newington Butts had closed, perhaps before the Privy Council order. All four inns that had become playhouses of a sort in the 1570s had apparently ceased to be so, the last two of them in 1594 and 1596. The Swan lay wounded on Bankside.[5] Only the Rose on Bankside and the other rival in Woodliffe's neighborhood, the old Curtain, functioned normally. It was the first time in more than twenty years that fewer than three public playhouses had done so, and the first time in ten that fewer than four had done so.

Woodliffe apparently meant his playhouse to be primitive and to cost no great sum. He may have thought that if the authorities left the place alone and it proved profitable he could enlarge it later. As his lease resembles the one that James Burbage had at the Theatre, so the scheme that Woodliffe chose for building and managing the playhouse in the Boar's Head resembles the scheme that Burbage and his partner, John Brayne, followed. Woodliffe's part would be that played by Brayne at the Theatre, and his partner's that played by Burbage. But the two parts would be neatly distinguished, as they were not at the Theatre, and Woodliffe would be infinitely better protected than Brayne was against bad luck and a conniving partner.

Woodliffe would be a silent partner who would provide some of the capital and take a share of the profits. An active partner would provide further capital and see first to the building and then to the management of the play-house. The partner whom Woodliffe chose was Richard Samwell, a yeoman evidently of means. Though they had not yet arrived at a formal contract, they had agreed well enough by Christmas 1597 to begin their contractual obligations to one another then, and Samwell and his family moved into Boar's Head.[6] They arrived at a written agreement on 13 April 1598, when at a little ceremony in the Boar's Head a notary's apprentice read the document aloud and Woodliffe and Samwell sealed it.[7] Then while Samwell contemplated the beginning of construction, Woodliffe went abroad, where he stayed for a year or so. He was, therefore, not only more or less invisible legally as the playhouse took shape and went through its first seasons, but literally out of reach.

The agreement between Woodliffe and Samwell was in the form of a lease that does not survive and evidently did not so much as hint at the theatrical enterprise—another of Woodliffe's attempts, perhaps, to become legally invisible. Yet this lease has caused one to know more about the legal and financial arrangements by which the playhouse in the Boar's Head worked than one knows about such arrangements at any other playhouse of the time. For the theatrical implications of the lease are thoroughly discussed and the lease itself cited and quoted repeatedly in lawsuits that do survive, argued from 1599 to 1603. The legal design was nice. Woodliffe simply leased to Samwell most of the buildings of the Boar's Head, including the upper parlor where Woodliffe lived, for his own rent, £40 a year, and for eighteen years from Christmas 1597 for, that is, all but the last three months of his lease from the Poleys. He kept for himself only the buildings along the western side of the yard on which he had contracted to spend £100. Samwell called them "certeyne Romes." Woodliffe meant to build there, among other things, a residence for himself (rather as the Burbages had done near their playhouse at Holywell), keeping, with Samwell's agreement, the upper parlor until he had done so.[8] The two men left the ownership of the yard vague, Samwell having specifically only "ingresse egresse and regresse" there.

The unstated idea was that this division of the real estate in the Boar's Head implied and made legally defensible the division of responsibility in the playhouse. Woodliffe, that is, would build a stage in the yard and develop his "certeyne Romes" into a tiring house and a gallery for spectators above the stage—the western gallery. Samwell would provide a lower and upper gallery along his building on the eastern side of the yard together with a small gallery along the northern side and another along the southern side, both these small galleries evidently leading from his lower eastern one. Samwell's galleries would have little to do with the yard because they would not be in it but over it, and people would be able to watch plays from under them (the lower eastern, northern, and southern ones, however, would be held up partly by posts resting in the yard). Woodliffe would have legal title to his western gallery and to the tiring house because the one would be attached to and the other part of his "certeyne Romes." He would have legal title to the stage because it stood in the yard. Samwell would have legal title to all four of his galleries because they were attached to or led from buildings to which he had title in his lease. Woodliffe would take half the profits of his gallery, "the gatherors beinge first payed."[9] The players would take the other half and use his stage and tiring house. Presumably, Samwell would make some such arrangement with the players for his galleries. The players would take all the profits of the yard. At first glance, therefore, all Samwell needed in the yard was what his lease gave him, the right to come and go so that he could have access to his buildings and galleries.

Samwell would see to the construction of both his and Woodliffe's parts of the playhouse. Once the place was functioning, he would manage both it and the inn. He would deal with the players and see to it that Woodliffe got the half profits of the western gallery. Samwell would see to repairs and improvements, but he would deduct the costs of those to Woodliffe's structures from Woodliffe's half profits. He would pay many of the incidental costs of keeping the place in business, like salaries of playhouse employees, taxes, and fees for licenses and legal maneuvers. He would not pay, it seems, the costs of such theatrical matters as costumes, scenery, and the like, nor would he pay the tax on new plays.[10]

All was much less tidy at the Theatre in Holywell. Brayne and James Burbage financed the place jointly, and Burbage came to manage it, but they had no written contract between them, much less separate title to different parts of the playhouse and separate income from those parts. Burbage held the lease of the site, and although he evidently promised to include Brayne in it, he did not keep the promise. Even with the best of intentions, it was nearly inevitable that such an arrangement should arrive in the law courts. The arrangement at the Boar's Head would not have got to the courts if Woodliffe and his successor had resisted the temptation to exploit what appeared (but no court ever found) to be a flaw in the lease-cum-contract with Samwell. At the Theatre, the owners began by taking all the profits of the galleries and leaving the players only those of the yard. By 1598, however, it had become customary for players to have a share of the profits of the galleries, as at the Boar's Head, and the people at the Theatre had recently made the chief players part owners, hence sharers in the profits of the galleries.

Woodliffe having left the country, Samwell got on with the building of the playhouse. Woodliffe's western gallery was built along his buildings.[11] It was a very narrow affair. It had a roof and was distinctly for spectators. Samwell built small galleries of his own along the northern and southern sides of the yard, and for an eastern one he used the existing gallery that ran along the upper story of his eastern building to give access to the rooms of that story.

He meant to build another gallery above this eastern one, but probably because such a project would inevitably be expensive, he put it off. He also saw to the building of Woodliffe's stage, which, compared to the other structures of the playhouse was massive. Curiously, it was out in the middle of the yard, like a boxing ring. It may well have lacked a roof.

The work was probably finished, except for the upper eastern gallery, in the summer of 1598. The playhouse was a slight and tentative affair. Samwell laid out only a bit more than £40 for his parts of it. His son remarked that these parts consisted of "certeine galleryes or roomes for people to stand in to see the playes." Samwell spent £12 to £14 of his own on Woodliffe's parts, but how much of Woodliffe's money he spent does not appear. This playhouse opened for business in the summer of 1598, probably, and it remained in business for nearly a year. However primitive they may have been, Samwell's galleries proved, it seems, a thorough financial success, and so, very likely, did Woodliffe's gallery.[12]

When Woodliffe returned to the Boar's Head in the late spring of 1599, he saw a builder and his foreman taking measure for Samwell's upper eastern gallery.[13] Suddenly Woodliffe was ready to spend a great deal more money. Perhaps his foreign ventures had been successful. Surely he was relieved to find that the place had been working profitably for many months without being blasted by lightning from the Privy Council, the lord mayor, or the authorities in Middlesex. Sunny prospects must have opened before him, too, when he found that Samwell had fallen in with an excellently connected player-manager named Robert Browne who was ready to move his company into an elaborated Boar's Head.

It occurred to Woodliffe, therefore, that more capital would bring in more profit, and that now was the time to spend the money, before carpenters went to work on Samwell's upper gallery. He would propose to Samwell that, in effect, they build a proper public playhouse involving a great deal more money than they had originally thought to spend. As he said to the builder, his foreman, and some of his workmen one day in the yard, "I would pull downe this older gallery to the ground, and buylde yt foure foote forwarder toward the stage into yᵉ yarde." He pointed with a lath how far that might be, and added, "yf yt were buylt so farr forwarder then would there be roome for three or foure seats more in a gallery, and for many mo people, and yet neu*er* the lesse roome in the yarde."

Later in this conversation, or in another in the yard soon after, Woodliffe put the matter to Samwell. He proposed that they pull down the three new galleries and one old one and build newer ones farther out into the yard. In addition to pushing up his and Samwell's profits, he was making the place more attractive to the players. Samwell agreed to the proposal, and, for some reason, he forgave the £12 to £14 he had spent on Woodliffe's structures the year before. Samwell and Woodliffe did not bother to reduce the new agreement to writing because, probably, if the lease of 1598 could protect them in the venture of that year, it could protect them in an enlargement of it now.

Rorbert Browne led the Earl of Derby's Men, who had been active in the country and were now moving, or had already moved, to London. Browne had some impressive strengths. He was financed by an apparently cooperative moneylender named Israel Jordan.[14] His sponsor, the earl, seems to have taken drama more seriously than any of the other noble sponsors of theatrical companies and was notably placed to do so. The earl's countess was niece to Cecil, the secretary of state who dominated the affairs of the Privy Council, and the earl was not above using his wife to protect a theatrical company. She wrote her uncle, for example, about Browne and his followers perhaps at about this time:

> Good vncle[,] being importuned by my Lo: to intreat your fauor that his man browne with his companye may not be bared from ther accoustomed plaing in maintenance wher of the[y] haue consumde the better part of ther substance, if so vaine a matter shall not seame troublesum to you I could desier that your furderance might be a meane to vphold them for that my Lo: taking delite in them it will kepe him from moer prodigall courses and make your credit preuaile withe him in a greater matter for my good[.] So commending my best loue to you I take my leaue
>
> Your most louing nece
> E. Derbye

Moreover, unlike other noble sponsors, the Earl of Derby had something directly to do with literature. As George Fenner wrote in a newsletter to a correspondent in Antwerp on 30 June 1599, "Therle of Darby is busyed only in penning comedies for the commonn Players."[15] No wonder that Woodliffe and Samwell were willing to build a much more expensive playhouse.

Once again Samwell set about building a playhouse, but this time with his partner, Woodliffe, at his elbow. Samwell hired the builder who had done some repairs during the first year of the playhouse and had begun the upper eastern gallery. He was John Mago, born between 3 February and 25 July 1548, whose name was evidently pronounced "Maygoe," since it was sometimes spelled so. He was a very experienced member of the London company of carpenters, in which he had done his apprenticeship from March 1569, to November 1575. Unlike his colleague who built the Globe and Fortune, Peter Street, he was literate. He led, it seems, a large squad of workmen.

He and his men took all the new work down and put newer up. They did the job, apparently, in July and possibly part of August, 1599, immediately after the Globe had opened.[16] Samwell timorously had them extend his galleries only about three feeet. Woodliffe's extension, no doubt, went the full four feet. If it had not had one before, his stage now got a roof, and his western gallery a new one. That stage was moved westward about six feet, where it joined whatever Woodliffe built under his gallery, probably an extension of those buildings which served as a tiring house. Stage and tiring house now adjoined, as they did in the other playhouses of the time for which evidence exists.

Mago and his men seem to have rebuilt the southern gallery first and then the northern one, possibly because those were the two under or around which wagons had to go in order to get to the various parts of the inn and, in the case of the southern one, to get to Mago's work in the yard. The men were working on the northern gallery when Woodliffe had them move his stage, partly to facilitate their next project, the eastern galleries. They then took on those eastern galleries, and, finally, turned to Woodliffe's western premises.[17]

When Mago set about moving the stage, he found a great deal of rubbish under it that he had to cast into the yard before he could move the stage. The stuff lay there until the workmen had finished or were finishing the eastern galleries, when Woodliffe hired a twenty-six-year old man, Richard Bagnall, to carry it away. When eventually Bagnall presented himself for payment, Woodliffe and Samwell had their first argument. Woodliffe refused to pay the man because, said Woodliffe, the stuff lay in Samwell's yard. Moreover, by now the rubbish from under the stage must have been joined by a fair amount from the rebuilding of Samwell's four galleries.[18] Samwell, in any event, paid Bagnall.

For Samwell's enterprise, Mago supplied on credit what Samwell's son (who kept the books) described as "the tymber nayles bords tyles lathes & other stuffe," and Mago simply as timber and nails. Mago said he spent on Samwell's enterprise £140 for the one and £20 for the other. Woodliffe and Samwell paid the workmen, Samwell spending, as Mago thought, about £100. With the work of the year before, Samwell said he was out of pocket £300 "and more."[19] With whatever Woodliffe was spending on his side of the yard, therefore, the playhouse in the Boar's Head must have cost more than the Hope, £360, less than the Theatre and Globe, about £700, and something like the Fortune, £520.

These sums were more than Samwell could afford. While the work was going on, Browne lent him £100 "and vpwards," partly, no doubt, toward a favorable contract for the use of the galleries. That left Samwell to find only £160 to keep Mago reimbursed and the men at work on the galleries. But Samwell could not or would not find it, and he decided that the project was financially beyond him. Mago finished the job at least partly unpaid. Heavily obligated to them, Samwell "sett the players" (doubtless Browne and company) "in possession" of his part of the Boar's Head "to play there," perhaps in August.[20] Then in rather mysterious circumstances, he withdrew from ownership altogether, probably in mid-October. He took £260 more from Browne and formally turned the lease over to him. Browne, therefore, came to hold it on the same terms as Samwell had done, except that Samwell, too, seems to have kept a dwelling for himself.[21] He still owed Mago £67 for timber on 2 February 1600, but his year and a half in the playhouse business had gained him some £60 and perhaps a residence.

Probably late in the summer of 1599, then, Browne had the use and to all intents the control of a new public playhouse closer to the City than any of the others. It was the only new public playhouse on the North Bank, indeed, the first one built there in some twenty-two years. It was one of the two new houses that opened that season, the other being its great rival on the South Bank, the Globe. Like the Burbages' men, Browne's could congratulate themselves on controlling their own house though Browne had Samwell somewhere in the middle distance, shared the gallery over the stage with Woodliffe, no doubt owed his moneylender, Jordan, a good deal of money at the inevitable 8% interest or more, and paid Woodliffe £40 a year in rent. As Woodliffe and Samwell had done, Browne probably moved his family into the Boar's Head. He had a young wife, Susan, aged twenty-one or twenty-two, the daughter, perhaps, of an actor in Worcester's company. She would soon bear the first of a succession of children. This ménage joined in the Boar's Head not only the Woodliffes, Jane Poley, and Richard Samwell, but Samwell's son, another Richard, who was also 21 years old and also had a wife and young family.[22]

CHAPTER 4
Autumn 1599–1600

Browne's playhouse was surrounded by a self-contained community, partly an old inn but increasingly a complex of permanent dwellings. The process had been going on at least since 1581, and by 1599 the scene at the Boar's Head must not have been greatly unlike the one that had existed at the Burbages' Theatre from inception to demise. When the Privy Council forbade acting in inns in June 1600, Browne might have wound up his inn trade quite willingly, if he had not already done so, content with a playhouse intimately set into a housing estate, most of which was also his. Certainly the inn had long since died in 1621 in favor of such an estate.

While Browne and his men were settling into their playhouse in the autumn of 1599, Woodliffe was worrying, as Samwell had done, about the amount of money he had in the place. He fell in with Francis Langley, whom he had known for only a few months. Langley was looking for an investment in the playhouse business, though he had already burned his fingers in it. He had built the Swan in the winter of 1594–95, the largest and fairest playhouse in or near London, only to see it ended as a licensed playhouse more or less permanently by the ferocious Privy Council order of 28 July 1597, the order that had probably worried Woodliffe but seriously affected only the Swan and possibly the old playhouse at Newington Butts.

Langley offered £400 for Woodliffe's gallery, tiring house, stage, and other parts of the Boar's Head—a vast and, as it proved, foolish improvement on Samwell's bargain with Browne. Langley was not willing to pay so much only because of the profits that Browne could earn for him in that gallery. For if they came to £2 a week or less, as Browne and Woodliffe hinted in their legal sparring of 1602 and 1603, Langley was offering at best two hundred playing weeks' purchase.[1] That was not a good bargain in a business so risky as that of the playhouses, because a London company would need five to eight years to play so many weeks in London. A more important reason for Langley's extravagant offer was no doubt the way in which their lease provided that Samwell and Browne could use the yard. It gave them only ingress, egress, and regress there (the right, that is, to come and go). Woodliffe, as Browne could argue, had implied that Samwell and his successors should have at least control of the yard, even title to it, when he and Samwell had agreed to be partners in the building of the playhouse. But no document specifically gave Samwell and his successors either.

Browne's customers standing in the yard to watch plays could probably be seen as his agents coming and going, but the posts standing in the yard to hold up his galleries obviously could not. They rested on ground that, according to the lease, belonged to Woodliffe. Hence Woodliffe could argue that those galleries were his because they were on his ground and that Browne should pay him rent for using either them or the yard. In addition to the right to come and go in the yard, as Woodliffe might have pointed out, Samwell should have negotiated into his lease control of the few square feet of the yard that he needed for his posts. Woodliffe and Langley could easily have seen this lapse as worth considerably more than the half profits of the western gallery, and for a time during the winter of 1601–2, Langley could have supposed that his offer was only eighty playing weeks' purchase.

Langley's arrival in the affairs of the Boar's Head would guarantee that the implied spelling out of responsibilities and rewards of 1598 could not keep the peace there. The Boar's Head would proceed as its organizational archetype, the Burbages' Theatre, had done, and for the same reasons—not so much a piece of bad legal writing, or in the Burbages' case, no initial legal writing at all, but not enough capital and owners too eager for quick profits. After twenty-three years of strife with the old way, the Burbages had just devised a new way of capitalizing and managing their playhouse that would last, despite storms, for nearly twice that long. The chief players, not merely their manager, became also the financiers and hence sharers in responsibilities and rewards. The people at the Boar's Head, however, had the lessons of the Burbages to learn over again and, unlike the Burbages, would not survive them.

Langley had already invested in "many" such cloudy titles, or so Samwell soon said. Some seven years before, as another antagonist said, Langley had bought and tried to exploit in the courts a bond that should have been worthless (the debt it recorded had been paid, but late). Now he was considering, or would soon consider, not just the cloudy title in the Boar's Head, but another in Shoreditch, until recently held by the Burbages, on which he would embark in a few months.[2] There he would deal with a title in dispute for some time. At the Boar's Head he would break new ground.

Langley and Woodliffe had first invested in playhouses in the same year, 1594. They were probably about the same age and both were City men.

Langley was free of the drapers after lengthy delays in 1576; Woodliffe was free of the haberdashers in 1572. Both were pursuing not their crafts but transactions in finance (Langley was often called "goldsmith"), and neither was a model of probity. Langley had begun at the top of the City ladder, however, and Woodliffe, evidently, well down on it. Langley's uncle was lord mayor. At the urging of Walsingham and the Privy Council, the City had made him an alnager in 1582. His wife was sister to the clerk of the Privy Council. Moreover, his dealings were much grander and more daring than Woodliffe's were, as his projects at the Swan and Boar's Head show, and his luck or skill was incomparably worse. By 1599, Langley and the other al-nagers had just been tried for corruption, and apparently he and they had been found guilty (though unlike some of the others he had not been fined); his brother-in-law had been discredited, his playhouse was in trouble, he was being harried by Cecil and the Privy Council over his part in the embez-zling of a diamond of great price, and he was wrestling with one judgment after another against him for debt in the courts of common law—three in 1599. He was on his way to a bankruptcy that the playhouses helped to cause. Woodliffe had a competency that his playhouse probably did little to advance.[3]

The way to turn a cloudy title to profit was simply to harass the apparent holder of the title, usually by violence, always in the courts, until he had to buy peace. Massinger has his characters Sir Giles Overreach and Jack Marrall discuss a rural version of the method in *A New Way to Pay Old Debts:*

Ouer.	. . . I'le make my men breake ope his fences;
	Ride o're his standing corne, and in the night
	Set fire on his barnes; or breake his cattells legges.
	These Trespasses draw on Suites, and Suites expences,
	Which I can spare, but will soone begger him. . . .
Mar.	The best I euer heard; I could adore you.
Ouer.	Then with the fauour of my man of *Law,*
	I will pretend some title: Want will force him
	To put it to Arbitrement: then if he sell
	For halfe the value, he shall haue ready money,
	And I possesse his land.

(1633, sigs. D^v–D2)

The man with a cloudy title to exploit in the high street would begin by seizing the property for a time, with the help of a few goons, or otherwise interrupting the business there. The apparent title holder then either negoti-ated with his antagonist or sued him at common law for trespass. If the latter, the antagonist stayed the suit by countersuing in one or several equity courts, where he made as much smoke as he could with whatever claim he had to the property. Litigation and its expenses and frustrations multiplied, time passed, and business suffered. Eventually, the apparent title holder would take his case to the Star Chamber, which specialized in cases involving violence. There he would argue that his antagonist had committed serious crimes and misdemeanors in resorting to violence and trespass and in acquiring and maintaining a cloudy title in the first place. The antagonist would reply, among other things, that it was no crime to seize his own property. Star Chamber might decree nothing, but it could drive the two men to some settlement because it dealt more freely than other courts in the difficult legal ground between common law and equity. It could punish the antagonist with a large fine or even imprisonment, and it could, in effect, take the title away from the apparent holder. The Star Chamber depended upon such cases for a large share of its business.

Woodliffe had to decide whether he could gain more from exploiting himself the lapse in his agreement with Samwell or from letting Langley do it. He decided to let Langley do it. Perhaps he felt that Langley could do it better, being an expert in the work, or that someone not involved in the original partnership could make the legal case with a straighter face. No doubt his instinct for being invisible in theatrical affairs had something to do with his decision. In any event, he accepted Langley's offer and gave him a lease dated 7 November 1599. He took £100 in cash and the rest in three bonds of £100 each, all dated 12 November, from a nephew of Langley's, Richard Langley, like Woodliffe a haberdasher. The bonds were due "at severall dayes specyfyed in the Condicions of the same bondes," the first a year hence, and were worth (as such bonds usually were) double if forfeit. For his security, Richard got the lease until Francis should pay off the bonds. Woodliffe and Francis drew the lease carefully so as to spell out the weakness of Samwell's and Browne's claim to the yard, "to avoide all Ambyguyties and doubts," as Woodliffe and Langley put it. Woodliffe evidently undertook to help in the inevitable lawsuits, and that was probably the meaning of a bond Langley extracted from him of a thousand marks "for his securitye of the same lease."[4]

Samwell and Browne, meanwhile, were keeping the ownership of their lease a mystery. Woodliffe and Langley did not know who held the lease. Samwell, Browne, and those who eventually testified for them were at best vague about when the lease changed hands, even nearly four years later. But in testifying about something else in June 1601, the younger Richard Samwell clearly implied that his father had held the lease "by the space of a yeere & a half or thereab[outs]," until, that is, about mid-October 1599, and young Samwell should have known, for as he said, he was present both when his father sealed the lease with Woodliffe and when he passed it to Browne.[5]

Samwell and Browne may have been saying little about the ownership of the lease partly to make harassment in the courts more difficult. Certainly

they would soon charge Woodliffe and Langley with champerty and mainte-
nance, the offense of buying and selling a property of which someone else
had had possession for more than a year. If Samwell did not still control this
lease, therefore, he and Browne soon wanted to be able to say that he did.
They could have destroyed one document conveying the lease and drawn up
another with a later date. With or without such a stratagem, the lease itself
might have been in the hands of neither Samwell nor Browne. Samwell could
have given it to Browne during the summer, not as a way of conveying the
property to him, but as security for the money he was borrowing from him
for the rebuilding of the playhouse. Once it had been passed permanently to
Browne, it could have found its way to Israel Jordan as security for the
money Browne may have been getting from him, the man "by whome,"
according to Woodliffe in May 1603, "the said Broune is directed & advysed
in all his indirect dealeings & vnlawefull Courses."[6]

Woodliffe and Langley could only assume in the autumn of 1599 that Samwell had the lease, and Samwell was willing to say that effectually he did.
The brunt of Langley's operations, therefore, fell on Samwell. Besides,
Langley could not trouble Browne with impunity. Thanks to his noble
sponsor, Browne must have amounted to the license by which the Boar's
Head stayed in business, and for every performance he could not or would
not give there, Langley would not get a sum of money for the half profits of
the western gallery. Browne, in any case, may have been in the country with
his company during at least part of the autumn, for they played at Wollaton
and Leicester on 7 and 16 October.[7]

It was Woodliffe who first brandished a sword in the war for the Boar's
Head. He demanded rent from Samwell for the yard in addition to the
money that the two had agreed Samwell should pay: the half profits of the
western gallery and the annual rent of £40. That must have been before 7
November, when Woodliffe sealed his new lease with Langley.[8] After that
sealing, Langley no doubt lost little time making the same demand of Samwell. Langley would accept either a regular payment for the yard or a share
of the profits of Samwell's galleries whose posts rested in the yard. If he did
not want to pay regularly for a property he did not (or would soon not)
own, Samwell had the choice of fighting Langley or Browne. He could re-
fuse to pay, and so fight Langley. Or he could pay Langley and sue Browne
for the money, arguing Langley's case and implicitly, at least, admitting his
own carelessness in dealings with Woodliffe and Browne. Needless to say, he
refused to pay Langley and braced himself to defend theatrical properties
apparently no longer his.

Langley soon sued Samwell in a court admirably suited to the purpose,
the Marshalsea Court. It was a minor court looking for business. It had no
clear jurisdiction but did have tipstaffs eager for the fees men had to pay
when arrested, in this case, 9s. 8d.[9] Samwell evidenty refused to attend the

court, for on 13 December (shades of Woodliffe in Gloucestershire) Langley arrived at the Boar's Head with two bailiffs of the court, Alexander Foxley and John Johnson;[10] two servants of theirs, Peter Boulton and Anthony Strayles; Langley's carpenter, Owen Roberts, who was handy for breaking down doors; and Woodliffe's wife, Susan, an enthusiastic amateur it seems. They probably meant to serve a summons on Samwell. According to him, they entered the inn "most forcybly wth Bills staves swordes and daggers," but soon left, having probably served their papers.[11]

Samwell rushed to the law for weapons of his own. He sued Langley in King's Bench for trespass and Woodliffe in Chancery for title to the yard. Langley persisted. On 15 December he leased part of the yard to a Thomas Wolleston, who on the same day leased part of that part to a Richard Bishop, who Samwell said was eight years old and Langley said was twenty or more, both, in any event, creatures of Langley who disappeared noiselessly when his need for them was over. This strategy multiplied Langley's opportunities for lawsuits several times and at the same time deflected Samwell's blows.

On the next day, the sixteenth, Langley and his team, minus Susan Woodliffe, arrived once more at the Boar's Head at seven o'clock of a dark night. They meant this time to arrest Samwell. Then and there, as Samwell protested, "wth theyre Weapons drawen" they "did assaulte" Samwell and his son and "verry sore beate and hurte" them "in theyre Armes and legges and diuerse partes of theyre bodyes . . . intendinge to murder and kyll" them. The invaders "did in the darke throwe diuerse daggers and other Wepons at" the Samwells, "wch weapons hardly myssinge . . . did stycke in the wales of the said house." The Samwells "hardly escaped theyre lyves by shiftinge and flyinge away." By flying away, Samwell meant that the Marshalsea men eventually arrested him, and as he was going with them, young Richard and some servants mounted a rescue in which they "did shrowdly beate the sayd marshalls men." It must have been as good a show as Browne's men could do on Langley's stage.

Langley hastened to bind young Samwell to the peace in the King's Bench. That was a device by which Langley convinced the court that he went in fear of injury and death at young Samwell's hands, and the court demanded a bond from young Samwell that would be forfeit if he offered Langley further violence. The move could also have blunted somewhat Samwell's suit in King's Bench for trespass. No sooner did the Samwells put up the bond in King's Bench than Langley bound old Samwell to the peace in Chancery "for verry vexacion," as Samwell said, and perhaps as a way of slowing down Samwell's other suit in that court.

Browne's men were back in the Boar's Head for the Christmas season, so Langley turned to the takings of Samwell's former galleries. He and his team, including Susan Woodliffe, appeared yet again at the Boar's Head on 24 December before a play was to go on. They had a writ for the arrest of young

Samwell because of the rescue, a writ that they said was the work of the Privy Council and old Samwell said was forged. Young Richard, in any event, was not at the inn. His father managed to get the door locked leading to his former galleries, that door being, it seems, where the gatherer usually stood, "at the stayres foot leading vp to the sayd Galleryes." Owen Roberts proceeded to his speciality. He and Langley "did set they[r] hands to the sayd dore and did thrust it open." Strayles then took money "of such as Came then hither to here the playe." Samwell said they got £4; warily, Langley said only "that they did gather soe much mony as their part Came to[,] v[s] or therabouts." Samwell's figure is probably exaggerated and Langley's mini-mized. The two, however, suggest the arrangement between owner and players about the takings in Samwell's former galleries, and they might not be wildly discrepant. Samwell meant his figure as a gross one and Langley his as a net one. Langley was demonstrating that the galleries belonged to him because their posts rested in his yard. Hence, whatever Strayles col-lected that was not the share of the owner of the galleries Langley may well have given the players, and Langley would certainly have subtracted his con-siderable expenses somewhere in the accounting.

In any event, when Langley and his people left they took with them young Samwell's wife, Winifred, in lieu of him, she having, as old Samwell said, "a yonge enfante then of the age of three weekes . . . suckinge at her Breste." The child was Rebecca, who was actually about six weeks old, hav-ing been baptized on 11 November.[12] The Marshalsea men locked Winifred and her child in Foxley's house in Southwark until the elder Samwell could find bail.

The team, with Susan Woodliffe again, went to another play at the Boar's Head two days later, on 26 December.[13] This time Langley was demonstrat-ing in another way that Samwell's former galleries were his. He had Roberts cut down part of a wall so as to make a doorway leading from Langley's "house into the said gallerye," from, that is, Woodliffe's former premises on the western side of the yard into Samwell's northern or southern gallery. As Roberts was doing the work, young Samwell tried unsuccessfully to stop him, and, according to old Samwell, Roberts cried "who dare denye the same." Langley and his people offered to take money again, but young Sam-well somehow got rid of them before they could. Within a day or two, however, they had arrested him twice.

Browne and his company apparently went on playing at the Boar's Head all winter, unmolested by the troubles there. They played at court on 5 Feb-ruary 1600, thanks, no doubt, to their patron and his wife's connections.[14] Samwell, however, spent the winter in the midst of Langley's battle plan. Langley launched lawsuit after lawsuit in the Marshalsea Court against the Samwells in the names of Woodliffe, Bishop, Wolleston, and maybe John Johnson. Presently, as Langley admitted, he and his creatures had no fewer than six lawsuits going against the Samwells there plus another in Bishop's name against Samwell in King's Bench for trespass. Langley saw to it that none of these lawsuits reached open court before a judge or jury. Yet he procured writ after writ to arrest Samwell, his son, and a servant of theirs, Edward Willys, mostly for trespass in the yard. The Samwells for a time feared to set foot out of doors. One of the tipstaffs said in April 1600 that "he hath often arrested" Samwell "at Many Mens suytes by Wrytts out of the Courte of the Marshalsye." Willys did a long spell in the Marshalsea Prison. By Samwell's count, he and his household were arrested seven times in less than five months by writs out of the Marshalsea Court and at least once, possibly more often, by writs out of the King's Bench. He reckoned he had paid £40 in fees and other legal charges, "nor any suyte prosecuted," as he bitterly complained, "nor any Costes vppon the nonsuyte of any accion cold be recoueryd."

Samwell pressed on with his lawsuit against Woodliffe in Chancery, trying to prove that his lease with Woodliffe had effactually given him title to the yard, and that Woodliffe himself until recently had thought so. He got Mago, Mago's foreman, Walter Rodes (who had served his apprenticeship with Mago from 1582 to 1591), and his own servant, Willys, to testify for him on 2 February 1600.[15] They swore that not only had Samwell spent a lot of money in the yard, but Woodliffe had collaborated in the venture and, more to the point, that Woodliffe had several times said things implying that he assumed Samwell had title to the yard—his remrks about the removal of the trash under the stage, for example. Indeed, Samwell actually asserted that the lease meant that it was he who had title there and Woodliffe who had merely ingress, egress, and regress so that Woodliffe could have access to the parts of the inn that he had kept for himself. The going with this argument, however, must have been difficult, for if Samwell did not eventually give it up, his successor in the lawsuit did.

The going in Samwell's case in King's Bench must have been equally difficult, for Langley's arrests continued. Young Samwell was arrested again on 4 April on another writ that Samwell thought forged. When Winifred and another of Samwell's servants, Rowland Rosse, demanded to see it, Langley's team refused to show it and "wth theyre wepons and fystes did then and there sore beate wounde and evyll entreate the said Rowland Rosse" and even Winifred. That was enough for Samwell. His son still in the Marshalsea Prison, he finally filed suit in the Star Chamber on 11 April against all his principal antagonists—Langley and his carpenter, Roberts; Woodliffe and his wife; and the two tipstaffs of the Marshalsea Court, Foxley and Johnson. Samwell insisted that his lease gave him title to the yard, or if not, that his possession of it since 1598 did, and he charged his opponents with illegal and unconscionable harassment. These people replied between 17 April and 10 May, and the court examined Langley and Roberts on 30 April and 1 May.

But all the replies and examinations came to the same thing. Langley insisted that he had title to the yard because his lease said so. As for harassing Samwell by a multiplicity of lawsuits, Langley patiently explained (and so did Woodliffe) that that was "not in his Judgment any offence for that multiplicytie of wrongs cannot otherwise be (to his vnderstandinge) righted." So Samwell's "Bill is Without all Cause exhibited against" Langley and his associates. Samwell did have one satisfaction, however. He managed to have a bailiff of Middlesex arrest Woodliffe for the case in King's Bench as Woodliffe was going to his lawyer to answer the Star Chamber lawsuit—"to his greate charge," as Woodliffe complained, "discreditt vexac*i*on and hinderaunce." The Star Chamber proceeded, as usual, to no formal judgment,[16] but evidently it began the process of driving Samwell and Langley to an agreement.

Deprived of Samwell as an opponent, Langley now boldly opened a new legal front against a new opponent, Browne. On 20 May, Browne and Samwell's builder, Mago, were possibly altering the posts that held up one of the galleries and so affecting the seats in the gallery. Bishop was there to charge them with trespass—breaking and entering his premises, throwing down posts and fixed seats, and making mayhem in the place to the value of £5, then carrying away the posts and seats and doing other enormities against the Queen's peace to Bishop's further damage of £15.[17] Bishop set about making these claims into another lawsuit for the King's Bench, but Browne continued in possession and presumably continued playing. When the residents of Whitechapel were taxed during the summer, Browne was there and in possession, for he gave his goods as worth £4, a sum many residents gave. Jane Poley gave her goods as worth £6.[18]

Langley proceeded against Browne without arrests or armed intrusions and without the urgency of the previous December. Late in the summer, probably, Bishop filed his lawsuit, and Browne and Mago had to bond themselves to appear when the court might require. Langley now settled down to his new opponent, Browne, as though certain that the laws and judges of the realm would sustain him in open court. Browne and Mago were nothing loath. They pleaded not guilty the first day of the new term, on 9 October. Bishop put in the requisite bond on 22 October, and trial was set for a month later.

Samwell, too, was busy in the courts in October. Star Chamber probably drove him and Langley to an agreement that cost Samwell something. For Langley troubled Samwell no more, and late in the month Samwell sued Browne and his moneylender, Jordan, in Chancery, probably to get out of them whatever Langley had got out of him. Meanwhile, on 22 October, Samwell kept his lawsuit against Woodliffe going in Chancery, but he did not urge his original argument (that his lease with Woodliffe gave him title to the yard). He had a deposition taken from the apprentice notary, Nicholas Moxlay (who had attended the sealing of the Woodliffe-Samwell lease), in which

Moxlay swore that Samwell had been more generous to Woodliffe than necessary.[19] It was as though some settlement were possible in Chancery, too, and Samwell wanted to establish that Woodliffe owed him something. Chancery, however, did not decide who had title to the yard of the Boar's Head, and although that crucial question would remain at issue, an even more important event in the history of the Boar's Head soon took place.

Langley did not pay Woodliffe the £100 that would redeem the first of the three bonds with which he had mostly bought his interest in the place. From 12 November 1600, that bond was forfeit and worth £200 to Woodliffe. There was now more at stake between Langley and Woodliffe than between Langley and the others. Fittingly, two days later, on 14 November, Samwell disappeared altogether from the arguments about the Boar's Head when he paid a mark in costs in Chancery to let his lawsuit against Browne and Jordan drop.[20] He died during the winter or spring following.[21]

On 21 November, Bishop's lawsuit against Browne and Mago arrived for trial in open court before Sir John Popham, chief justice of the King's Bench, but Bishop did not. Langley's confidence had vanished. So Popham ordered Browne and Mago released from their bonds and Bishop charged with making a false claim.

CHAPTER 5

1601

As the year 1601 began, the Samwells were no longer concerned with the Boar's Head save as knowing bystanders and probably residents. Langley could think about harassing Browne again, but his recent defeat must have been cautionary, and he had much more urgently to think about defending himself from Woodliffe, whom he owed a great deal of money. Woodliffe was not a man to humor such lapses, and Langley's deteriorating affairs outside the Boar's Head prevented him from settling with Woodliffe in the ordinary way, by paying him. During that winter it must have occurred to Langley that the Boar's Head might not be worth the trouble it had already been and was sure to go on being. Browne, however, was securely and even grandly at the Boar's Head with his company. They played at court with the other great companies in the festivities on New Year's Day. They played there again in those on Twelfth Night when they shared the bill with the Burbages' company on their first night of *Twelfth Night*.[1] Despite people like Woodliffe and Langley, the Boar's Head had joined some of the finest company that drama in English has kept.

Such triumphs of the spirit, however, would not slow the march of business. A week or two later, Woodliffe sued Richard Langley in Common Pleas for £200 plus £40 in costs and damages.[2] Richard Langley, as we have seen, had given Woodliffe three bonds of £100 each toward Francis Langley's buying Woodliffe's part of the Boar's Head. The first bond due was now forfeit and so worth £200. As the custom was, Richard Langley pleaded not guilty and said that he had paid the £100. Trial was set for the end of April. Business proceeded, too, in matters of the spirit, though slowly. Browne and his men were paid the usual £10 at the end of March for each of their performances at court.

A great cultivation of lawsuits took place in the Boar's Head during the last days of April 1601. The Langleys planted two, Browne planted one, and Woodliffe watered his Common Pleas lawsuit, now a term old. Two were to withstand the vicissitudes of ensuing seasons, and their growth was to constitute much of the history of the Boar's Head during the next two years.

Francis Langley had decided to get out of the Boar's Head if he could do so without losing much money. He and his brother, Richard, therefore, sued Woodliffe in Chancery at the end of April, trying to get that Court to approve some formula for their extrication from the Boar's Head and at the same time to stop Woodliffe's operations in Common Pleas. So they sent no one to represent them when Woodliffe's lawsuit came to a hearing in Common Pleas at about the same time, and they took some grim satisfaction, perhaps, when they learned that even without opposition Woodliffe got judgment for only £100 plus only £7 in costs and damages, the court ignoring the penalty of £100 that forfeiture was supposed to add to the value of their bond and £33 of the costs and damages that Woodliffe claimed. Possibly as a way of dealing with Woodliffe from a position of some strength, the Langleys also sent their creature, Richard Bishop, back to King's Bench toward the end of April to file a new lawsuit against Browne. It was the old one there with some changes. Bishop now ignored the builder, Mago, and claimed, curiously, that he held his lease on the yard not only from Thomas Wolleston but from Browne. He also claimed as he had not done before that Browne had expelled him from ownership as well as damaged and carried off property.[3]

Browne resolved to confront Bishop in open hearing as he had tried to do six months before. He also resolved that defensive tactics were not enough. He sued Woodliffe, the Langleys, and Bishop in Chancery also late in April. In effect, he was taking up Samwell's old lawsuit in that court, trying to prove that he had got title to the yard from Samwell, who had got it from Woodliffe, and hence that the Langleys and their creatures were irrelevant. Browne made one significant change in Samwell's argument. Instead of insisting that the original lease had included title to the yard, he argued that the discussions between Samwell and Woodliffe in July 1599, during which they had agreed to rebuild the playhouse, amounted to a new document, a verbal lease, or "lease paroll." In this "lease," as Browne said, Woodliffe gave Samwell title to the yard for as long as Samwell's lease ran on his other parts of the Boar's Head, "in consideracion for" Samwell's rebuilding his galleries.[4] Samwell, in effect, had bought the yard. His claim to it, therefore, was no legal trifle. The argument proved durable, for Browne was still using it two years later and even expanding it to include other parts of the Boar's Head.

In their lawsuit against Woodliffe in Chancery, the Langleys protested that they had no quarrel with Woodliffe, except that he had done them an "Incombraunce" so that they could "not quietly enioye the said lease," meaning, probably, that they had never fully possessed the place. They did have a deal that they said Woodliffe had approved and that they wanted the court to sanction—so as to bind Woodliffe, but above all, so as to stop Woodliffe's lawsuit in Common Pleas. They would return the Boar's Head to where it had been before their negotiation with Woodliffe in the autumn of 1599. They would give back Woodliffe's lease and cancel his bond for a thousand marks for their "securitye of the same lease." Woodliffe would cancel Richard Langley's bonds, including the forfeit one, return Francis Langley's original investment of £100, and pay Francis for some work he had done in the inn. The Langleys, presumably, would keep whatever they had got from Samwell and the half profits Browne had paid them for the western gallery. They asked the court to appoint a master in Chancery to help. On 6 May the court stopped the case in Common Pleas and appointed John Hunt.[5]

Woodliffe, however, shrank from canceling bonds, giving up a judgment for £107, and giving back £100 in cash, all in exchange for the future half profits of the western gallery and whatever could be got out of Browne for the yard. Yet he had to be careful. The time allowed in the Poley lease for his spending £100 on various projects in the western part of the premises would be up in six months, when, if the work were not done, the lease would be forfeit. The Poleys would then sue Woodliffe for a bond of £300 and everybody else connected with the lease would sue him for various other sums. Woodliffe had built the tiring house and stage, but he had not done all the rest that he had bonded himself to do. He had to find a way of getting work done on ground for which Langley held a lease. Browne, moreover, saw no reason why he should be inconvenienced while Woodliffe or Langley carried out work that had nothing to do with the playhouse. So on 20 May, Woodliffe did not deny that he would consider a settlement by which Langley would get out of the Boar's Head, but he did object to Hunt and demanded that he be allowed to get on with his judgment in Common Pleas. Chancery did not agree. It insisted that Woodliffe and the Langleys attend Hunt and refused to let Woodliffe proceed in Common Pleas.[6]

On the same day, Bishop and Browne confronted each other in King's Bench, Browne to plead not guilty and both men to demand trial. But Langley's courage failed him this time even sooner than it had the previous autumn. Bishop did not put in the bond required, and his lawsuit collapsed.[7] Browne continued triumphantly in possession of the Boar's Head, all the more secure because he could see his two main antagonists, Woodliffe and Langley, struggling with one another in Common Pleas and Chancery.

Woodliffe refused to attend Hunt in Chancery and demanded again on 22 May that the court let him get at the Langleys in Common Pleas. Chancery, however, appointed two other masters in Chancery to adjudicate instead of Hunt, Dr. Matthew Carew and his nephew, George Carew, and continued to stop the lawsuit in Common Pleas. The court did make one significant bow to Woodliffe that the Langleys no doubt deplored. It suggested that the two Carews ask the Langleys to deposit in court the £100 they should have paid Woodliffe the previous November for the now forfeit bond.[8]

With the appointment of the Carews, the Boar's Head fell into interesting hands. Both were Cornishmen, both were distinguished, and both were Middle Templars. The antagonists at the Boar's Head might have expected Matthew Carew, however, to take a stricter and more wary view of proceedings in playhouses than George, and a stricter view of the law involved in their quarrel. Matthew Carew had acquired his mastership many years before, after being a fellow at Cambridge (1551), a student at Louvain, and a lawyer in the Court of the Arches, the ecclesiastical court. He had already served an apprenticeship in theatrical squabbles, having been an adjudicator of the quarrel at the Theatre between James Burbage and his former partner's widow, Margaret Brayne, from 1589 to 1591. He was now one of the oldest and most experienced of the masters in Chancery, given to moralizing and "acid and cantankerous writings" about his cases. His wife was the daughter of a lord mayor of London, and his son, now six or seven years old and very much the child of his father's old age, was Thomas Carew the poet. In George Carew, the people at the Boar's Head perhaps looked for something different. He was much younger. He had reached his mastership only a year and a half before, after being a courtier, frequently an M.P., and a traveler abroad, sometimes as the queen's ambassador (King James eventually made him ambassador to France). His brother was Richard Carew the antiquary. Scaliger called George Carew, "vir amplissimus et sapientia et eruditione, et pietate praestantissimus."[9]

Woodliffe and the Langleys set about negotiating with each other and with the Carews in Chancery. Browne, for his part, pressed his own lawsuit against the lot of them in the same court. On 10 and 11 June, he had five people testify for him—young Samwell, William Hoppdale (one of Mago's carpenters, who gave his age as thirty-one), Richard Bagnall (who had carried away the trash under the stage in the summer of 1599), Jane Harryson, and Alice Saunders (two wives who lived in or near the Boar's Head and gave their ages as thirty-four and forty-three). Young Samwell, Hoppdale, and Bagnall sought mainly to support Browne's new argument, that old Samwell's agreement with Woodliffe to enlarge the playhouse was a verbal lease that gave Samwell title to the yard, and that the money Samwell put into the rebuilding was payment for that lease. The two ladies sought mainly to refresh Samwell's old argument, that the original lease had given him title to the yard from the beginning, for, as they testified, Woodliffe himself had once thought so.

Browne evidently did not drive the lawsuit on to judgment, and Woodliffe and the Langleys were content to leave it at that. Browne probably thought it enough to use the lawsuit as a kind of shield against the more serious business between Woodliffe and the Langleys in the same court. Browne's witnesses spoke, coincidentally, of current building in the yard. Browne, it seems, had been carrying out at least a few finishing projects in his part of the playhouse, for Hoppdale said he "hath almost finished" his galleries. Wood-liffe, however, had not yet begun his work on the western side and so still had possession of Samwell's, now Browne's, upper parlor, though (according to young Samwell) it was now locked up, and Woodliffe, presumably, was living elsewhere.[10]

So confident did Browne become watching the struggles between Wood-liffe and Langley in two courts that on 22 August he actually stopped paying the half profits of the western gallery to either of them, though he continued to pay the annual rent of £40.[11] He said that he did not know with which man he shared that gallery.

Shortly after, it seems, he leased the Boar's Head to another company and took his own on an extended tour of the provinces. They were recorded in Coventry, Norwich (twice), Faversham, and perhaps Ipswich during the next year.[12] The new company at the Boar's Head was the strong one formed by the union of the earl of Worcester's and the earl of Oxford's men, known usually as Worcester's until they became Queen Anne's in the next reign. Its ranks numbered more than a half dozen men who were well known then or were to become so: Will Kempe, John Duke, Thomas Heywood, John Lowin, Christopher Beeston, Robert Pallant, and Richard Perkins. An agreement between this company and Browne's (Derby's) was probably the easier because Derby's countess was Oxford's daughter, and Browne's wife had some connection with Worcester's going back at least to 1593 (she could have been the daughter of one of its members). Browne's rent for his play-house was "shares due in their playes," no doubt a share of the profits in the galleries. He took bonds from six of the new company, among them Duke and Heywood (the other four unnamed) as guarantees of payment.[13] On these terms, Worcester's men set up in the Boar's Head late in the summer or early in the autumn of 1601, probably playing, among other things, the mel-odramatic works of Heywood.

If Browne leased his playhouse and left London because he thought he had little to fear from Langley by this time, he reckoned without his man. Early in the autumn, Langley again appeared at the Boar's Head with "a company of rude fellowes." They broke "into the tiring house & on the stage swearing & thretning to kill any that shold come there." They found Mago and a carpenter of his, John Marsh, at work in the yard. One of Lan-gley's men struck at Marsh with "a holberd or such like weapon" (Marsh said) and "allmost maymed" him in the thigh, "but" (Mago added) "as god wold he hurt him not." Langley invaded only his and Woodliffe's structures on the western side of the yard, demanding that Worcester's men pay rent for the use of them. Because, as Mago said, Worcester's men "for that wynter had no other wynter house licenced for them to play in," they entered into yet another bond, this one to pay Langley £3 a playing week from Michaelmas 1601 until the Shrovetide following (14–16 February 1602), twenty weeks.[14] Langley and his men then, presumably, left the Boar's Head, having achieved at last a major success there. For these payments were to be in addition to the half profits in the western gallery, the paying of which continued to be the responsibility of Browne, who would have figured them into the "shares" he demanded as rent.

In limiting himself to his or Woodliffe's structures, and in demanding more for their use than the half profits, Langley was taking up a new legal stance that would prove useful to the end of the struggle. Effectually, he was abandoning the argument about the ownership of the yard, which perhaps seemed implausible on the face of it, or even fraudulent, and in any case had not been very successful. The new stance certainly seemed at least from a distance to have better ground under it. Langley was arguing that because he or Woodliffe unquestionably owned the stage, tiring house, and western gallery, they could rent them out for as much as they pleased and namely for more than the half profits. Browne could reply that Woodliffe had once agreed that the rent should be only the half profits but could not produce a document to that effect signed by Woodliffe, though he could produce witnesses to the agreement.

Worcester's men, of course, were not enthusiastic about paying Browne's exactions as well as Langley's. If they wanted to resist, they had, like old Samwell before them, the choice of siding with Langley or Browne. Unlike old Samwell, they chose to side with Langley, fearing, perhaps, the nearby danger of rude fellows more than the remote one of an actor. So they soon defaulted in their payments to Browne. That actor, however, seems to have taken them, or threatened to take them, to common law for his six bonds as swiftly as Langley would have done. Worcester's men replied as men usually did when they had no case at common law. Like the Langleys the previous spring, they countersued in Chancery, hoping to stop Browne at common law and to drive him to a compromise. Later, at least, they were using a lawyer associated with the Langleys, Staverton. Browne made a "sufficient" answer, but rather than proceed to judgment he arrived at an agreement with his tenants in which he must have made allowance for the contract they had made with Langley.[15]

Woodliffe and the Langleys, meanwhile, were weaving legal tapestries with their adjudicators, the Carews. Driven by his need to finish building on the western side of the Boar's Head by 28 November or pay the Poleys £300 and see the Poley lease, on which all the others depended, collapse, Woodliffe was not in a mood to dally. Yet neither was he ready to let the Langleys be gone from the Boar's Head for the mere return of his lease. He tried to maneuver them into doing the building for him, but apparently the adjudicators convinced him that because the Poley lease was only his affair (like, for that matter, the £300), he should carry out its terms. Besides, Browne refused to let the Langleys do the work.[16] For their part, the Langleys were no longer sure that they wanted to be out of the Boar's Head, encouraged, no doubt, by their success with Worcester's men and sobered by Woodliffe's unwillingness to let them off cheaply. Both sides were annoyed by Browne's not paying the half profits (or simply profits, as they preferred to call them) for the western gallery. So they arrived at a deal. If it was the same as that to which they nearly agreed some months later—as it probably was—it went something like this. Woodliffe would do the work on the western side of the place and try with the court's help to get the money for it out of Browne from the half profits, which, technically at least, still belonged to Langley. He would let the Langleys out of the Boar's Head for £100 or so, or let them stay in it for a new promise to pay the full purchase price of £400, secured by new bonds guaranteed by one of the Langley's more reliable associates, Hugh Browker, a successful financier, a prothonotary in Common Pleas, and a land owner in Whitechapel.[17]

Inevitably, everybody would protect himself, and the legal design would not be simple. Langley would draw up a lease for his parts of the Boar's Head and give it to Woodliffe. Langley would also give Woodliffe the new bonds for the unpaid balance of the purchase price, £300. For his security, Browker would buy the lease from Woodliffe for £12 supplied by Langley (which may have represented interest on the forfeit old bonds). Woodliffe would give Browker a bond for £8 (which may have represented money spent by Langley for repairs in the Boar's Head). If (option #1) Langley should pay Woodliffe the balance of the purchase price, Browker would give the lease back to Langley and also give to Langley Woodliffe's bond for £8; the new bonds would be worthless. Woodliffe would have sold his part of the Boar's Head for the original price, plus a little for interest on the old bonds. If (option #2) Langley decided not to pay and so leave the Boar's Head, Browker would give the lease to Woodliffe, and Woodliffe would give the new bonds to Browker, who would pass them, along with Woodliffe's bond for £8, to Langley. Woodliffe would again own the stage, tiring house, and western gallery and have for his pains Langley's original down payment of £100 plus some interest on the old bonds. In either option, Woodliffe would give up the old bonds (more than one of which were now forfeit) at completion.[18]

This agreed to in a preliminary way, Woodliffe commissioned the work on the western side of the Boar's Head and early in November received a bill for £16 18s. 8d. He did not have that much ready money, he said, and so he made an astonishing pact with Browne and Jordan. He borrowed £4 toward his building costs from Jordan, and Browne guaranteed the loan. Whenever Woodliffe should get Chancery to order Browne to pay the building costs, Browne was supposed to repay Jordan and deduct that much from the money he would have to pay Woodliffe. Woodliffe and Browne gave Jordan a bond worth £8 if forfeit, and to protect Browne should Jordan sue him, Woodliffe gave Browne a bond worth £16 if forfeit. Perhaps the thing looked all right at first glance. Jordan was protecting himself as customary by having a bond worth double his risk, and Browne was similarly protecting himself. But Woodliffe was risking *four* times the money he was borrowing, and, worse, whether he would have to pay the sum depended not on himself, but on two others who had no reason to love him.

If Browne chose not to pay Jordan, Jordan would sue Browne for £8, and Browne would sue Woodliffe for £16—and that is exactly what eventually happened. For the moment, as Woodliffe said, Browne agreed to forbear taking Woodliffe's bond to common law should it become forfeit, pending the order from Chancery. They put these bonds into writing on 18 November. So silly did the transaction look a year and a half later that Woodliffe insisted first that he had agreed to it only because Browne threatened his life and limb, and then, two or three weeks later, that he had agreed to it only because he was "drawne in by the indirect practise & senister dealing of the said Jordaine & Broune."[19] One must suppose, however, that Woodliffe could not have been so maladroit. Perhaps he thought that he was committing Browne to pay the half profits to him rather than the Langleys for the period during which he and the Langleys carried on their negotiations.

There was some sense in that, for as the year 1601 ended, the Langleys were not sure that they wanted either option of their deal with Woodliffe. So they simply did nothing. They did not press the deal to formal acceptance in Chancery, and Chancery still denied Woodliffe the chance of suing them at common law for the forfeit bonds. Woodliffe came to see these wavering negotiations with the Langleys as yet another example of "the practise & indirect dealinge" of Browne and Jordan.[20]

CHAPTER 6

1602

Worcester's men, not Derby's, went to court from the Boar's Head to play during the Christmas season of 1601–2. Unlike Derby's men the year before, however, Worcester's were there only once and on neither New Year's Day nor Twelfth Night, but 3 January. Moreover, they played at the Boar's Head only some nine to thirteen weeks of the twenty (from Michaelmas 1601 to Shrovetide 1602) involved in their contract with Francis Langley.[1]

Woodliffe began his year in another court, Chancery. His lawyer went there on 15 January to make two declarations before the court rather than just the adjudicators. The Langleys had not proceeded to formal acceptance of their deal with Woodliffe, and Browne was paying nothing for the use of the stage, tiring house, and western gallery. Woodliffe wanted the court to let him get at the Langleys in Common Pleas for the forfeit bonds and to order Browne to pay for the work on the western side of the Boar's Head out of the profits of the playhouse. The court directed the adjudicators to find whether the Langleys were delaying and directed Browne to pay for the work on the western side or to say in court within a week why he should not.

Three weeks later, on 3 February, the Langleys responded to Woodliffe in Chancery by asking for "publication," and the court responded as it regularly did to such requests. It agreed, if Woodliffe "shewe no cawse" to the contrary within seven days. Because publication did not take place and Woodliffe is not reported as saying anything in court, he must have shown cause in meetings with the adjudicators. Publication signified that both sides had finished examining witnesses and so were ready for a hearing and an end of their case. The Langleys would seem to have been edging their deal with Woodliffe toward formal acceptance, though no doubt they were also fending off Woodliffe's attempt to return to Common Pleas. They might well have decided to get out of the Boar's Head after all. Shrovetide (14–16 February) was less than two weeks off, when Worcester's men would no longer have to pay them £3 a playing week, and they may have doubted whether another band of armed intruders could achieve another such success.

Browne, however, did nothing to fend off Woodliffe, who had his lawyer tell the court of this effrontery on the sixth. Chancery promptly ordered the sheriff of Surrey (where Browne must now have been staying) to attach him. The sheriff did so, and Browne freed himself by giving the sheriff a bond for appearance. Browne appeared in Chancery with his lawyer on the tenth "for savinge of his bonde." They duly protested that Browne was no party to the argument between Woodliffe and the Langleys. They did not protest, however, that Browne should be spared from paying for Woodliffe's work on the western side from the half profits of the western gallery. They only asked that Browne "might not be compelled to paye the said money before proof be made thereof." They probably added that those half profits so far due did not amount to so much as Woodliffe had spent, £16 18s. 8d. The court ordered the two adjudicators to consider Browne's remarks and report whether "they thinke meete that the said some . . . ought to be payed by the said Browne." In the meantime, the court freed Browne from the claims of the sheriff of Surrey, and Browne may soon have left for Norwich and then Faversham, where his company played on 27 February and 10 March.

Presently, the adjudicators did think meet that Browne should pay Woodliffe's costs on the western side of the Boar's Head, if so much money had accumulated from the profits due to Woodliffe or Langley. If not, they thought that Browne should make an oath saying so.[2] Browne again did nothing, partly, perhaps, because he was with his men in the provinces.

The Langleys must have agreed to the adjudicators' decision that Browne should pay at least some of these profits to Woodliffe rather than to them. Moreover, they did not try to force Worcester's men into a new contract of weekly payments for the stage, tiring house, and western gallery. Hence they must have decided by now to carry out the version of their deal with Woodliffe that would let them out of the Boar's Head. For a time, Woodliffe did not object, and the two sides came perilously close to formal agreement. Francis Langley actually drew up a lease passing his part of the Boar's Head to Woodliffe, who accepted it. Browker actually gave to Woodliffe Langley's £12 for the lease. Woodliffe actually gave the lease to Browker along with a bond for £8. The transaction, however, stopped there. Woodliffe decided, apparently, that there was more to be got from the Langleys' forfeit bonds in Common Pleas than from this intricate deal in Chancery. So Woodliffe did not give up the old bonds, the Langleys may not have drawn up new ones, and Chancery sanctioned nothing save Browne's paying for Woodliffe's costs on the western side.

Freed in mid-February from paying Langley £3 a playing week, and apparently having settled on a reasonable rent with Browne, Worcester's men set about formally legalizing themselves and making the Boar's Head their permanent house. Two other theatrical enterprises had recently received formal permission to play and at specific houses: the Burbages' at the Globe and Henslowe's at the Fortune. Permission for these two was in the form of a letter from the Privy Council to the lord mayor and the justices of the peace of Middlesex and Surrey dated 22 June 1600 and another, reinforcing one of 31 December 1601. Both letters were couched so as to seem harshly restrictive, but both greatly liberalized the rules about acting by erecting it into a business officially and specifically allowed (or tolerated, to use the Privy Council's word) by the queen herself. One of the restrictions more apparent than real was the Privy Council's repeated insistence that only two enterprises were to be allowed in this way.

Now, exactly three months after the second letter, Worcester's men got one of their sponsors, the earl of Oxford, to lay their case before the queen, which is to say the Privy Council, and to specify that the Boar's Head was "the place they haue especially vsed and doe best like of." Their other sponsor, the earl of Worcester, was a privy councillor, present and voting when the matter came up, as was Browne's connection with authority, Cecil. Not much daunted, apparently, by a foolish consistency, the Privy Council duly "thought meete" to grant the queen's "tolleracion" also to Worcester's men, "notw^thstandinge the restraint of o^r said former Orders." The letter went to the lord mayor on 31 March, couched like the others so as to seem restrictive. The Privy Council prayed and required that the lord mayor *assign* Worcester's men to the Boar's Head, "and that they be verey straightlie Charged to vse and exersise there plaies in noe other but that howse." Worcester's men henceforth were formally the third company and the Boar's Head the third playhouse. From the point of view of the people at Guildhall whom the Privy Council expected to enforce the contents of the letter, however, its effect may have been mainly to license the playhouse rather than Worcester's men, for someone at Guildhall summarized the letter as "to ye l. Maior for the Bores head to be licensed for ye plaiers."[3]

Browne by 21 April had done neither of the alternatives proposed by the Langleys' and Woodliffe's adjudicators in Chancery, the Carews. He had not paid Woodliffe £16 18s. 8d., nor had he made an oath that the half profits did not amount to that much. Woodliffe, therefore, complained before the court (not the adjudicators) on that day, and the court gave Browne until the thirtieth to do either. It added that if Browne made an oath, then he "shall forthwth pay to" Woodliffe "soe much as he shall charge himselfe wthall by his said oth." If Browne was still with his company in the country, he set about returning to London. As he did so, the Langleys again, on the twenty-ninth, asked Chancery for publication in their lawsuit against Woodliffe, and they achieved the same result as before.[4] The court granted it, if Woodliffe "shewe noe cause" to the contrary within a week, and because he seems to have said nothing in court and publication seems not to have taken place, he must have shown cause before the adjudicators. Woodliffe was probably now intent on finding a way to get at the Langleys in Common Pleas for their forfeit bonds and not on agreeing to the deal of the previous autumn.

If not before, Browne was probably back in London early in May. He made an oath in Chancery agreeing that he had to account for the profits of the western gallery and agreeing, presumably, that he had to pay out half those profits, but adding that to whom he accounted and paid depended on to whom the court decided the stage, tiring house, and western gallery belonged. He produced, however, neither accounting nor money just yet.

So long as he had to be in London and in Chancery to deal with Woodliffe, Browne took the occasion also to ambush his tenants, Worcester's men. Perhaps he did not see their tenancy as so permanent a thing as they did, and was looking for a way to move his own company back to London. He had replied to their Chancery lawsuit during the autumn in such a way that they should have put in a reply to him, but because he and they had arrived at an agreement, they had simply abandoned their lawsuit. Now, on 13 May, Browne reminded the court of this lapse and asked for costs and a formal end to the lawsuit. He got both, costs being £2. When Duke and Heywood had not paid a week or two later, Browne had them attached by the sheriff of London and given until 7 June to do so. Perhaps Browne then left for East Anglia, where his company may have performed on 4 June at Ipswich and six days later was not allowed to perform at Norwich. Meanwhile, Worcester's men consulted a lawyer about how to deal with Browne—Staverton, who would be, perhaps already was, counsel for the Langleys in their case against Woodliffe.

Staverton appeared in Chancery for Worcester's men on 8 June to argue that the court should reopen the case. The court agreed, and it appointed one of the Langleys' and Woodliffe's adjudicators, Matthew Carew, to see if Browne's reply of the autumn "be sufficient or not," and if not, to subpoena Browne "to make a perfect and direct Answere."

Two weeks later, Woodliffe managed at last to get around the order in Chancery that forbade him from proceeding against the Langley's in Common Pleas. He asked Common Pleas for a writ that would allow him to execute his year-old judgment against the Langleys for £107. (The money was for one of the now forfeit bonds that the Langleys had given Woodliffe toward the buying of their part of the Boar's Head.) On 23 June, the last day of the current term, Trinity, the court awarded Woodliffe an "elegit," the writ by which the authorities could seize half the delinquent's goods, sell them, and give the proceeds to the creditor. Specifically, the court directed the sheriffs of London and Middlesex to seize half Richard Langley's freely held goods in their jurisdictions and to report in court three weeks after Michaelmas (20 October) what they had done.

How Woodliffe got around the order in Chancery is a puzzle. He may have convinced the adjudicators that the Langleys were dallying about carrying out the deal of the previous autumn, despite the impression the Langleys had given in February and April by asking for publication. Chancery had decreed on 15 January and confirmed on 10 February that if the adjudicators decided the Langleys were dallying the order "shalbe cleerely dissolved." Or perhaps Woodliffe simply ignored the order and risked being thrown into the Fleet prison for contempt of court if the Langleys chose to protest in Chancery. He made his move in Common Pleas on, after all, the last day of the term, and judges would not sit in Chancery again until 9 October, when the next term began. In the event, the Langleys did not protest, but neither did Woodliffe put his elegit into operation, for the sheriffs reported in the autumn that they had done nothing.[5]

That Woodliffe now had not just a judgment but an elegit, though not acted upon, meant that he had managed to raise his price for letting the Langleys out of the Boar's Head. An elegit must have been considerably more trouble for the Langleys, hence worth considerably more to Woodliffe, than a judgment. In effect, not only could Woodliffe keep the Langley's down payment of £100, which he had convinced Chancery he should have some eight or nine months before, but now he could demand up to £107 for his elegit. So the deal to which he and they had nearly agreed was no longer available.

Browne and Worcester's men arrived before Chancery again on 28 June, or at least their quarrel did, and this time the lord keeper himself, Egerton, took a hand. He was told that these litigants were "players," not, presumably, sober men of affairs like the Langleys and Woodliffe, and that their quarrel was about the "shares due in their playes" that Browne chose to accept as rent rather than regular payments of a fixed amount. Players and plays, his lordship thought, were "noe meete matter for this Co^rt." He threw the case out of his court, therefore, and bade Duke and Heywood "to take their Remedies for the same els where."[6] Because the adjudicator, Carew, found Browne's reply sufficient, Browne got costs. Duke and Heywood had not wasted their time, however, for Browne's costs this time were 13s. 4d. less than before.

Francis Langley soon left the Boar's Head without Woodliffe's leave or Chancery's. He died early in July and was buried in St. Saviour's Church on the ninth. His last view of the Boar's Head could have done little to cheer him on his way, nor could that of his other affairs. He left no will, but he did leave a widow with six children. He also left at least ten people clamoring with judgments against Richard Langley alone for his debts.[7] One of those ten was, of course, Woodliffe, whom Richard Langley now confronted single-handedly in the quarrel about the Boar's Head.

As Browne may have hoped they would, Worcester's men looked for a way to leave the Boar's head. By 17 August they had joined Henslowe's enterprises, and presently they were mentioned as belonging to his original but by now lesser playhouse, the Rose, on the South Bank. Browne, presumably, moved his own company back into the Boar's Head.[8]

Soon after, Browne finally produced an accounting of the half profits in the western gallery and paid Woodliffe £6 8s. 8d. for the period beginning on the previous 22 August (1601) and ending, it seems, at the end of September (Michaelmas) 1602. Woodliffe thought the sum derisory.[9] Browne would have deducted everything remotely allowable from the true half profits, including the £3 a week the Langleys had exacted from Worcester's men (because Worcester's men would have deducted that much or something like it from the rent they had agreed to pay Browne) and money he had spent repairing Woodliffe's structures. But the reckonings of the two men in the autumn of 1602 are obscure. Seven months hence both would give a few more details that allow one to see better into their reckonings for the period from August 1601 to March 1603.

Richard Langley negotiated to escape the Boar's Head, and by 15 October, he, Woodliffe, and their adjudicators in Chancery, the Carews, had arrived at a new and simpler arrangement. They would leave the former deal out of it, except that Browker (apparently in trust for Francis Langley's widow) and Woodliffe would keep the artifacts of that deal. Woodliffe would keep the £12 that Browker had paid him for Francis Langley's new and now (if all went well) meaningless lease. Browker would keep that lease along with Woodliffe's bond for £8—both of which could be embarrassing to Woodliffe if the new arrangement should fall through and Browker should go to law. Otherwise, the new arrangement was in its obvious features the one that Woodliffe had more or less established in June. They would simply exchange the old documents. Richard Langley would return the old lease free of incumbrances, and Woodliffe would return the two old bonds he had not taken to common law. Woodliffe would keep the down payment of £100. Langley would either pay him something, yet to be agreed upon, to give up his elegit and the bond on which it was based, or deal with the elegit in the courts as best he could along with the other judgments against him for Francis's debts. One way in which Richard Langley could do that was to sue Francis's widow in Chancery, ostensibly to demand money to pay the debts, more usefully to prevent for the time being those people (including Woodliffe) who had judgments from proceeding with them. Richard Langley soon set about that work.

With this revised arrangement by which he would reacquire the Boar's Head and Richard Langley escape it, Woodliffe contrived to include a less obvious but significant new idea. Langley would have to turn over to Woodliffe not just the old lease, but possession of the structures it conveyed: the stage, tiring house, and western gallery.[10] That is, Langley would have to prevent Browne from using them with, no doubt, a view to getting somebody into the Boar's Head who would pay more for them than the half profits, or to reforming Browne so that he would pay more. Woodliffe was pressing on with Francis Langley's new argument of the year before: that the owner of the stage, tiring house, and western gallery could demand what rent he pleased for them and that the half profits were not enough. He was not arguing as of old that he owned the yard hence also owned Samwell's galleries above it because their posts rested in it.

Getting Browne out of those structures, however, or getting him to pay more for them, would be no easy thing for Richard Langley to do in an ordinary lawsuit. He would have to prove that Woodliffe had not agreed with Samwell about the half profits, or that the agreement did not apply to Browne. Yet Woodliffe had never denied the agreement; there had been many witnesses to it; and he had accepted the half profits since 1598. He argued now and later, therefore, simply that Worcester's men had once paid more than the half profits and so should Browne. For the moment, Woodliffe was fixing his rent at "better then" £4 a week because, he said, that is what Worcester's men had paid. He would soon revise that figure upward.

Woodliffe, however, did not expect Richard Langley to dislodge Browne, or make him pay more money, as the result of an ordinary lawsuit or any other maneuver. He devised not on but two devious schemes by which he might do it himself without tackling Browne head on in a lawsuit. One of them would profit from Langley's cooperation, hence, perhaps, the as yet unfixed amount Woodliffe would take to give up his elegit and forfeit bond.

The first scheme depended on Common Pleas. Before Woodliffe and Langley exchanged documents—while, that is, Langley still owned the stage, tiring house, and western gallery—Woodliffe would press the sheriff of Middlesex to seize them from Langley, according to the elegit granted by Common Pleas, and Langley would do nothing to stop the seizure. The sheriff would hold the structures until he could raise £107 from them by collecting the profits in the western gallery (probably the full profits, on the ground that Langley owned the whole structure), or by selling the goods he found in them, or by both. Langley could further help by not saying that only half the profits and none of the furnishings were really his. Browne would be greatly inconvenienced in the playhouse and expensively engaged in the courts to get his half profits and goods back, unless he stopped playing or sued for peace.

Woodliffe's other scheme depended on Chancery, where he tied it to his negotiations with Richard Langley. On 15 October, after announcing the new arrangement with Langley, Woodliffe's lawyer declared that Browne no longer paid for the use of the stage, tiring house, and western gallery, and that Browne had made an oath in Chancery confessing that he had to render an account to whoever should win the lawsuit between Richard Langley and

Woodliffe. So the lawyer asked for an injunction that would deprive Browne of possession and give it to Woodliffe. The court directed Matthew Carew to investigate and "make report whether he thinke fitt an Iniunction shall goe against the said Browne." If Carew thought fit, Browne was to be sub-poenaed to show cause why an injunction should not be granted.

No doubt Woodliffe preferred the scheme in Chancery to that in Common Pleas, if only because it did not require Richard Langley's cooperation. He did nothing about his elegit in Common Pleas, therefore, except to keep it current, while he waited to see what Matthew Carew would do in Chancery. On 20 October, a week or so after the agreement in Chancery, the sheriffs of London and Middlesex reported to Common Pleas, as they were bound to do, how they had dealt with the elegit and said that they had done nothing. Woodliffe simply got the elegit renewed until 12 November, when the sheriff of London reported again that he had done nothing and Woodliffe got the elegit renewed again, this time until 21 January 1603.[11] The elegit now covered the Christmas season, which was, it seems, a likely time to discomfit a playhouse, for Francis Langley and his team had twice raided the Boar's Head at Christmas in 1599. As Christmas came on, Carew had still made no report to Chancery, and that court had issued neither subpoena nor injunction against Browne.

Woodliffe, therefore, now got the sheriff of Middlesex to do something. Armed with the elegit, the bailiff of Stepney appeared at the Boar's Head about Christmas and took possession of the stage, tiring house, and western gallery. Browne and his playhouse were at last in serious trouble. Browne seems to have saved his goods but stopped playing. No company went from the Boar's Head to play at court that Christmas, and Browne was furious. He was sure that Richard Langley not only had cooperated with Woodliffe, but had helped pay for the elegit. Browne had beat back all the lawsuits Woodliffe and the Langleys could level at him in three courts. Now he suffered a defeat in a lawsuit that Woodliffe leveled not at him but at Richard Langley, "because," as he said bitterly, "they could not Recouer the premises by due course of Law."[12]

Whether or how much Richard Langley did cooperate is not clear. Whatever he had the chance to do, he probably did. For everything the bailiff could get out of those structures at the Boar's Head was so much less that Woodliffe could get out of Langley toward the judgment for £107.

CHAPTER 7

1603

Serious though the elegit was to Browne and to the Boar's Head as a theatrical enterprise, it demolished neither, but it did in effect begin the final stage of the legal struggles there. The sheriff of London (who was also sheriff of Middlesex) reported in Common Pleas on about 21 January 1603, as he had been doing since the previous October, that he had done nothing about Woodliffe's elegit. Woodliffe renewed the elegit, as he had also been doing since October, this time until Easter. The bailiff of Stepney's intrusion at the Boar's Head must have yielded no money, probably because Browne stopped playing and managed to get his goods out of the tiring house before the bailiff could seize them.

A week later, on the twenty-eighth, Woodliffe's and Langley's lawyers said in Chancery that they had agreed about all the details of the bargain by which Langley would leave the Boar's Head, except one: they had yet to "determyne the sume." The court ordered Woodliffe's lawyer, Ayloff, and a Mr. Towse (no doubt for Langley) to decide if they could what the sum would be. If they could not, Mr. Justice Thomas Walmesley would hear both sides and fix the sum, which both sides agreed to accept.[1] Because Walmesley was a judge of Common Pleas, "the sume" probably had to do with Woodliffe's lawsuit there. It should have been the amount Woodliffe would take to give up his elegit and the bond behind it, but if so, either they did not agree to a sum, or Richard Langley did not pay it, for Woodliffe continued aiming the elegit at him.

Soon the Langleys left the Boar's Head once and for all, giving their lease back to Woodliffe and getting in return two of their three bonds. On 3 February, Francis Langley's widow, Jane, demanded the documents that Browker still held presumably to protect the Langleys' interests in their dealings with Woodliffe, and on 13 May Browker said he was willing to give

them to her.[2] The departure of the Langleys from the Boar's Head also allowed the Carews to depart, and as though in expiation, both were soon
knighted.

Soon, too, Browne seems to have been using the stage, tiring house, and
western gallery as usual.[3] Once Richard Langley had given his lease to
Woodliffe, Browne had nothing to fear from the sheriff of Middlesex or the
bailiff of Stepney, because the elegit applied only to Langley's possessions.
Browne had paid Woodliffe the half profits due at the last time of payment,
Michaelmas. Woodliffe was dissatisfied with the amount of money he had
received, but mainly because he thought that he should have more than the
half profits. Hence, unless Woodliffe could bring himself to launch a new
lawsuit about that very vexed matter of how much he should receive for the
use of his parts of the Boar's Head, Browne was reasonably secure from him,
too. When Woodliffe's lawyer spoke in Chancery on 28 January, he said
nothing about Browne at all, his first omission of that kind in his appearances for Woodliffe in over a year.

Early in February, some sizable stretches of the public highway in Whitechapel, apparently the sidewalks, were hazardous to persons passing by. The
civic authorities called upon the occupants of adjacent buildings to repair
them. One stretch, it seems, lay outside the Boar's Head, for the occupant
ordered on 8 February to see that his share of the work was carried out was
Robert Browne, "Stage Player."[4]

All the playhouses closed on 19 March because the queen was mortally ill.
She died on the twenty-fourth and was not buried until 28 April. The playhouses presumably remained closed in mourning. If they reopened
promptly after the queen's burial, they could have been open for only a week
or two before they had to close again, this time because one of the worst
sieges of plague had begun, which would keep them closed until April of the
following year. Woodliffe had regained his stage, tiring house, and western
gallery in time for a disaster, and people like Browne must have confronted a
very lean time. Thanks to the departure of Worcester's men in the summer of
1602 and the closing at Christmas, Browne may have been having a lean time
for some months already, for he soon said that Woodliffe's half profits for the
western gallery from Michaelmas 1602 to the closing of the playhouses were
less than £6, "yf there be any."[5]

Browne did not pay Woodliffe the half profits of the western gallery due at
Lady Day 1603. If Browne was unable to pay, he was soon able to begin a
new and final round of lawsuits. He sued Woodliffe in April in Common
Pleas about the bond of £16 that he had extracted from him in November
1601.[6] That bond, as we have seen, had to do with Woodliffe's borrowing £4
from Browne's backer, Israel Jordan. It must have been forfeit for some time,
and Browne must have delayed taking it to the courts. Moreover, as far as
Woodliffe was concerned, the £4 might actually have been repaid, because

Browne could, indeed should, have deducted it from the half profits paid to Woodliffe the previous Michaelmas (1602). But the bond did not depend on anything Woodliffe had to do. It depended on Browne's repaying Jordan, and Browne had not done so. Jordan had successfully sued Browne for Browne's and Woodliffe's bond of £8. Browne had now paid this £8 and so could sue Woodliffe for £16. The affair sounds more like a devious stratagem by Browne and Woodliffe than a genuine commercial transaction. Whichever it was, Browne probably marshaled it against Woodliffe now in order generally to recoup some of the money lost as a result of the elegit, and specifically to diminish the half profits he owed Woodliffe at Lady Day 1603.

Woodliffe defended himself briefly in Common Pleas. He said that he had agreed to the bond for £16 only because Browne had threatened him with violence. Browne, of course, disagreed. The court ordered the sheriff to produce Woodliffe on May 8 so that it could make an inquiry. Seeing little profit in that, Woodliffe did what men usually did when confronted by difficult lawsuits at common law. He countersued at equity, this time not in Chancery but in the Court of Requests, where justice was supposed to be simpler, swifter, and cheaper. He filed his bill against Browne on 20 May.[7] He insisted that he had effectually paid the £4 for which the bond was security, because Browne had withheld that much, and he offered as a reason for getting into so feckless an arrangement not any threat of violence from Browne, but Browne's and Jordan's indirect and sinister practice. To show how sinister the practice was, and coincidentally how feckless his own part was, he added a new suspicion: he thought the original £4 was Browne's money and not Jordan's!

This business of the bond, however, was probably no more Woodliffe's real purpose now than the loan of £4 had probably been in 1601. He wanted the court to do what Matthew Carew and Chancery had not done the previous autumn: either throw Browne out of the stage, tiring house, and western gallery, or make him pay for them what Worcester's men had paid Langley. According to Woodliffe now, that was "better then" £5 a playing week (the previous autumn it had been "better then" £4).[8] Moreover, now as then he preferred not to get into the old argument about the ownership of the yard. So he said nothing about who owned the yard and nothing, of course, about the half profits.

Woodliffe was taking Francis Langley's new argument of the autumn of 1601 to its final point. He said not only that Browne had once paid better than £5 a week for the use of the stage, tiring house, and western gallery, but that Browne had sworn as much. As part, that is, of his accounting for the half profits due the previous Michaelmas, Browne had probably shown that the £3 a week Langley had for a time exacted from Worcester's men together with the half profits of the western gallery could amount to something like that much. Woodliffe did not, of course, go on to say that Browne had deducted the exactions from the half profits at Michaelmas, so that in effect nobody had ever paid £5 a week for the use of those structures. Woodliffe also ignored the £6 8s. 8d. he had received for the half profits due at Michaelmas, probably thinking the money quite inadequate. He added that Browne had got Samwell's property "by indirect meanes" and the stage, tiring house, and western gallery "by force," which he held "without any right title or interest," which is to say, probably, without paying as much for their use as Woodliffe wanted. He calculated that Browne owed him "better then" £200, at, presumably, more than £5 a playing week, from August 22, 1601, when Browne stopped paying half profits to either the Langleys or him, until the closing of the playhouses in March 1603.

Exaggerated as more than £200 must be as a statement of Browne's and Woodliffe's affairs in the Boar's Head, it is probably not an exaggerated indication of how much the players had used the place. It suggests that plays took place there for about forty weeks in nineteen months, and when in his reply Browne came to challenge Woodliffe's figures, he did not argue that the players had used the Boar's Head less than Woodliffe had inferred. Probably the forty playing weeks would have been more but for the elegit.

Woodliffe asked Requests, finally, to subpoena Browne and Jordan so that it might look into the bond and, more importantly, no doubt, Browne's not paying better than £5 a playing week to Woodliffe's "great losse & hinderance & vtter vndoeing foreuer vnlesse" the court of its "pittie & clemency" relieve him. He also, of course, asked the court to stop Browne's operations in Common Pleas.

Browne replied ten days later, on 30 May. He denied that he had withheld £4 from his payment to Woodliffe. Hence Jordan's lawsuit against him and his against Woodliffe in Common Pleas were quite proper. So was the way in which he held Samwell's part of the Boar's Head and used Woodliffe's. If Woodliffe preferred not to quarrel about the yard, Browne was nothing loath. He advanced his argument of 1601 for his ownership of the yard, except that what was a verbal lease then was by implication an ordinary one now. He explained that he used the stage, tiring house, and western gallery in return for paying to Woodliffe and his successor half the profits of the gallery. (No one had explained before this basic part of the arrangement among the owners of the Boar's Head, though Woodliffe had hinted at it four times in Chancery in 1602). By implication, he elevated this arrangement, too, into a regular contract rather than merely an oral understanding. Browne pointed out that Woodliffe had accepted the half profits, hence the arrangement, until the previous Michaelmas. He confessed that he had not paid the half profits since then and that £6 might be due. He denied owing Woodliffe £5 (he omitted "better then") a playing week from August 1601, or £200 altogether, as Woodliffe "hath most ympudently surmysed."

The two men's accounting here must go something like this. Woodliffe arrived at "better then" £5 a playing week and more than £200 altogether for the playing weeks from 22 August 1601 to 19 March 1603 by reckoning as he had been doing for months: Browne should have paid not only the half profits of the western gallery for each of the forty playing weeks but the extra sums the Langleys had for a time exacted from Worcester's men. Browne took it for granted that this was Woodliffe's method, and he and his witness, Mago, would soon say that the extra sums were £3 a playing week. So Woodliffe supposed that the half profits could reasonably be seen to come to £2 a week, and he had Browne's accounting at Michaelmas 1602 before him. Browne, however, would insist that he had to account now only for the half profits during the forty playing weeks—something like £80. He would deduct from them the £30 to £40 that, as he would also soon say, he had spent for repairs to Woodliffe's structures.[9] He would deduct, too, the £6 8s. 8d. that he had paid Woodliffe for the half profits from 22 August 1601 to Michaelmas 1602. He was evidently ready now to pay him £6 more for the half profits from then until 19 March 1603. These sums substracted from £80 leave from about £27 to about £37 that Browne was also deducting but nowhere said for what. The money must have represented the sums the Langleys had taken from Worcester's men over and above the half profits. Worcester's men would have deducted those sums from the rent they had agreed to pay Browne for the Boar's Head, and he would try to recoup them now from Woodliffe.

Of, therefore, the twenty weeks during which the Langleys took this money (from Michaelmas 1601 to Shrovetide 1602), Worcester's men played at the Boar's Head nine to twelve or thirteen. The net half profits of the western gallery for forty weeks of playing over nineteen months were about £40 to £50, and but for repairs to that gallery, the stage, and tiring house they could have been as much as £80. Woodliffe's earlier claim (in 1602) that he should have only £4 a week suggests that he then thought the half profits could sag to about £1 a week.

The day after Browne's reply, on 31 May, the court appointed an adjudicator to see if there was reason to stop the lawsuit in Common Pleas. A week later, on 6 June, Woodliffe offered to deposit in court the amount of the original loan, £4, if the court would stop Browne in Common Pleas. The court took Woodliffe's money and stopped Browne until "further order to the contrarie vpon the hearing of the sayd cause."

The Court of Requests, however, did not order to the contrary and did not hear the cause. Browne took the quarrel back to Chancery toward the end of June by suing Woodliffe and Richard Langley there.[10] He probably thought that a lawsuit about a bond of £16 and a debt of £4 was no place to argue his claims to the Boar's Head. He may have found some wry amusement in combining Woodliffe and Richard Langley against him, because those two were now struggling furiously over Woodliffe's judgment and elegit for £107 (the sheriff having, as usual, done nothing about the elegit by Easter, and Woodliffe having, as usual, renewed it). Langley had sued Francis's widow, Jane, in Chancery and was trying to get all ten of the lawsuits against him for Francis' debts stopped, "especially" Woodliffe's. Woodliffe and some of the others were trying hard to have Langley arrested. On 27 June, Langley got the order to stop the lawsuits, "And," as Chancery added, "the sd Woodlyffe ys forthw[th] to haue this order shewed vnto him for stay of the proceedings vpon the Ellegett by him sued out against the said Richard Langley for the debt of the sd ffrauncis Langley."[11] Yet Browne was just then assuring the same court, among other things, that the elegit was really a "Conspiracye" between Woodliffe and Langley by which they had meant to seize possession of Woodliffe's parts of the Boar's Head.

Browne meant his new lawsuit to show directly that he owed Woodliffe only the half profits of the western gallery for the use of that gallery, the stage, and tiring house plus the annual rent of £40 for the use of the rest of the Boar's Head. He pointed out that he and Samwell before him had paid both the half profits and the annual rent, which Woodliffe had accepted.[12] He devoted himself mainly to the original quarrel that Francis Langley had abandoned in 1601 and Woodliffe a year later, about the ownership of the yard, and to the one that had replaced it, about rent for the use of the stage, tiring house, and western gallery. He ignored the bond of £16 and the debt of £4.

After rehearsing Samwell's lease, therefore, Browne claimed the yard by running out again his argument of 1601, but not in the misleading words he had used a few weeks before in the Court of Requests. The discussion of the yard between Woodliffe and Samwell when they had agreed to the rebuilding of 1599 amounted to a separate lease, which Browne called now, as in 1601 but not as in Requests, a "lease paroll," or verbal lease. As he had argued in 1601, that lease gave Samwell title to the yard for the period of his principal lease on the Boar's Head, and Samwell had paid for it by rebuilding his galleries. Browne then turned to the arrangement by which he used Woodliffe's stage, tiring house, and western gallery. His "lease" of the case in Requests was now merely an "agreemente," but it was of the same kind and force as the verbal lease by which he claimed the yard (his witnesses called this a "lease paroll," too). Woodliffe and Samwell, Browne urged, had also made this arrangement when they had agreed to rebuild the playhouse, and Samwell had paid for it, too, by rebuilding his galleries. Samwell was, moreover, also to have this arrangement for the period of his principal lease on the Boar's Head. In short, Browne simply refined and developed his claim to a verbal lease of the yard of the Boar's Head and expanded it to include the arrangement by which he used the stage, tiring house, and western gallery.

Most of the rest of the lawsuit is a series of arguments to support this case, including at last details of the money Browne and Samwell had spent and of the responsibilities of owner and players in the playhouse (see appendix 4). Browne also challenged Woodliffe's elegit (which he thought a kind of fraud) four times and Francis Langley's exacting £3 a playing week from Worcester's men (which he thought extortion) once.

On 25 July, Browne had his builder, Mago, and one of Mago's carpenters, his former apprentice, John Marsh, testify for him. It was, however, a rather thin turnout, because neither could say much for Browne's claims except rather vaguely to agree with them. Indeed when asked (interrogatory no. 8) to confirm that Woodliffe had got his elegit by a "synister" conspiracy with Richard Langley, Mago confused that episode with Francis Langley's getting £3 a week from Worcester's men, and Marsh could only say that whether "the same was done by coven & vppon a plott & practise to get awaie the possession" of the stage, tiring house, and western gallery from Browne "is more then he knoweth." Neither could be so convincing and helpful as young Samwell had been to Browne in 1601 or even as Mago had been to old Samwell in 1600. Minds fumbled at the complexity the quarrel had acquired and the four years that had passed since some of the most important events had happened.

As Requests did not hear Woodliffe's lawsuit, Chancery did not hear Browne's. For Woodliffe abruptly left the Boar's Head long before the court could conclude anything. He died of the plague a few days after Browne's witnesses had testified. He was buried in Whitechapel with no fewer than twenty-seven others on 30 July, one of the worst days.[13] Like Francis Langley, he left no will.

The lawsuits about the Boar's Head stopped and never recommenced. Maybe Susan Chaplyn Woodliffe grew content with the half profits, reckoning that it was a doubtful, expensive, energy-consuming business to try to get more because the posts of Browne's galleries rested in a yard of dubious ownership, or because for a time the Langleys had got more. She might have reflected, too, that no matter how Browne might calculate the half profits or how her husband would have added to them, there weren't any payments coming from playing at the Boar's Head now, hadn't been any since March, and wouldn't be any for many months to come. Browne had, therefore, won his case at last, but the victory had been a pyrrhic one. For he possessed an empty and no doubt disease-ridden shell, and though his company seems to have gone into the provinces with the others to escape the plague,[14] Browne stayed behind impoverished at the Boar's Head.

On 26 August, a Susan Samwell was buried in Whitechapel, having died of the plague. Susan Woodliffe, however, got her husband's part of the Boar's Head on that day, having applied to the London Commissary Court a second time for the administration of a husband's goods. She posted a bond for Woodliffe's goods that was about a twenty-eighth of the one she had posted for those of her first husband, Chaplyn. With the prospect of receiving the half profits of the western gallery at the Boar's Head for some twelve and a half years among her assets, she married a third husband, James Vaughan, seven months later at Whitechapel. He was, it seems, her third financier, who was living at his "howse in white Chappell," perhaps the Boar's Head, in February 1608.[15]

Browne died of the plague in mid-October when the disease was waning. He and only two others joined Woodliffe in Whitechapel churchyard on the sixteenth. Five days later, on the twenty-first, Joan Alleyn wrote her husband, the famous actor, Edward, that for ought she knew all the players were well, "but that Browne of the Boares head is dead & dyed very pore, he went not into the Countrye at all." Browne, like Langley and Woodliffe before him (and for that matter, Chaplyn), left no will. Perhaps death took them all by surprise. In any event, Browne's part of the Boar's Head, like Woodliffe's, was now owned by a woman, another Susan, and she like Susan Woodliffe probably grew content with whatever she could peaceably get out of the place. It was none of the great courts of record in London that finally lifted the Boar's Head clear of legal mazes but the great plague of 1603. Susan Browne applied to the Prerogative Court of Canterbury for administration of her husband's goods and got it on 9 January 1604.[16] She was then twenty-five or twenty-six years old.

The Langleys must have lost a fair amount of money in the Boar's Head. For their three years and three months or so there, they could probably show something paid by Samwell in the autumn of 1600, £27 to £37 or so paid by Worcester's men, and the half profits of the western gallery for a year and nine and a half months (from 7–12 November 1599 to 22 August 1601)— all in all probably less than £150. They lost their down payment of £100, probably the amount of Woodliffe's judgment and elegit, £107, and sizable amounts in legal fees and money paid to people like Bishop and Wolleston. They also lost a great deal of energy and time. The Boar's Head, however, was just one of many nasty tangles Francis Langley left behind to resolve themselves into lawsuits, like those between his widow, Jane, and Richard Langley, Hugh Browker, and her bother, Sir Anthony Ashley, and those between Richard Langley and numerous of Francis's creditors.

Woodliffe had done much better at the Boar's Head. He had spent some hundreds, perhaps, putting up his stage, tiring house, western gallery, and other structures, and he, too, had had great legal fees, though probably not on the Langley's scale. In return, however, he had Langley's down payment of £100, probably the amount of his judgment, £107, the half profits of the western gallery for some nineteen months, and his original investment, which he could leave to his wife.

If Browne's acquaintances thought he had ruined himself in the Boar's Head, as Joan Alleyn seems to have thought, the ruin they saw was more apparent than real. He had paid £360 for his part of the place, £30 to £40 in repairs (which he had deducted from money due to Woodliffe), great legal fees, and whatever the help of Jordan had cost. Marsh thought he had spent £500 to £600 "at least."[17] He had also paid £120 in rent. In return, however, he had used one of the newest playhouses in London and most of a sizable inn for almost three years, he had a share of the profits made by Worcester's men during the year or so when they were in the Boar's Head, and above all, he, too, had his original investment to leave his wife. It was more secure in her hands, in fact, than it had ever been in his, and it saw her into old age. Or reckon his operations another way. He needed to earn only some £4 a week clear from the playhouse and inn during three years to pay for his original investment, his rent, and other capital charges. A main reason for his poverty when he died must have been a lack of ready money caused by his not playing for seven months and his having had a difficult time playing for some months before that.

Browne and his wife prospered in one way at the Boar's Head. Their household grew rapidly to include five children, four baptized in Whitechapel from December 1600 onward with intervals of sixteen, nine and a half, and eleven months between them. They were Robert, Susan, William, Elizabeth, and a child with whom their mother was six months pregnant when her husband died, Anne. All were alive in 1612. William, baptized on 25 April 1602, became a player and must now join the handful of Elizabethan and Jacobean colleagues for whom a date of birth is known.[18]

CHAPTER 8

1604–1615

With her five small children and the Boar's Head among her attractions, Susan Browne soon married another actor, Thomas Greene. He was in the process of joining the company that might have included her father when she was a child and that had recently spent a year in the Boar's Head, Worcester's men, now called the Queen's men. While the plague kept all the companies from playing in London, the Queen's men had a shuffling of members in which they acquired, among others, Greene, a clown,[1] to replace their famous clown, Kempe, who had probably died in the autumn of 1603. They also had a reorganization of their affairs in which they left Henslowe's undertakings, including his playhouse, the Rose. They seem to have arranged to move into the Curtain when playing should begin again. That ancient playhouse, lying in Shoreditch, north of Whitechapel and not far from the Boar's Head, was supposed to have been pulled down in 1600 but was to remain standing for many years. Inevitably, with their acquisition of Greene and Greene's acquisition of Susan Browne, the Queen's men again took an interest in the Boar's Head, the more so because Browne's company, Derby's, now moved permanently to the country. Equally inevitably, Thomas Greene became at once one of their principal members.

They played at court during the Christmas festivities and just after, on 2 and 13 January 1604, and it was John Duke who procured their warrant for payment on 19 February. They took part in the coronation procession on 15 March as "officers to the Queene," Greene's name appearing toward the bottom of their list. During the next three weeks, perhaps, still waiting for the plague to diminish enough so that they could play again in London, they tried to improve their standing as the Burbages' company (now the King's men) had recently done, and, perhaps, to steal a march on Henslowe's main company (now Prince Henry's men), as the King's men had also done. The

Privy Council, as we have seen, had legitimatized both the Burbages' and Henslowe's companies in a letter of 22 June 1600 (and in a reinforcing one of 31 December 1601), and Worcester's men in a letter of 31 March 1602. Soon after James became king, the King's men got themselves legitimatized in a much grander way, typical of many things in the new dispensation, and without Prince Henry's men doing the same. They acquired a patent on 19 May 1603. Now, Prince Henry's men still not having done as much, the Queen's men sought the same patent, except that they inserted their own particulars, conspicuous among which were Greene and the Boar's Head.

The patent would allow them to play not at one playhouse in Middlesex as the Privy Council's letter of 1602 had done, but at "other conveinyent places, w^{th}in the liberties and freedomes of any Cittie, vniversitie, Towne, or Boroughe whatsoeue*r*," and it would bear not the signatures of a few councillors, but the Great Seal of England. It would be addressed in the king's name not merely to the lord mayor of London and the justices of the peace in Middlesex and Surrey, but "To all Justices of peace Maiors, Sheryfes, vice-chauncello^{rs}, of any our vnyversities, Bailiffs, Head boroughes, Constables And to all other o^r Offycers mynisters and lovinge subiectes to whome it may appertaine." When the plague should abate, the company, Greene's name first, would "freely . . . vse and exercise, the art and faculty of playinge Comedies, Tragedies, Histories, Enterludes, Morralls, Pastoralls, Stage plaies, and such other lyke." They would play these works "Aswell w^{th}in there now vsuall Howsen, Called the Curtayne, And the Bores head, . . . as in any other play howse not vsed by others, by the said Thomas Greene, elected, or by hym hereafter to be builte."[2] This splendid document reached only the draft stage somewhere in the labyrinth of government. It did not, apparently, pass the signet, privy, or great seals.

When on 9 April the Privy Council at last allowed playing in London, therefore, the Boar's Head was probably back in business, and Susan Browne, now Greene, was probably in residence. The Privy Council, however, now specifically allowed only three playhouses, the Globe, the Fortune, and the Curtain, so that the Boar's Head once more functioned in some less secure way, as it had until the letter of March 1602. Greene and his colleagues may have divided their time between the Boar's Head and the Curtain for a year or two, until they moved into a large new playhouse in Clerkenwell, built in another inn-yard, the Red Bull. Then they probably left the Boar's Head forever, though for a while they continued to appear occasionally at the Curtain. They played without formal authority at the Red Bull until 15 April 1609, when at last they got the patent they had not got in 1604. It was almost word for word the same as the draft of 1604, except that a remark about the Red Bull replaced the one about Greene and the Boar's Head. Prince Henry's men, however, had got the same patent three years before, so that in a sense Henslowe had lost ground on the Burbages, and the

Queen's men had lost ground on both.[3] Greene died in August 1612 and was buried not at Whitechapel, but Clerkenwell. He left a will in which he provided for all Browne's children and one of his own, Honor, baptized in Clerkenwell on 17 April 1609. He also left an appreciative audience, several of whom wrote epigrams for him, like W. R., who wrote, presumably in the autumn of 1612:

> How fast bleake Autumne changeth Floraes dye,
> What yesterday was *(Greene)* now's seare & dry.

and admiring colleagues like Heywood, who wrote:

> As for Maister *Greene*, all that I will speake of him (and that without flattery) is this (if I were worthy to censure) there was not an Actor of his nature in his time of better ability in performance of what he vndertooke; more applaudent by the Audience, of greater grace at the Court, or of more general loue in the Citty, and so with this briefe character of his memory, I commit him to his rest.[4]

Susan Browne Greene married again in June 1613 a James Baskervile, not, it seems, a player, but a bigamist, who in 1617, having taken up "diuerse commodityes in & about London vpon Creditt, and beinge taxed for having two wieves lyving both at one tyme," fled to Ireland. Susan carried on in Clerkenwell. She remained interested one way and another in the Queen's men at least until 1626. She lent them money in 1615 and 1616, and her son and Browne's, William, was playing with them in 1616 as a fourteen-year-old hired man. She died a widow of some seventy years in January 1648 and was buried in Clerkenwell. She was, it seems, only semiliterate.[5]

When the Queen's men left the Boar's Head, the place did not fall desolate. It was conspicuous among those playhouses on 12 April 1607, where "comon Stage Plaies . . . are daylie shewed and exercised and doe occasion the great Assembleis of all sortes of people." For on that day the lord mayor wrote the lord chamberlain and by implication the Privy Council asking them to order the justices of Middlesex to close the playhouses, or, as the lord mayor put it, "to put in due execution such ordenaunces as are formerly . . . recomended vnto them" and "especially that there may be a better care hade of White Chappell Shorditch Clarken-well and such other remote Partes then formerly hath ben accustomed."[6] He meant, no doubt, the Boar's Head, the Curtain, and the Red Bull. One may guess that the company at the Boar's Head was the Duke of Lennox's men, who in 1608 could have become Prince Charles's men. The one company vanished, in any event, about when the other appeared, and they shared one member, John Garland, who became the leader of Prince Charles's men. An early allusion to Prince Charles's men is a payment for a performance at Leicester in the summer of

1609, and then they were of Whitechapel: "Item given to the Princes Players of the White Chapple london—xxˢ."⁷ These Prince's men must have been Charles's, because the other Prince's men, Henry's, were thoroughly settled at the Fortune in St. Giles Without Cripplegate.

It is imprudent to suggest that the company that became Prince Charles's men followed the Queen's men at the Boar's Head and continued to use the place for many years. Other than the allusion of 1609, no evidence puts any company in the Boar's Head after the Queen's men. Yet such a suggestion has some curious justifications.⁸

Prince Charles's men, for example, shadowed the Queen's men for many years. If they followed them at the Boar's Head in 1605 or 1606, they also followed them at the Red Bull in 1617 and at the Cockpit in Drury Lane in 1619. Prince Charles's men got the same patent as the Queen's men, and next after them, on 30 March 1610, so that if the Queen's men may be considered the third company, Prince Charles's men must be considered the fourth. For their London playhouse, the patent of Prince Charles's men reads merely, "such vsuall howses as themselues shall provide." Two of the principal men among the Queen's men eventually became Prince Charles's men, Christopher Beeston when Queen Anne died, in 1619, and Robert Pallant in 1616, after two years with Lady Elizabeth's men.

Although they made extensive tours of the provinces, Prince Charles's men must have played often to ordinary audiences in London, at least during the five seasons from 1610 to 1615–16 when they were there to play at court, but no playhouse in London is associated with them until the leases were running out at the Boar's Head in 1615. Then, in June, they joined a consortium to build Porter's Hall near Puddle Wharf in Blackfriars. It was an abortive venture, however, and neither they nor any other company played there in 1615. So on 20 March 1616, Samwell's and Browne's lease having run out at Christmas and Woodliffe's grand lease from the Poleys having less than a week to run, they drew up a contract to play at the Hope, where they stayed until 1617.⁹

In 1660 or so, the marquess of Newcastle remembered eleven playhouses in London where one could see plays "In my Time."¹⁰ One of them was the Boar's Head. His time probably began between 1600 and 1606, when one of the enterprises he mentioned, Paul's Boys, functioned, and it ended at the earliest in 1630, when another, Salisbury Court, began. He was eight years old in 1600 and thirty-eight in 1630. He put the Boar's Head first in a list of playhouses that occurred to him after he had run through those he thought the main ones. The others in this second list were the Curtain, which housed plays until 1627 or thereabouts, the Hope, which opened in 1614, and Whitefriars, which opened in 1608. It would seem, then, that whether it was Prince Charles's men who were at the Boar's Head or not, memorable theatrical events were in train there well after those executed by the Queen's men.

CHAPTER 9

1616–1676

Of the five great public playhouses built in the momentous decade that began with the building of the Swan and ended with that of the Red Bull, the Boar's Head was the first to fall silent. Even the ill-fated Swan survived it, as did the ancient Curtain. Contrary to what one might have expected at Christmas 1599 and at almost any time during the next three years and more, the demise of the Boar's Head had nothing to do with legal quarrels, the great yard, the Samwells, the Woodliffes, the Langleys, or the Brownes. The place operated quite successfully in the face of all that, at least until the elegit, the Queen's death, and the plague of 1603. It probably operated successfully in the face of the calm that overtook it in 1604, too, but thanks to that calm, there is almost nothing certain one can say about the Boar's Head during the last dozen years.

It is not even possible to say who held the leases as they fell in. Browne's widow, or as she then was, Susan Baskervile, was very much alive at the time, across the City in Clerkenwell. Woodliffe's widow, who was probably old enough to be Susan Baskervile's mother, could well have been dead. In any event, Samwell's and Browne's lease ran out at Christmas 1615, when whoever held Woodliffe's grand lease took over Samwell's and Browne's part of the Boar's Head. The whole playhouse now belonged to one person for a quarter of a year. Then on Lady Day 1616, he or she surrendered the playhouse and much else in the Boar's Head so that the whole place was now entire and in one man's hands for the first time since 1594.

That man was Sir John Poley, Jane Poley's second son and heir. He had spent his youth as a soldier. In about 1613, when he was forty-eight years old or so, he married Ursula North, the sister of a friend of his, Sir Roger North, a squire in Suffolk. Then he settled down to emulate not his father, who had been a magnate of Whitechapel, nor his mother, who had aspired to own a

playhouse, but his cousins, those Poleys who were squires of Badley in Suffolk. He began amassing an estate at Columbine Hall in Stowmarket, Suffolk, and fathering the children who would live there and inherit it. He must
have thought occasionally that he did not have a great deal of time. When the
Boar's Head leases fell in, he was fifty years old and had no heir. He need not
have worried, however. By 1628, when he was past sixty, he had eight young
children, two sons (John, born in 1621, and Edmund, born in 1628) and six
daughters, all baptized in Suffolk. He died when he was sixty-nine years old,
on 13 or 14 February 1635, leaving his daughters the competent if far from
magnificent portions of £200 each, though his executors (one of whom was
Sir Roger North) had trouble raising that much from his estate.[1]

When Sir John Poley assumed ownership of the Boar's Head at Lady Day
1616, then, the place fell into a scheme of things very different from the one
that had prevailed there. He could have had no interest in living in the Boar's
Head and none in managing it, either as an inn or as a playhouse. It was
useful to him simply as a way of financing his concerns in Suffolk, and the
ways in which he might reap the value of the place were about to change.

Many properties in Whitechapel, including the Boar's Head, were
copyholds belonging to the manor of Stepney rather than freeholds. Manors
exercised control over how the owners of copyhold properties used them
and especially over how they sold, leased, and bequeathed them. Just then
the lord of the manor of Stepney, Lord Wentworth, and his copyhold tenants
were negotiating new and more liberal terms, or "customs," by which those
tenants could hold and dispose of their properties. One new custom, already
and separately agreed upon, was that such tenants could "enfranchise" these
properties. They could, that is, buy nearly all the manorial rights over their
properties and so hold them not as copyholds but as freeholds of a kind.
Having enfranchised their properties, they could dispose of them as they
pleased—divide them into parcels, for example, and sell each parcel as a
freehold or let each on a very long lease (copyhold tenants could not make
leases longer than thirty-one years). They still paid the manor, however, the
small annual "quit rent" that copyhold tenants paid, for their freeholds were
in "free and common socage" rather than "fee simple." Lord Wentworth got
a patent in July 1615 that allowed him to sell his rights. He finished his
negotiations with his tenants in June 1617, got a decree in Chancery for-
malizing the new customs a month later, including the right to enfranchise,
and allowed them to be printed before the end of the year.[2]

Evidently, Poley had made up his mind long since that the Boar's Head
was worth more as a collection of small holdings than as anything else. The
playhouse, therefore, probably died promptly on Lady Day 1616. If the inn
business had survived the Privy Council order of 1600 that forbade acting in
inns, it, too, probably died on Lady Day 1616.[3] Soon Poley seems to have
sold a strip of the great yard between the stage and the eastern building as a

copyhold to one Samuel Rowley,[4] leaving himself a thin slice of the yard in front of the eastern building for access to that building. (The eastern building was a long, narrow structure that formed the eastern side of much of the Boar's Head.) Probably he rented out every other useful square foot of the place on short leases, up to the three years the manor allowed without a fee under the old customs. For though Rowley did subscribe to the new customs in 1617, Poley did not, perhaps because he had resolved to enfranchise the place and so was no longer interested in the rights of copyholders. Only subscribers were supposed to take advantage of the new customs, but the one that allowed enfranchising must have been an exception.[5] Poley, in any event, concluded a contract with Lord Wentworth on 23 June 1618 to enfranchise the Boar's Head, except, presumably, for Rowley's strip. In the contract the Boar's Head is "All that mesuage or Tenement called or knowen by the name of the Boores Head now devided into seuerall Tenem^{ts} or Cottages, And one Barne therevnto adioyneing or belonging." By June 1618, that is, the playhouse had been dead for some time, and the name Boar's Head as referring to any coherent enterprise was already an anachronism.

Poley now dismantled the stage and pulled down Woodliffe's buildings on the western side of the yard that had contained the tiring house and supported the western gallery, which also disappeared. Probably he pulled down Samwell's northern and southern galleries, too, and if he did not pull down Samwell's two eastern ones, he adapted them. For apparently he left standing the eastern building that supported them, as did his successors well into the eighteenth century.[6] In place of the stage and Woodliffe's buildings he meant to create a group of small holdings and a narrow lane leading to them. Then, toward the end of 1621, before he had gone further, he decided that he preferred cash to an investment in a scheme for redevelopment. So he sold two large pieces of the Boar's Head as freeholds, one of which included the site of the stage and Woodliffe's buildings.

William Browne, citizen and cooper of London (no relation to Robert Browne, it seems), bought one of these pieces for £200, and this piece included the site of the stage and tiring house. Thomas Needler, citizen and merchant tailor of London, bought the other for £120. Poley and his buyers drew up their deeds on 27 December (Browne) and 29 December (Needler) 1621, and Poley put a copy of both on the Close Roll on the twenty-ninth. Both Browne and Needler had already paid the full price before the deeds were drawn up. Poley would not repeat Woodliffe's dealings with Langley. For their parts, Browne and Needler had Poley attach to their deeds a copy of his contract with Lord Wentworth enfranchising the Boar's Head and to say in the deeds that he had done so.[7]

The quit rent for the whole Boar's Head was 16d. a year, of which Browne was to pay 4d. and Needler 2d. Hence they and Poley must have reckoned that these two pieces comprised about three-eighths of the value of the Boar's

Head. If pieces worth three-eighths could be sold as freeholds for £320, then perhaps the whole Boar's Head could be sold so for £860, which, presumably, was more than it would have been worth with a twenty-two-year-old playhouse in its midst.

Poley may also have disposed of the rest of the Boar's Head about now. In any event, he had none left when he died. One of the original copies of Browne's deed survives, as do the copies of the Close Roll of both his and Needler's deeds. Quotations from two more of Poley's deeds occur in eighteenth-century deeds that survive. These quotations describe two small pieces of ground in the Boar's Head without buildings, and they show that it was Needler who bought them from Poley but not for how much or when. I have not found anything to explain Poley's giving up other parts of the Boar's Head. He may have sold his parents' great garden plot north of the Boar's Head to John Wood and Anne his wife in 1632. If so, it then comprised two messuages, fourteen cottages, and a quarter acre of land.[8] Rowley, Browne, Needler, and Wood all owned properties adjacent to the Boar's Head when they dealt with Poley.

The two full deeds and the two quotations are maddeningly inexplicit for the person who would know what the Boar's Head was like at the time of Poley's sales and cannot walk through the place as it was then with a tape measure in hand. They are, however, vastly better than nothing. Taken together with remarks in the lawsuits from 1599 to 1603 and the later history of the site, especially maps from 1676 onward, they lead to many conclusions not only about Poley's operations but about the playhouse. More about the playhouse in later chapters—here I continue with the history of the site from 1621.

In effect, Poley gave up the Boar's Head in four main pieces, each related to one of the three parts of the yard. That yard, as we shall see, began behind the buildings of the Boar's Head in Whitechapel High Street and stretched northward along the eastern building of the Boar's Head. The southern part of the yard was relatively small. The yard then bulged westward to form a large central part where the playhouse had been, and it narrowed again in the north to form a northern part much like the southern one in size. Unlike the southern and central parts, in Poley's scheme of things this northern one was to remain open and public, and it did so until 1882.

Browne bought the central part of the yard (excluding Rowley's strip and the land on which two alleys were to be made) and the central part of the eastern building alongside it. His part of the yard included the narrow piece between Rowley's strip and the eastern building, to which, evidently, it provided access. He meant to carry out Poley's plan in the central part of the yard—create a collection of small holdings where the stage and tiring house had been and make an alley leading to them on land there set aside for the purpose. In his parts of the eastern building he meant, it seems, to organize something grander, "houses" or a "messuage." By means of several transactions, Needler eventually acquired everything in the Boar's Head north of the northern part of the yard. He already owned the property immediately north of the Boar's Head, around what in 1676 was called Tripe Yard. He collected a large domain there so that one of his successors eventually joined the northern section of the Boar's Head to Tripe Yard.

The pieces of the Boar's Head that Browne and Needler did not acquire were the northern part of the yard and the buildings on its eastern and western sides—the properties, that is, lying between Browne's and Needler's pieces—and the southern end of the Boar's Head. The northern part of the yard had on its eastern side the northern section of the eastern building and on its western one the buildings (or their successors) that had once housed among other matters the Poley family and now housed Thomas Milles, a butcher. The southern end of the Boar's Head comprised the buildings of the inn in Whitechapel High Street, the southern part of the yard, the entrance, and the southern end of the eastern building. These southern premises must have been worth most of the five-eighths of the value of the Boar's Head that Browne and Needler did not buy.

When he dealt with Poley, Browne already owned the building in the High Street that was immediately west of the buildings of the Boar's Head there.[9] It or its successor was the fourth building east from the corner of Hog Lane in 1676 and perhaps long before. Luckily, the properties along Whitechapel High Street from Hog Lane to the entrance of the Boar's Head kept their north-south lines (except for the entrance itself, which eventually disappeared) from then until the latter part of the nineteenth century, and one such line still exists. The site of Browne's building was no. 145 when the properties in the High Street came to be numbered in the eighteenth century, and it remained so until modern times. The sites of the three buildings between it and the corner of Hog Lane, none of which belonged to the Boar's Head, were nos. 146, 147, and 148. The sites of the buildings belonging to the Boar's Head were nos. 141, 142, 143, and 144. The back garden of Browne's building had the southern part of the Boar's Head yard on its eastern side and the central part on its northern one. So, in buying the central part of the yard of the Boar's Head, Browne bought the land just over his back garden wall.

By selling the central part of the yard to Browne and Rowley and, probably, the southern part to someone else, Poley cut off much of the Boar's Head from the old entrance in Whitechapel High Street. He had, therefore, to provide a new way for people, especially, Needler, to get into and out of the northern end of the place. He did this by opening, or having one of his unknown purchasers open, an alley from Hog Lane east across the top of the central part of the yard and into the northern part of the yard. It remained a piece of the public highway until 1882, and both Browne and Needler specifically had the use of it, Browne at least partly because the alley that he was to make was to lead into it. I call it Needler's alley, though he did not build it nor did it touch any of his property. I call the other alley Browne's.

Poley's reorganization of the Boar's Head meant among other things that only the southern end of the place could still be described as in Whitechapel High Street. The rest was henceforth in Hog Lane, or Petticoat Lane as that thoroughfare became known. It also meant, of course, that if the old Boar's Head had died in 1616 and had been pronounced dead in the enfranchise-ment of 1618, it was buried in Poley's transactions of 1621.

William Browne passed some copyhold lands in Whitechapel to his heirs in 1630. He wrote his will in 1633, "sicke in body by reason of age," where he described his part of the Boar's Head as "my said lands Tenem^ts and houses in the Boars head yard in the parish of White Chappell." They must have been worth at least the £12 a year that his heir had to pay various legatees out of the income from them. He died a year later, leaving his free-hold properties in Whitechapel to his nephew, John Browne,[10] who sold them in 1637, describing those in the Boar's Head, it seems, as one messuage (his uncle's part of the eastern building?) and nine cottages (new structures on the site of the stage and tiring house?). Robert Dixon and Humphrey Browne bought the premises in the Boar's Head and Thomas Abraham the messuage and garden in the High Street.[11]

Needler, on the other hand, soon overreached himself. He leased property immediately north of the Boar's Head in 1625 to John Needler, tiler and bricklayer, for 205 years.[12] He mortgaged eight houses in or near the Boar's Head in 1632 for £250 and in 1637 for £150 more. The man who provided Needler the money, along with another £600 on a property in Kent, was Nicholas Parker, merchant tailor. In the mortgage, the houses are "Eight mesuages or Tenements now in thoccupacion of the said Thomas [Needler] . . . in or neere a Courte ground or place commonly called the Boares head." Poley seems to have referred to the northern part of the yard, which he left open and public, as the courtyard. Needler kept up the interest payments, but he died in 1650 still unable to pay the principal. His widow turned the keys over to Parker's son and heir, Francis, in 1651 so that he might manage the houses and take interest and principal out of the rents. Needler's son, Samuel, and his grandson, another Samuel, sued Francis Parker in 1658 and 1659 to get the houses back, having found that they were then worth more to sell than was owing on the mortgage.[13] In these lawsuits, the houses are repeatedly described as in Boar's Head Alley, perhaps that passage shown in Ogilby and Morgan's map of 1676 as running along the eastern side of the eastern building.[14]

The first reliable sight we have of the Boar's Head we owe to the great fire of London of 1666. No map before then shows the suburbs east of the City accurately if one is curious about matters more particular than such things as the layout of the main thoroughfares. Soon after the fire, the City hired a group of surveyors to make the first accurate map of London. They finished early in 1667. Their map was not printed and is probably lost, but Wenceslaus Hollar drew and published a picture map in 1667 based on it and, it seems, on an abortive "Great Map of the City" that he had been divising since 1660.[15] The Boar's Head, unburned in the fire, appears on the right-hand edge of Hollar's map, forty-five years after the deeds of 1621. Because of Hollar's scheme of perspective and his purpose, which apparently was not to be accurate in a detailed way about ordinary buildings, one probably cannot depend on his map for the size, shape, and number of buildings in the Boar's Head, much less for accurate dimensions. It must, however, be suggestive.

The fire eventually produced a much better map for our purposes, that of John Ogilby and William Morgan, begun in 1673 and printed in 1676.[16] It is not a picture map but a flat one of the modern kind. It is incomparably the best map of London at least until Horwood's in the 1790s. Ogilby and Morgan tried to show not just every street and lane, but every yard and every building, every property line and even important divisions of buildings. Their scale was huge, 100' to the inch. They took elaborate pains to get their measurements and angles right. But they did their work when surveying on such a scale was in its infancy, and some of the information they show may be guesswork. Still, what survived around the Boar's Head until the first large-scale Ordnance Survey maps, like the little that survives yet, was and is close to what Ogilby and Morgan show. On sheet 15 (the one that shows the Boar's Head), at least, they seem often to have been accurate to 6% or 7% or better in their measurements, and probably they were at least reasonably accurate about the old yard of the Boar's Head.

In both Hollar's map and Ogilby and Morgan's, the eastern building still forms the whole eastern line of the yard, and in both the northern part of the yard is open and has two buildings on its western side. Otherwise, the two maps generally differ. Hollar shows Needler's part of the Boar's Head as mostly open space and Browne's part of the yard also as open space. Ogilby and Morgan, however, show both places covered with buildings and small yards, and this scheme of things must be close to the truth. In the central part of the yard, for example, Ogilby and Morgan show nine small holdings and an alley leading to them, along with a narrow rectangle of property that should be Rowley's, and a narrow strip of open land beside the eastern building—all more than reminiscent of Browne's deed and his nephew's sale. Ogilby and Morgan show Needler's alley lying where the deeds suggest and later maps specify that it did, leading straight from Hog Lane into the northern part of the yard. Hollar shows it farther south and apparently leading into the central part of the yard.

In the High Street, Ogilby and Morgan also show what later maps do—eight buildings from Hog Lane east to the end of the Boar's Head and the old entrance to the Boar's Head still open among them. They show the eastern four of these buildings as having either the eastern building or the yard behind them, rather than gardens of their own. Hence they suggest what must be right, that these were the four that, as the old lawsuits specify, once belonged to the Boar's Head. Hollar shows no entrance in the High Street and only six buildings from Hog Lane to the end of the Boar's Head, none with gardens behind them. The easternmost of the six is about as wide as three of the others, and it could represent the four once belonging to the Boar's Head; the ridge pole of its roof runs east and west rather than north and south as most of the other ridge poles along the High Street do.

Being a picture map, Hollar's shows some things that Ogilby and Morgan's cannot. His eastern building is actually two buildings joined end to end, the ridge poles of their roofs running north and south. The ridge poles of the roofs of his two buildings beside the northern part of the yard run east and west. His buildings in the High Street, his eastern building, and his two beside the northern part of the yard are all of two main stories, as they are in the lawsuits sixty-five years before.

Evidently, the redevelopment of the Boar's Head suggested in Browne's and Needler's deeds was carried out and still largely obtained there fifty-five years later. In 1676, the eastern building was probably the ancient one, and the buildings on the western side of the northern part of the yard and those in the High Street may have been. One building in the place in Elizabethan times, however, was gone: the great barn that according to the lawsuits had stretched west from the northern end of the eastern building and so formed the northern side of the northern part of the yard. For in their different ways neither Hollar nor Ogilby and Morgan show it.

CHAPTER 10

1676–Present

One should not stop the pursuit of the Boar's Head playhouse with Ogilby and Morgan's map. The history of the site from that time to the present contributes significantly to what we know about the playhouse by, for example, defining some of the earlier evidence, like Thomas Needler's deed and the map. Ultimately it reveals exactly where in the London of our time the playhouse was. It also provides a minor piece of urban sociology.

The quest for the playhouse would probably be easier if we had the documents by which Poley disposed of the parts of the Boar's Head that William Browne and Thomas Needler did not acquire. I have not been able to find any of them nor, except for a few scraps about Browne's part, any documents by which anybody else disposed of parts of the Boar's Head during the seventeenth century. I have, however, found deeds for both Browne's and Needler's parts beginning in the 1720s: a run of deeds for Browne's part from 1723 to 1786 and a run of deeds for Needler's part from 1721 to 1882. I have also found deeds for the entry on Whitechapel High Street and the eastern building behind it from 1781 to 1882, and some titles for the whole site from 1882 to the present. Though even the oldest of these documents was drawn up a hundred years after Browne's and Needler's deeds, they prove instructive. Let us begin with Needler's property, because the evidence about it is clearest.

All Thomas Needler's pieces of the Boar's Head fell into the hands of a French weaver of Spitalfields, Adrian Denise. Presumably, that would have been after the revocation of the Edict of Nantes in 1685, which prompted many men like him to settle in such places as Spitalfields and Whitechapel. Denise also acquired the property north of the Boar's Head that Needler had leased to John Needler in 1625 for 205 years. This collecting of Needler's pieces probably caused the Boar's Head to be extended northward. For the yard north of the Boar's Head, which Ogilby and Morgan show as Tripe Yard, was part of Boar's Head Yard by the time of Rocque's map (1746). Someone had narrowed the old entry to Tripe Yard, which was on the northern side and led to an alley running westward into Hog (now Petticoat) Lane, and opened a new entry on the southern side leading into the Boar's Head. The name, Tripe Yard, continued, but only for the alley into which the old entry had led.[1] By the nineteenth century the old entry had been closed off and a still newer one opened directly into Petticoat Lane. The entry into the Boar's Head remained, however, and the yard and its entries continued to share the name, Boar's Head Yard, with the surviving parts of the ancient yard of the Boar's Head until 1882.

Denise died early in 1721 or before, leaving his property in the Boar's Head to three children, John, Jane, and Mary Ann, and his property north of the Boar's Head to his executors for sale. Within eleven years, the Denise family had washed their hands of the Boar's Head. The children and the executors disposed of their pieces separately, but by 1749, ten transactions later, Sir Clifford William Philipps owned them all. He was "a noted justice of peace," as *The Gentleman's Magazine* (1754, p. 340) called him, who lived across Whitechapel High Street in Mansell Street. In these transactions, the piece of the Boar's Head that Needler had bought in 1621 is regularly described word for word as in Needler's deed. Also, two of Needler's other pieces of the northern end of the Boar's Head and his and John Needler's property on the other side of the northern boundary of the Boar's Head are described in language that must belong to the same times, for the people mentioned are also mentioned in the deeds of 1621.[2]

Sir Clifford William Philipps died in 1754, leaving his whole fiefdom in and north of the Boar's Head to his cousin, Sarah, the wife of the Rev. John Sarraude, rector of Sutton upon Derwent in Yorkshire.[3] She died before her husband, and he died in 1800, leaving the properties to his executors for sale. They sold them in 1802 to William Cordell, who already owned six houses next to the Boar's Head in Goulston Street.[4] Cordell died in 1826. He left his properties in and north of the Boar's Head together with those in Goulston Street not just to his children, but to their children as well. Presumably, these people suffered the property north of the Boar's Head to pass into other hands when Needler's lease ran out in 1830. They took the income from the rest of the place until 1860, when they set about selling it. Because they were by then scattered from Australia and New Zealand to Liverpool, it was not until 1865 that they could get the papers and a purchaser together.[5] He was the Rev. John Oakley, who owned the properties in the Boar's Head until 1879. Both the transaction of 1865 and that of 1879 were accompanied by maps that allow one to locate Needler's properties on modern maps.[6]

Unlike Needler's properties, Browne's part of the Boar's Head did not hang together very long, and the old deeds were soon abandoned as guides for new ones. None of the later descriptions of Browne's premises that I have found refers even by implication to the events of the seventeenth century, much less to Browne's deed of 1621. The language of that deed must have been thoroughly inappropriate by 1738 when the first of these appears (in a mortgage).

Browne had joined the central part of the yard and the adjacent section of the eastern building to a property in the High Street. Although his heir seems to have sold these pieces of the Boar's Head and the property in the High Street to different people, the logic of what Browne had done was irresistible. The owners of the slender properties in the High Street must have looked constantly over their back garden walls for a way to extend their properties, especially when what they owned in the High Street came to be business enterprises rather than houses. In the 1730s the people who paid taxes for nos. 145 (Browne's former property) and 146 Whitechapel High Street also paid taxes in the southern section of the Boar's Head. In 1740 no. 146 had an entrance through its back wall into the Boar's Head. From 1765 to 1783 the people who paid taxes for no. 145 paid also for a group of premises in the southern part of the Boar's Head, and from 1784 until well into the nineteenth century, it was the people who paid for no. 141 (the old entrance to the inn) who paid also for the same premises.[7]

Some decades after Browne's time, much of, if not all, the southern part of the Boar's Head belonged to William Gregory. John Oswin, a baker of Spitalfields, bought it as a freehold from Gregory, and when Oswin died in 1708, he left it to his four younger children, Amos, Katherine, Elizabeth, and Joseph. In his will Oswin wrote of having to pay the parish £2 a year for the poor out of his property in the Boar's Head, alluding to Browne's bequest in his will of 1633.[8] Oswin's son, Amos, apparently died young, so that the property was owned in three shares. Elizabeth, who remained a spinster, acquired Joseph's share in 1742.[9] Katherine married a man named Weston and had three sons, Richard, John, and Thomas, the first and last being clergymen. When Elizabeth Oswin died in 1766, she left her two shares to her nephews, Richard and John Weston.[10] After her death, the history of ownership becomes obscure. Thomas Weston probably had by then, or would soon have, his mother's share, for he began appearing in 1768 as owner of part of the place in the yearly tax returns. Richard Weston died in 1783, leaving his share to his brother, John, and John died in 1786, leaving his two shares to his daughter, Frances Brudenel Weston, who had married Joseph Sibley. Yet in 1781, Thomas Weston began appearing in the tax returns as owner of the whole place, and he continued to do so until 1797. He was replaced by Mary Long, spinster of Walthamstow, who owned no. 141 Whitechapel High Street as well.[11] Moreover, in 1801 and 1802 a Henry Sibley appears in the tax returns as owner of part of the property, and in 1807 Mary Long said in a deed that she had owned no. 141 in the High Street and the buildings in the Boar's Head behind it since at least 1781.[12] Those buildings would have been on the site of the old eastern building. One suspects that Mary Long was a relative of the Westons and Sibleys, and that the conflicting evidence is the result of some family arrangement.

Mary Long sold the southern part of the Boar's Head in at least two parcels. She sold no. 141 Whitechapel High Street and the buildings ranged behind it in 1807 to Joseph Ager, an apothecary and surgeon who had rented no. 141 from her since 1804. Ager's descendants sold these buildings in 1841 to William Thirtle, grazier of Wimbledon. In the 1870s the buildings belonged to Jane, wife of Edwin John White and probably daughter of Thirtle. She also owned no. 142 Whitechapel High Street and about two-thirds of the rest of the southern part of the Boar's Head, all of which she passed in 1880 to a trustee, George Thirtle.[13] The other third of the southern part of the Boar's Head went by this time with no. 145 in the High Street and lay behind that place and behinds nos. 146 and 147 as well. The piece belonged to people who certainly owned four houses adjoining it in Petticoat Lane and no doubt no. 145 Whitechapel High Street. They were Isaac Polley, Frederick Richards, and Sarah Fisher, widow, which is to say, probably, Sarah Fisher with the help of two trustees.[14]

As a result of Poley's sales, the Boar's Head became a tangle of small holdings, the northern group of them attached to the properties north of the Boar's Head and the rest attached to those south of it in the High Street. The dividing line was eventually the northern edge of the northern part of the yard. The site of the stage and tiring house in Ogilby and Morgan's map has no fewer than seven buildings, two open plots, and an alley. The 39′ 7″ of the stage front was room enough for the fronts of three buildings in a day when thousands of buildings in London were twelve or thirteen feet wide. Though the new entry from Petticoat Lane (which I call Needler's alley) had been created by Ogilby and Morgan's time (1676), the old one from Whitechapel High Street remained open at least until the end of the eighteenth century. The new one, at 8′ wide, was spacious compared to the old one at about half that in Ogilby and Morgan and later perhaps even less, for neither Rocque (1746) nor Horwood (1792–99) shows the old one. Once the new entry had been built, the Boar's Head was and long remained postally as well as proprietarily in two parts, that served by the new entry and that served by the old. But the two postal parts were not quite the same as the two proprietarial parts. One postal part comprised not only the northern section belonging to Needler and his successors but the places surrounding the northern part of the yard, including much of what had been Browne's property. These premises were usually given as in Boar's Head Yard, Petticoat Lane. The other postal part comprised only the southernmost places in the Boar's Head, given usually as in Boar's Head Alley, Whitechapel High Street.[15]

In Restoration times, the southern section of the Boar's Head began a long history of having to do with the making of tobacco pipes. In 1665 a Richard Price of Boar's Head Yard, Whitechapel, tobacco pipe maker, had to appear before the Middlesex justices because an apprentice, Anne Tutchbury, accused him "of tyeing her with a line by the wrists and thumbs upp to a beame and there [he] unreasonably beate her." Pipe makers paid taxes in the Oswins' part of the place in at least the 1730s and 1740s. A pipe maker's premises occupied part of the site of the eastern building (also, of course, in the Oswins' part) in the latter half of the eighteenth century, and from 1765 until 1784 a family named Price paid taxes for it.[16] From about 1743 until about 1779, much of the northern part of the place was a brewery, and from 1779 until well into the nineteenth century a hat dyer's works.[17]

The most lasting enterprise in the place, however, was religion. There was "a Meeting House or Place of Religious Worship" in Needler's part of the Boar's Head from at least 1723 until 1743, when it probably gave place to the brewery.[18] At the same time there was another, more durable one in Browne's part, called the Boar's Head Yard Meerting. In 1738, Elizabeth Oswin described it as "all that large Structure or building then [presumably in her father's time] and for many years before used for a Religious dissenting meeting House . . . and . . . all Rooms Vaults [and] Cellars under the same."[19] The place was an Independent meeting for many years, then an Anabaptist meeting from about 1765, and finally a Calvinist meeting in the nineteenth century. It is shown on Rocque's map (1746) as squarely, if perhaps uncomfortably, on the northern half of the site of the stage and tiring house, and it was still functioning in 1832, when it must have been one of the oldest dissenting churches in the country.[20] About when that enterprise ceased, yet another such began. For a synagogue occupied the upper floor of a building in the northern part of the Boar's Head from around the middle of the nineteenth century, or before, until 1882.[21] Perhaps a couple hundred years of organized religion atoned for whatever Browne and his fellows had done on the stage of the Boar's Head.

Late in the eighteenth century, such places as the Boar's Head were too small for manufacturing, so that Mary Long and the others set about doing what Sir John Poley had begun doing in 1616—turning the place back into a tangle of small residences. The pipe maker's premises and a brewer's warehouse then standing on the site of the eastern building became five small cottages in 1784, and a property nearby became five or six in 1804.[22] As the years went by, these places housed more and more people in increasingly unsanitary conditions, and most of the people were Jewish (the first person of Jewish name in the Boar's Head was Levi Moses, who appears in the tax returns as early as 1759).[23]

Through all this, probably not a stone of the inn or playhouse survived until 1882, but quite a few property lines did. One could still trace in 1882 much of the shape of the yard where the playhouse had been and even most of the site of the stage and tiring house. The lines of the northern half of Samwell's eastern building were probably those of the building there in 1882. The northern part of the yard was still open and had probably kept much of its shape, though the fronts of the buildings standing on its western side in 1882 might have been built a few feet behind where those of the buildings in Ogilby and Morgan had been—possibly to allow for a sidewalk in the yard and coincidentally to make that part of the yard a few feet wider than it had been. Otherwise, the lines of the buildings in 1882 might not have been much different from those of their Elizabethan predecessors (which had probably contained the hostry and the quarters of the Poleys). The properties along Whitechapel High Street were also within their old north-to-south lines, though their back fences had all marched northward into what had been the yard of the Boar's Head.

Most of the site of the stage and tiring house was traceable in 1882 because of Needler's and Browne's alleys. With Needler's alley, most of the north line of the stage and tiring house survived. Browne's alley itself (along the western side of the site) was half gone in Rocque's time (1746) and all gone in Horwood's (1792–99), but its eastern side, running north and south behind the western side of no. 146 Whitechapel High Street, is probably a property line in Rocque, because the Boar's Head Meeting lies alongside it, and probably a property line in Horwood. The same arrangement appears in much greater detail in a map drawn to accompany a surveyor's report of 15 June 1849 of the Metropolitan sewers in and around Goulston Street.[24] It was the best map of the area so far: to a large sacle (1:500) and the first detailed map since Ogilby and Morgan. It shows what a plan of William Browne's old premises, no. 145 Whitechapel High Street, to a vast scale (1:120) also makes clear in 1860.[25] The owners of that property had acquired all the land behind them to Needler's alley, and all the land behind nos. 146 and 147 to that alley as well. They had enlarged no. 145 by extending its western and eastern lines to Needler's alley and building between those lines a yard, two warehouses, and a stable. Behind no. 146 and beside their buildings behind no. 145, they had built a stable, a chaise house, another stable, and a "chaff" house. The western walls of these buildings kept to the eastern line of Browne's alley. By 1882 these buildings had been rebuilt and reorganized. One of the stables had been made into a house and sold to the Thirtles, and much of the rest had become a business called Adkins' Stables, though still owned, apparently, by the people who held no. 145 Whitechapel High Street.[26]

Enlightened government, at length, put an end to the Boar's Head. In 1875, Parliament passed the "Artisans and Labourers Dwellings Improvement Act," which encouraged cities to pull down slums and erect in their places ranges of flats for "the working class." London pounced on the Boar's

Head almost without waiting to breathe. The Metropolitan Board of Works condemned the place as unfit for habitation in 1875 and started legal proceedings in 1876 to seize virtually all of it, along with all its neighbors on the east, west, and north, and two of those on the south, nos. 147 and 148 Whitechapel High Street. Only the most southerly parts of the place escaped, and they did so because they belonged by now to nos. 141 to 146 Whitechapel High Street, which also escaped. The Board of Works held hearings in 1877 in which one witness said that "the locality is of extreme wretchedness containing abodes certainly unfit not only for . . . human beings, but even for dogs."[27] By 1882 the Board of Works had acquired the last properties. Oakley gave up Needler's parts of the place in 1879, and Jane White and Sarah Fisher gave up Browne's and other parts in 1882.[28] The Board of Works set about obliterating tangles of courts, alleys, passageways, and yards that had been breeding there since Transfeild's time, among them the strip that had served for access to the eastern building and its successors since William Browne's time, Needler's alley, the northern part of the Boar's Head yard, the yard north of that (which Ogilby and Morgan had called Tripe Yard), the passage between the two yards, and the entrance from Petticoat Lane (now Middlesex Street) to the more northerly one. In short, the Board of Works cleared the whole complex called Boar's Head Yard since Rocque's time, including every vestige of Transfeild's inn.

The Board of Works also cleared the first two buildings in Whitechapel High Street east of Middlesex Street (nos. 147 and 148). It used the land where they had stood and all the land in a line north of them along Middlesex Street, where the Boar's Head's neighbors on the west had once stood, to widen Middlesex Street.[29] The western line of no. 146 Whitechapel High Street, therefore, became the eastern line of Middlesex Street, and the Boar's Head site came to front that street. Hog Lane had moved over the Boar's Head. The Board of Works also cleared the two buildings in Whitechapel High Street east of Goulston Street and the premises north of them, in order to widen that street.

The Board of Works divided the land between Middlesex and Goulston Streets into, roughly, eastern and western halves. It built a great range of very solid and very typical council flats on the half along Goulston Street, some of which are still there. In 1884 and after, the city sold these buildings to people who agreed to keep them decent and use the property for nothing else for eighty years from 1884.[30] On the half along Middlesex Street, a vast warehouse appeared in the south and a row of private premises stretching north. The Board of Works built, finally, an alley between this warehouse and the properties along Whitechapel. It lay parallel to where Needler's alley had been and some 27' south.[31] The city called it Boar's Head Yard, an appropriate name because it ran over the southern half of the site of the stage and tiring house from Middlesex Street to a point about 3 or 4 feet into the site of the eastern building.

Soon after these operations, another arm of the city acquired most of what remained on Whitechapel High Street, nos. 140 to 144 (nos. 141 to 144 had once belonged to the Boar's Head), cleared the buildings away, and built there the Aldgate East station on the Metropolitan Railway. By 1894, only nos. 145 (the site of William Browne's house) and 146 survived as separate entities, with their south line and at least parts of their east and west lines as they had been in 1882 and, probably, for upward of three hundred yards before that.

This dispensation continued unchanged for half a century, nos. 145 and 146 Whitechapel High Street continuing to go by those numbers. What enlightened government had spared in 1882 and after, the Luftwaffe at last destroyed in 1940 and 1944, together with some of the council flats to the north and much else in the district. Everything where the Boar's Head had been and the whole frontage on the High Street (including the old Aldgate East station) were bombed flat. After the war, much of the place, including the site of the Boar's Head, was used for a car park for nearly twenty years, and the city's new alley, still called Boar's Head Yard, remained a piece of the King's highway leading into the place.[32]

In 1964, when, coincidentally, the eighty years exacted by the Board of Works were up, builders took the place in hand again, so far for the last time. The city acquired the sites of nos. 145 and 146 Whitechapel High Street and added to them the piece of the alley called Boar's Head Yard directly north and a piece of the site of the warehouse directly north of that. It used these pieces as the Board of Works had used nos. 147 and 148 in the High Street and the land north of them eighty years before—for the widening of Middlesex Street. The new widening, however, was mainly of the widewalk at the southern end of the street. North of that Middlesex Street and its sidewalk were realigned and widened again, but only marginally.[33] So a great new rectangle of sidewalk appeared extending north from the corner of Whitechapel High Street, in the middle of which is the spacious entry to a new subway for pedestrians under the High Street and Middlesex Street. If Hog Lane had moved over the western edge of the Boar's Head in 1882, a short stretch of it now moved over to the middle of the great yard. For the eastern line of no. 145 Whitechapel High Street, slightly straightened and extended north, is that of the fronts of the southernmost buildings now in Middlesex Street. Another result of this enterprise was that the alley called Boar's Head Yard disappeared, and with it the name Boar's Head from that corner of the kingdom after the better part of half a millennium.

One single-story shop went up in Goulston Street and three along what frontage remains in Whitechapel High Street between Middlesex and

Goulston Streets, the one on the corner of Middlesex Street being a clothier's. North of these shops rose a large building and a smaller one attached to it. The large building contains Cromlech House and United Standard House, the small one the premises of the Sheepskin and Leather Discount Centre. Cromlech House, which is in the north, is open at its street level, and it is here that the Petticoat Lane Market takes place on Sundays. United Standard House is in the south and lies over most of the site of the Boar's Head. Its southern extremity is a single-story appendage stretching along the new sidewalk in Middlesex Street to the clothier's on the corner of Whitechapel High Street. This appendage houses the Carpet Supermarket of the Mercantile Carpet Company.

These fronts on Middlesex Street of the clothier's and the Carpet Supermarket lie almost exactly along the ancient eastern line of William Browne's old property, no. 145 in the High Street.[34] If one may believe Browne's deed of 1621, Ogilby and Morgan's map of 1676, and the later maps I mention, that line runs through the whole length of Woodliffe's and Samwell's stage, parallel to the front edge and a few feet behind it. Where along that line does the 39' 7" of the stage begin and end?

The northern side of the stage lay along what became the southern side of Needler's alley. The plan of no. 145 Whitechapel High Street of 1860 shows the distance along the eastern line of that property from the front on the High Street to the southern side of Needler's alley as about 118' 6". The Ordnance Survey shows a few inches less, and Ogilby and Morgan show about a foot and a half less. The fronts on Whitechapel High Street did not change in the Ordance Survey maps of 1894, 1913, and 1938, nor in those of 1952 and 1971. Presumably, then, the southern side of the stage was about 79' and the northern side about 118' north of Whitechapel High Street along that line. The shops in Middlesex Street extend for about 147' from the High Street, the clothier's about 61' and then the Carpet Supermarket about 86'. The stage, therefore, lay along the front of the Carpet Supermarket from about 18' north of its southern end to about 58' north of that end. If anyone is minded to commemorate the third playhouse of the great queen's time, he may fix his plaque in the sidewalk in front of the Carpet Supermarket, 4' or 5' south of its center. For it was about here that Robert Browne, Will Kempe, Thomas Heywood, John Duke, John Lowin, Christopher Beeston, Thomas Greene, and their like for a time earned their living. The national grid reference for this spot would be about TQ33829/81309.

Looking at the site now, one cannot really bring himself to believe that it once contained, among other things, numerous dwellings, several sizable open places, a great barn, and a large stage with galleries on all four sides—especially when one remembers that he must subtract from the site the footage on the eastern side that once belonged not to the Boar's Head but to premises along Goulston Street.[35] Much of the Boar's Head and all its west ern neighbors are now, of course, part of Middlesex Street and its sidewalks. It is, however, the scale of things belonging to the last half of this century that renders the Elizabethan scale of things absurd. It is as unbelievable in the shadow of Cromlech House and its adjuncts that a man's castle could be 13′ square or even less, as it would have been in the shadow of the eastern building that men could live and work hundreds of feet in the air, or that a shop front could be 86′ long.

CHAPTER 11

The Yard in Which the Playhouse Was Built

A great deal of information survives to explain what both the playhouse in the Boar's Head and the rest of the place at the time were like, more for the playhouse than for any other public playhouse save the Fortune and, perhaps, the Hope. This information does not come from direct sources like contemporary pictures, maps, builders' contracts, or deeds, but mainly from three indirect and disparate sources. None the less, much of it is quite specific, and the numerous pieces fit readily into a coherent whole with very few (and no fatal) discrepancies. The indirectness and disparateness of the sources, therefore, must as a matter of logic help to establish the reliability of the information. The three sources are:

1. The lawsuits about the Boar's Head, which began in 1599 and ended in 1603;

2. William Browne's deed of 27 December 1621, with which he bought much of the part of the Boar's Head that had been used for the playhouse;

3. Ogilby and Morgan's map of 1676.

The lawsuits describe the function and location of various buildings of the Boar's Head, including those that stood around the yard, but give neither dimensions nor shapes. They also describe the transformation of the place into a primitive playhouse in 1598 and into a regular public playhouse in 1599 fit to compete with the Curtain, Globe, and Fortune; and they explain the contractual arrangements between the two owners and between them and the players. The deed gives some of the dimensions of the part of the yard in which the playhouse had mainly been, and specifically those of the plot of ground on which the stage and tiring house had stood. It only hints, however, at the nature of adjacent buildings and at the shapes of things in general, and it was written after much of the playhouse had been pulled down. The map shows nothing of the playhouse, but it does show buildings, dimensions, and shapes in the part of the Boar's Head where the playhouse had been. Where its dimensions are for things also measured in the deed, the two figures are similar. The map shows the place as it was sixty years after the playhouse and fifty-five after the deed, by which time some things there—fewer, it seems, than we might have expected—had changed. None of these sources of information on its own can be used to define substantially and in detail what the playhouse was like, but the three together can be.

We must first find what those parts of the inn were like among which the playhouse was built. As the lawsuits explain, the Boar's Head playhouse was not a single free-standing building, like the Globe, Fortune, and others, but, except for the stage, mostly a scheme of additions and alterations to existing buildings originally meant for very different uses.

The lawsuits contain six summaries of what stood on the Boar's Head property before the playhouse was built. Two describe the place briefly as it was when Oliver Woodliffe leased nearly all of it from the Poleys in 1594. One describes even more briefly and three describe at length the major part that the elder Richard Samwell leased from Woodliffe in 1598. These summaries probably relate to, even quote, the summaries that would have appeared in the two leases. They must be reliable, because they were presented in courts that could and probably did see the leases. Moreover, people sharply at odds with one another about much else agreed about these summaries.

The elder Samwell declared in April 1600 that at the time of the Woodliffe-Poley lease six years before, the Boar's Head had consisted of the following: "edyfyces Barnes buyldings stables yardes wayes and passages wth the appurtenances vsed wth the said" Boar's Head, "together wth one garden and Backyarde occupied and vsed to and w^th" the Boar's Head, "together wth the wayes and passages occupied wth the said garden and yarde." Woodliffe agreed with the summary a month later and used another very like it himself in May 1603. Both, obviously, are too general to be much use here. In the same document of April 1600, Samwell described his own part of the Boar's Head as "diuerse Chambers a Hall an Hostry a Barne and diuerse stables a Pryvy and the said Gardeyne and Back yarde." Despite his brevity, Samwell made one point here that appears nowhere else—there was a privy in his part of the Boar's Head—and clarified another left doubtful by longer summaries—the whole of the great barn belonged to him and not just its eastern end.[1]

The three longer summaries are admirable for our purpose. They are nearly identical, sometimes even in spelling, though presented by people on opposite sides of the quarrels about the Boar's Head: Robert Browne (in June 1601); his ally, the younger Richard Samwell (also in June 1601); and their foe, Woodliffe (in May 1603). They describe the elder Samwell's part of the Boar's Head systematically, beginning with the buildings in Whitechapel High Street and proceeding to those lying around the yard behind. The method is counterclockwise. The buildings in the High Street are described from west to east and those around the yard on the eastern side first, then the northern side, and finally the western side. As the younger Samwell put it in the best of these summaries, his father's part of the Boar's Head included along the High Street, "a hall, parlo^r and kitchin being of one flower wth a celler vnderneath part of the hall, twoo chambers ou^{er} the said hall a chamber ou^{er} the kitchin, a chamber ou^{er} the entry going into the said Inne, on the west side of the same entrye and on the east side thereof [for "thereof," the other two summaries helpfully read "of the yarde"] a roome to drinke in three parlo^{rs} a celler & three stables, one gallery wth seven seuerall chambers or roomes ou^{er} the said drinking roome parlo^{rs} Cellors & stables together wth the east end of the barne [Woodliffe has "great barne"] there, and on the west side of the said yarde [Woodliffe has "great yarde"] the ostry wth a lofte ou^{er} yt to laye hay in, one back roome behinde the said ostrye and a stable vnder the twoo houses or roomes (wch were reserved by the said Mrs Pooley) and also one garden & one back yard to lay dunge in."[2]

These three summaries were not much concerned, of course, with the parts of the Boar's Head that Woodliffe had not leased to Samwell—the two "houses or roomes" of the Poleys alluded to in the summaries, the yard, and a place on the western side of the yard, apparently south of the Poleys' quarters. This place seems to have included an area where Woodliffe meant to build a residence for himself; it certainly included structures that, as we shall see, he used in the building of his western gallery and the tiring house. Samwell called these structures "Romes by the yard" (in February 1600) and "certeyne Romes" adjoining the yard (in April 1600). Woodliffe called them "the Larder the Larder parler the well parler the Cole house the oate loaft" in May 1603, after he had improved them. They must have amounted to a building of two stories (because it had a "loaft")—perhaps a larder, a room with a well, and a coal storage on the ground floor, and a parlor over the larder, another over the well, and an oat loft over the coal storage.[3]

According to the lawsuits, then, along Whitechapel High Street was a row of two-story buildings. Beginning in the west they had on their ground floors a hall, a parlor, and a kitchen and on their upper floors three chambers. These structures, as we have seen, probably stood on plots that from the eighteenth century until World War II were numbered 144, 143, and 142 Whitechapel High Street. Then came the entry to the inn with a chamber above. Beside the entry was another two-story structure that was not, like the hall, parlor, and kitchen, part of a row of buildings along the High Street, but the southern end of a building that stretched northward, at a right angle to the High Street, and, in effect, faced the yard rather than the High Street. Its southern end and the entry occupied the plot that was eventually numbered 141 Whitechapel High Street. It was a long building that formed the whole eastern line of the yard and, presumably, most of the eastern boundary of the Boar's Head itself. Beginning in the High Street, it contained on the ground floor a drinking room, three parlors (into one of which the Woodliffes moved), a cellar, and three stables. On the upper floor were seven chambers and a gallery running the whole length of the building (save, no doubt, where the room over the entrance was), along which people must have walked to get to the chambers. Several witnesses in the lawsuits called that gallery in 1600 the "long" gallery. The premises in the High Street must have been where the innholder fed his guests and the eastern building where he mainly housed and entertained them.

Because the northern end of the eastern building was associated with the eastern end of the great barn, that barn must have stretched east and west; and it must have formed the northern line of the yard. Several more two-storey buildings stood along the western side of the yard. Presumably beginning in the north, these were first the hostry, with a loft over it and a room behind,[4] and then premises that housed the Poleys above and had a stable below. Next must have come Woodliffe's "certeyne Romes." The garden and backyard for dung could have been south of these "Romes," more or less behind the buildings in the High Street west of the entry. Or perhaps at least the backyard for dung was at the end of the summaries because it was a miscellaneous item rather than part of the systematic description of buildings and so was elsewhere in the inn—north of the yard, for example, near the great barn.

Two deeds of 1621 and two eighteenth-century quotations from other deeds of about the same time survive to explain what the Boar's Head was like when Sir John Poley disposed of it.[5] If, however, we are trying to define not the whole Boar's Head but the yard and adjacent buildings, which in turn defined much of the playhouse, we may ignore both quotations and most of one of the deeds. They describe, as we have seen, the parts of the property that Thomas Needler acquired, extending from the northern line of the yard to the northern line of the Boar's Head. The deed to which we must attend closely is William Browne's.

Before laying Needler's deed aside, however, we must notice that several of its provisions allude to the yard as it was in 1621. The northern part of the yard duly appears as adjacent to part of his property. It is called simply "the Court yard" several times. The word "Court" implies that in 1621 the northern part of the yard was rather small, roughly quadrangular, and surrounded by places not for common use. That part of the yard itself, however, was to remain unsold and open, and Needler was to have the right to come and go through it. Or, as his deed has it, he could "at all tyme & tymes hereafter with carte & carriage . . . passe & repasse . . . by the said Court or common yard of the said Boares head." We have seen that it remained a public thoroughfare until 1882.

William Browne's deed, put simply, explains that he was buying eight "roomes & dwelling places" in the Boar's Head and two pieces of the yard. These premises were evidently part of a single scheme, for, according to the deed, at least two of the rooms and dwelling places were adjacent to one of the pieces of the yard, and that piece was at least for a short distance adjacent to the other piece. Hence, to locate one of the premises is probably to locate the others, indeed to locate the playhouse, because the deed has it that the stage and tiring house had stood on one of the pieces of the yard.

Browne's eight rooms and dwelling places comprised six described as such, plus "one roome called a chamber roome" built over one of the rooms and dwelling places and another "roome" evidently related to them but in an unspecified way. Or as the deed describes them: "All those severall roomes & dwelling places parcell of . . . the Boares head as the[y] now be or late were in the seuerall possessions of Elizabeth Mitchell widowe John younge John Price William Bowyer Thomas Gawen Nicholas Jones together with one roome called a chamber roome builded over the tenemente wherein the said Elizabeth Mitchell now dwelleth now or late in the possession of Roger Meggs together alsoe with one roome late in the occupacion of one ffrancis Pleyvie." That these premises are not described as buildings, edifices, messuages, houses, or cottages suggests that they were not buildings on their own but parts of a large building, and that the large building contained other parts that Browne did not buy. Because the deed says nothing of the High Street, these premises were not parts of the Boar's Head buildings there. What other building in the Boar's Head could have had so many significant parts? Only, surely, the long eastern building described in the lawsuits.[6]

One of Browne's pieces of the yard is described in his deed as 53' from the south side of the widow Mitchell's section of this building "right downe into the said Boares head yard," evidently north to south. For we are told next that at the bottom of the 53' the piece was 22'5" "in bredth . . . east vnto the west." At this southwestern corner, the piece met the northern end of a garden that Browne already owned. Otherwise the deed is silent about what lay at the sides of the piece, and it is also silent about its shape. Browne's other piece of the yard was that on which the stage and tiring house had been. It was 36'6" "in breadth," east to west, and 39'7" north to south. Its southern side was "next" to Browne's garden and its eastern side to a strip of the yard that Samuel Rowley had already bought. The deed describes this second piece as "soe much of the said Boares head ground As lately was builded & knowne for a tyreing house or Stage & twoe tenements late in the severall occupacions of humphrey Plevy & John Walford and haue ben lately pulled downe to be reedified and builded in a better forme." It measured "at the north end . . . in breadth from the pale belonging to the Coppyhold tenements of Samuell Rowley west . . . thirty six foote & a halfe of assize & in breadth at the south end next the garden of the said William Browne the like assize . . . & . . . on the east & west side thereof thirty nyne foote & seauen ynches." (I shall say more about the "north end" in a moment.)

For a start, these descriptions of Browne's two pieces of the yard confirm the implication of the lawsuits that the yard lay beside and west of the eastern building, since the measurement north to south of his first piece begins at a section of what must be the eastern building and the other measurement specifically extends east to west. The two pieces were roughly in a line east to west, because both had the northern end of Browne's garden just south of them. The first piece was the eastern one, because it was beside the eastern building, and the second, that on which the stage and tiring house had stood, was the western one. Here the lawsuits are confirmed again, for they put the buildings in which the tiring house was on the western side of the yard. Because the eastern piece measured 53' north to south and the two together at least 59' (22'5" + 36'6") east to west, they belonged to a part of the yard surely much bigger in both directions than the part that Needler's deed says was to remain unsold and open. Being for Needler's use, this smaller part should have been the northern end of the yard; hence the part out of which Browne's pieces were taken should have been south of it.

That garden of Browne's lying west of his eastern piece of the yard and immediately south of both his pieces is a clue not only to which part of the yard his pieces were in but, among other things, to how it was that he arrived in the Boar's Head in the first place. If Browne's pieces could not be in a northern part of the yard, and if one of them measured 53' north to south, a garden south of them must have been near the High Street. Such a garden would have to be the back garden of a building in the High Street. If Browne already owned the garden, he already owned the building to which it belonged.[7] If the garden was at the back of a building in the High Street, the building was not one of the buildings there belonging to the Boar's Head, because presumably they would have had part of the yard behind them, not individual gardens. If the building did not belong to the Boar's Head, and if its garden was west of Browne's eastern piece of the yard (as his deed says), it was the building immediately west of the Boar's Head buildings, on the property eventually numbered 145 Whitechapel High Street. Because Browne's two pieces of the yard were north of this garden, they were in a central part of the yard, and this central part extended farther west than the part of the yard south of it.

So the yard of the Boar's Head consisted of a small northern part that remained open, a small southern part behind the Boar's Head buildings in the High Street, and a bigger central part that extended farther west than the others. The playhouse had been in the central part. In buying the two pieces of the yard described in his deed, Browne was investing in the property on the other side of his back garden wall.

How did these two pieces of Browne's relate to one another and to the rest of the inn? Since the deed does not explicitly say what lay alongside the eastern piece, the information is probably implied in the descriptions of the rest of his property in the Boar's Head—his sections of the building and his other piece of the yard. These descriptions suggest that the eastern piece was shaped like a backward L, the upright (53' long) lying between Browne's sections of the eastern building (except for that of the widow Mitchell) on the east and Rowley's strip on the west, and the bottom extending west across the southern end of Rowley's strip to the garden Browne already owned and his other piece of the yard. Inside the L would have been Rowley's strip. Browne would have bought the upright for access to his sections of the eastern building. His other piece of the yard lay immediately west of the L and stretched to the western end of the Boar's Head, where, as we shall see, land was set aside on which he was to make an alley running north to south. Browne bought in his deed, that is, the central sections of the eastern building and the central part of the yard lying in front (west) of these sections, except for Rowley's strip, the space left in the west for his alley, and, as we shall also see, space left across the top of that part of the yard for another alley, this one running east to west. His 53' of the eastern piece could have begun south (hence not in front) of the widow Mitchell's section of the eastern building because that section did not need special access. Being the northernmost of his sections, perhaps it fronted the lower reaches of the northern part of the yard, which was to remain open.

Both alleys were necessary to the scheme for reorganizing the Boar's Head as envisaged in the deeds. Neither had existed in the time of the playhouse or even in 1621, since the deeds say that they were to be made not that they had been made. Both were to be 8' wide. One was to allow people having to do with the northern part of the Boar's Head, specifically the northern part of the yard, to get into and out of the place through a more or less public thoroughfare. Such people could not use the old entrance in Whitechapel High Street if Browne and Rowley owned a great segment of the central part of the yard stretching from the eastern building almost to the western end of the inn. This alley must have been mainly for Needler, and I call it Needler's alley. The other alley was to give Browne access to the buildings he was to put up where the stage and tiring house had been. I call it Browne's alley.

Needler's alley was to run east to west from the northern part of the yard out into Hog Lane. Evidently it occupied the northernmost 8' of the central part of the yard. The position of Browne's alley suggests as much, as we shall see, and so does that of the central part of the yard, whose western side would have been closer to Hog Lane than any other part of the Boar's Head. To the size north to south of Browne's western piece of the yard (39′7″), therefore, we should apparently add 8′ to find the size north to south of the central part of the yard. Needler was not to make the alley, nor was his property to touch it, but his deed explains it. He had the right to come and go "with carte and carriage" through the "Court or common yard of the said Boares head by & through a passage way of eight foote in widenesse to be made leading from the said Court yard west into the common way or streete called hoggelane." The court yard, as we have seen, was the northern part of the yard. Needler could use "the said way . . . into & from hogge lane aforesaid" forever. The alley was made and remained in public use until 1882.

Browne was both to build and maintain the other alley, but he was not to own the ground it would occupy. That ground had belonged to the place on which the stage (and presumably the tiring house) had stood, as had Browne's western piece of the central part of the yard. Browne's alley was to begin at Needler's alley and run north to south. Along its whole length it bordered Browne's western piece, as his deed clearly implies when it requires him not only to make and maintain the alley but to keep it "passageable" to an "altitude" of 9′. He could not prevent buildings being extended over the alley at any height unless the buildings were his, and the real purpose of the stipulation must have been to allow him to extend his buildings over the alley if the extensions were high enough. Coincidentally, unlike Needler's alley, Browne's is not said to be suitable for cart and carriage. It did not run along the eastern side of this piece of Browne's because his deed has Rowley's strip there. Nor did it run through the piece, because it would have divided the piece, the alley not belonging to Browne, and the deed would have said so. It ran, therefore, along the western side of the piece, and we may guess that it marked the western boundary of the Boar's Head. Since Browne did not own the alley, its width was not counted in the dimensions of the property he bought in his deed. So we must add 8′ to the size east to west (36′6″) of the piece of the yard on which the stage and tiring house had stood (= 44′6″).

Browne's deed is quite specific about this alley. "Except & alwaies reserued out of this bargaine & sale," it reads, "one passage way of the breadth of eight foote & from the ground the altitude of nyne foote to be made laid out & mayneteined passageable by the said William Browne . . . in & through the said parcell of ground where the stage was builte." It was to be "right discending from" Needler's alley, "the way alonge out of hogge lane to be made of equall breadth into the said Boares head yard." This is not the only time a north-to-south dimension is seen in the deed as extending downward. The north-to-south dimension of Browne's first (eastern) piece of the yard extends "right downe into" the yard. Browne was to "enioy free & quiett passage" through Needler's alley forever, as were Poley and his tenants through Browne's alley. Browne's alley was built, too. It disappeared as a passageway in the eighteenth century, but most of it remained as a property line to 1882.

The deeds also mention three parts of the Boar's Head that Needler, Browne, and other inhabitants shared: the pump, which was on Needler's property;[8] a watercourse used for carrying away waste, which ran through Needler's property and had its "sink" in the garden of John Needler to the north; and somewhere in the inn a piece of "wast ground," 39' on the east and west sides and 34' on the north and south sides.

These deeds, then, explain some important things. The playhouse was in the central part of the yard. That part was probably a good deal bigger than the northern or southern parts, because while all three had a common line on the east, the central one extended farther west than the others did. The central part had on its southern side not just the southern part of the yard but, farther west, the garden behind at least one of the buildings in the High Street that did not belong to the Boar's Head. The central part measured 66'11" east to west—22'5" belonging to Browne's eastern piece of it, 36'6" to his western piece, and 8' to his alley along the western side. Moreover, his western piece and the alley constituted the plot on which the stage and tiring house had been, so that the distance between the eastern side of the yard and the stage was 22'5", and that from the front of the stage to the western end of the property was 44'6".

The deeds do not, however, leave us bereft of questions, especially about the dimension of the central part of the yard, hence the playhouse, north to south. On its eastern side, this part could have measured 53' north to south, for Browne's eastern piece of it did. The plot where the stage and tiring house had stood measured 39'7" north to south, so that the stage measured that much across its front. (It is, incidentally, only the second professional stage of the time for which we have a measurement, that of the Fortune being the first.) The deeds say fairly clearly that Needler's alley (8' wide) was to be made between this plot and the northern side of the central part of the yard. Because we must suppose that the stage was centered in its part of the yard, we must guess that if there was 8' north of the stage there was 8' south of it. So we arrive at 55'7" for the dimension of the central part of the yard north to south along the two-thirds of it that lay west of the front of the stage. But what of the garden evidently belonging to a building in the High Street that Browne's deed firmly puts south of the stage plot rather than a strip of yard 8' wide? And how does 55'7" relate to 53'? Moreover, though suggesting in one place that Needler's alley was to be made north of the plot where the stage and tiring house had been, Browne's deed explains in another that the existing matter there was a dwelling, not a strip of land for an alley. The north side of the plot was "next the tenemente wherein Thomas Milles butcher now dwelleth" and extended from Rowley's fence "west to the corner of the said ten*emen*ts wherein the said Thomas Milles now dwelleth." Did Milles live in an 8'-wide structure between this plot and the former quarters of the Poleys, part of which had been the northern gallery of the playhouse? Whatever the structure, we must guess that eventually it was cleared away so that the alley could replace it.

We should turn, then, to Ogilby and Morgan's map seeking first to confirm the general scheme of the inn and its yard as found in the lawsuits and deeds. We should next look closely at the central part of the yard in which Browne's deed implies the playhouse was. We should look especially for the things that would define the plot on which Browne's deed says the stage and tiring house stood—the garden that his deed says he owned south of the plot, the alley that he was required to build on part of the plot, and Needler's alley out of which Browne's was to lead.

The map nicely confirms the general scheme. The eastern building, the three parts of the yard, and the buildings in the High Street are all on the map as the lawsuits and deeds would have them. The central part of the yard extends much farther west than the other two parts, so that the two pieces of the yard that Browne's deed has him buying could belong only to that part. Moreover, the central part of the yard is built over as Browne's deed, his will, and his heirs' transactions provide that it should have been. Above all, south of the plot on which the stage and tiring house would have stood, the map shows a garden. It is, as the deed suggests it should be, the one behind the building in the High Street just west of the four there that have the southern part of the yard or the eastern building behind them and hence belonged to the inn. Browne's alley is on the map, too, "right discending," as his deed says, along the western end of the Boar's Head. The alley turns east for a few feet toward its bottom to serve both the southern side of the plot on which the stage and tiring house must have been and the northern side of the garden—confirming, probably, that the two properties and the alley once had to do with the same man. Needler's alley is on the map exactly as the deeds suggest, running east to west through the top of the central part of the yard, and Browne's leads south from it. Because it became a property line in Browne's deed, the front of the stage is also on the map. So is Rowley's strip.

Except for one, the dimensions on the map are not greatly different from those given in the deeds. The dimensions north to south are somewhat bigger, at most 4.4%, and those east to west are usually smaller, at most 6.7%. Such differences over such distances are quite within what we should expect of the map and of our ability to measure it. A scarcely measurable distance on the map, like a sixty-fourth of an inch, works out to more than a foot and a half of actual real estate. Where a piece of ground is 22'5" wide, for example, a deviation of a sixty-fourth of an inch in the placement of the *two* defining lines on the map will produce an error of about 7.1%. Moreover, lines that probably should be parallel on the map rarely are exactly so.

For the dimensions north to south, the map does more than reasonably confirm the deeds. It probably solves our problem about the dimension north to south of the central part of the yard by showing the shape of what must have been Browne's garden south of the plot on which the stage and tiring house had been. The garden reaches into the central part of the yard about 8′ beyond the garden west of it. So we may well guess that before Browne bought the pieces of the central part of the yard described in his deed, he had bought a small piece to extend his garden northward about 8′.⁹ The map shows Needler's alley about as the deeds have it, occupying the northernmost 8′ of the central part of the yard and running straight west into Hog Lane. (In the Ordnance Survey map of 1848–50, the alley begins at about 10′5″ and narrows to about 7′3″.) Ogilby and Morgan show the plot on which the stage and tiring house had been as about 1′4″ more across the stage front than the 39′7″ given in Browne's deed (+3.4%), some 1′9″ more across the back of the stage (+4.4%). So in the time of the playhouse, the central part of the yard, hence the playhouse itself, very likely measured 55′7″ north to south, the distance taken up by the stage and strips of the yard 8′ wide north and south of it. The distance can be accurately measured on the map only across the middle of the stage, where it is about 2′3″ more (+4%).

What, then, of the 53′ that Browne's deed gives for the measurement north to south on the eastern side of this part of the yard? As we have seen, it was probably the length of a narrow piece of the yard along the eastern building and used for access to it. The map clearly shows such a piece. The deed has the 53′ reaching south to a point that was east of the northern "end" of Browne's garden. Perhaps the 53′ began at the northern line of Needler's alley and finished some 5′6″ south of the line of Browne's garden, "end" being understood in a general rather than a precise sense. The narrow piece was probably the ground under the gallery along the upper floor of the eastern building. On the map the piece is about 8′ wide.

While they also confirm Browne's deed in crucial ways, the dimensions east to west shown on the map for the central part of the yard create a problem. The distance from the eastern building to the eastern side of the plot on which the stage and tiring house had been is what one would expect. The deed gives it as 22′5″. On the map the distance is about 22′1″ in the north (−1.5%), about 20′11″ in the south (−6.7%). The plot of the stage and tiring house is 36′6″ east to west in the deed. On the map the distance in the north is about 36′2″ (−0.9%), about 37′4″ in the south (+2.3%). These northern measurements were easy for the mapmakers because they were between obvious points along an open alley. The southern ones, however, involved measuring through buildings and fenced-off properties. The problem concerns Browne's alley. The deed says that it was to be made 8′ wide and that the ground had been part of the plot of the stage and tiring house, so that the whole plot was 44'6" east to west. The map shows the alley as only about 4' wide, and it was the sort of thing that Ogilby and Morgan should have had no trouble measuring. They ought not to be wrong by 50%.

As we have seen, the ground on which Browne was to build the alley belonged not to him but to Poley. So he and his successors, in theory, at least, could not use half of it for their buildings. Could there have been less ground in the plot of the stage and tiring house than the makers of the deed thought, so that when Browne and his successors built their buildings they took the 36'6" of their deed and left only 4' for the alley? Or could Browne *et al.* have built upper stories over the alley (as they had the right to do) by 4', so that either the mapmakers measured from the overhang or by their time someone had illegally built under the overhang? It must be possible that the central part of the yard was only 63' east to west, not the 66'11" of the deed, and that the full plot of the stage and tiring house was 40'6" rather than 44'6". Ogilby and Morgan show the distance from the eastern building to the western side of Browne's alley as about 62'3" along Needler's alley and about 61'10" along Browne's garden, 7% and 7.6% less than the deed. Given the allowance that we must make for the map and our reading of it, however, and given that fifty-five years elapsed between the deeds and the map, we should use the map to confirm the deeds and add to them but not to alter them.

CHAPTER 12
The Playhouse Proper

When Woodliffe leased the Boar's Head in 1594 so that he might develop it as a playhouse, the place was an inn part of which had long been used for permanent residences. It comprised a group of four two-story buildings on the north side of Whitechapel High Street and behind them a great yard and other two-story buildings. The entrance was, in effect, through one of the buildings in the High Street. Much of the inn occupied the land behind the buildings strung around the corner of Hog Lane (later Petticoat Lane and now Middlesex Street) and the High Street. Except for those in the High Street that belonged to the Boar's Head, these buildings belonged to people who evidently had nothing to do with the inn in early times but who took a lively interest in the place as the years went by and, long after the days of the playhouse, came to own nearly all of it.

The great yard consisted of three adjacent parts all bounded on the east by the straight line of a long eastern building. There were a small part in the north, eventually called the court yard; a large one in the center stretching farther west than the others, where the playhouse mainly was; and another small one in the south, to which the entry led. The northern part had a great barn on its northern side and evidently the hostry and quarters of the Poleys on its western side. The central part had Woodliffe's "certeyne Romes" on its western side; on part of its southern side it had two of the gardens behind buildings in the High Street that did not belong to the Boar's Head. The southern part had one of these gardens on its western side and the backs of the Boar's Head buildings in the High Street on its southern side. (Here and throughout, I give these locations as they are in nearly all the evidence, but they are actually simplifications. Whitechapel High Street does not run east to west but northeast to southwest. The Boar's Head, therefore, lay not east and west, north and south, but northeast and southwest, northwest and southeast.)

The Boar's Head had commended itself to a company of players as early as 1557, but it did not become a playhouse, at least in any formal sense, until Woodliffe and his collaborator, Samwell, set about converting it in 1598. It became a playhouse partly because of where it was—just outside the City of London. It was accessible to a great many people who lived in London, yet it was a few feet beyond the ordinary jurisdiction of the lord mayor and his aldermen, which ended with the City in Hog Lane. It was not, however, outside their jurisdiction when they acted with the approval of the national government, as the players of 1557 found. It became a playhouse, too, because of its yard and some of the surrounding buildings.

The central part of the yard, it seems, was nearly square. As we have seen, the deeds of 1621 make it about 67' east to west, from the eastern building to the western end of the property, but from this figure we must substract the width of Woodliffe's "certeyne Romes" along the western side, perhaps 12'6" as I shall explain in a moment.[1] It measured 55'7" north to south, according to the deeds and a suggestion in Ogilby and Morgan's map. So the central part of the yard measured some 54'6" east to west and some 55'7" north to south, more in area than the room in which the Second Blackfriars had just been built and almost exactly the same as the yard soon to appear at the Fortune (55' square). Woodliffe and Samwell would have seen the central part of the yard of the Boar's Head as big enough for an Elizabethan theatrical enterprise.

The deeds say nothing about the size of the northern and southern parts of the yard, but the map shows the northern one as about 30'6" square and the southern one as about 35'4" along the eastern building and 27'9" east to west. The whole yard, then, stretched perhaps 121'5" along the eastern building (the map shows about 122'10"—+1.2%), and its central part was a good deal bigger both north to south and east to west than the two extremities. Other inns in Whitechapel High Street have yards of similar shape on Ogilby and Morgan's map, like the Blue Boar (in which Robert Miles, one of the disputants at the Theatre, had a share),[2] but by 1676, at least, their dimensions east to west were smaller.

The Boar's Head had at least one other prime inducement to drama. Along the whole length of the upper floor of the eastern building was a gallery giving access to the rooms on that floor. It suggested a theatrical gallery, and it may have been as wide as about 5'. The inn had other useful amenities from a theatrical point of view, like a privy, "a roome to drinke in," and places for cooking and dining.

In such a yard as that of the Boar's Head, it is obvious why Woodliffe meant that the playhouse should be mainly in the central part and why he kept the western side of it for his tiring house. The northern and southern extremities were too narrow for an Elizabethan stage, much less for the usual arrangement of stage and "wedges" of the yard at left and right for spectators. Moreover, had Woodliffe put his stage at either extremity, some customers would have been nearly a hundred feet away, and much of the gallery along the eastern building, together with a great piece of the central part, would have been useless for spectators. By putting his tiring house on the western side of the central part, he made the best use of the gallery. By putting the stage in the central part he had much more room for it, and he provided that people in all three parts could see at least a significant share of it and none of them from much more than 40' away.

When in the summer of 1598 Woodliffe and Samwell converted the Boar's Head into a rudimentary playhouse, Woodliffe had a roofed gallery built along his "certeyne Romes."[3] It was, of course, on the western side of the central part of the yard, facing the existing gallery along the eastern building, and it was for spectators. In a codicil to their lease, he and Samwell had agreed that he would have 3' of the yard "nere adioyninge to" his certain rooms "to buyld on." Hence, probably, the gallery was only 3' deep, and the space under it could not be considered part of the yard. Either, that is, the space under the gallery was boxed in and made part of the certain rooms, or the gallery was too low for people to walk under it. As for the certain rooms themselves, they became, among other things, Woodliffe's tiring house.

Woodliffe also had a large stage built in the middle of the central part of the yard, placed like a boxing ring. The stage measured 39'7" across its front (north to south), according to William Browne's deed of 1621. If, as we shall soon see, the stage might have been about 25' east to west, the "certeyne Romes" about 12'6", and the existing eastern gallery about 5', the stage would have been about 11'5" in front of that gallery and about 10' in front of the western one. It would have been about 16'5" in front of the eastern building itself and 13' in front of the "certeyne Romes." The stage was about 8' from the northern and southern sides of the central part of the yard. It may well have lacked a roof, hence pillars and machinery above for flying people and things onto and off it. Professor Wickham has recently argued that before 1595 or so stages generally lacked such things.[4]

Writers have occasionally speculated that stages were placed like boxing rings in inn yards,[5] but the stage at the Boar's Head in 1598 is the first anywhere that we have found clearly placed so. Moreover, though the Boar's Head was an inn, it was being converted into a public playhouse, and its stage was no portable thing carried by migrant players from inn to inn. Presumably spectators stood all around the stage, and presumably actors and props got through these spectators from their tiring house to the stage, but of how there is no hint. Perhaps they used a long ramp. In placing their stage, Woodliffe and Samwell may have been thinking of putting on such things as boxing matches and fencing exhibitions as well as plays. Mainly, however, they must have been thinking of getting the stage far enough east so that the northern and southern parts of the yard would be suitable for spectators. Given that those parts were as Ogilby and Morgan show them, even the most disadvantageously placed people there could see the front two-thirds or so of the stage as it was in 1598. The number of people who could be induced to pay their money to watch from the yard was no doubt very important, because Woodliffe and Samwell were building tiny and primitive galleries.

Samwell built galleries of his own along the northern and southern sides of the central part of the yard, hence along the sides of the stage. They may have been 3' deep to match Woodliffe's western gallery, a figure that seems about right in view of the 8' available for each and the extensions made to them later. Both these galleries stood well above the yard on posts so that they did not diminish the amount of the yard available for spectators. The existing gallery along the upper story of the eastern building became Samwell's eastern gallery and, probably, the main gallery of the playhouse. His northern and southern galleries probably abutted Woodliffe's gallery at their western ends (eventually they certainly did) and led into the eastern gallery. Samwell meant to build another gallery over the eastern one, but probably because such a project would involve complicated engineering and be expensive, he put if off. Whether any of Samwell's galleries of 1598 had roofs does not appear, though Woodliffe's western gallery certainly did. The playhouse of 1598 was primitive and evidently cost considerably less than £100 to build.[6] Samwell's son described his father's structures of 1598 four times as "little galleryes" and, lest we equate them with theatrical galleries of later times, once as "certeine galleryes or roomes for people to stand in to see the playes."

A year later, in 1599, Woodliffe and Samwell pulled down the playhouse of 1598 and put up a new playhouse fit to compete with that playhouse just opened across the water, the Globe. They spent something like the amount soon spent on another competitor, the Fortune, £520. The four galleries of 1598 were replaced by four bigger and no doubt better galleries, and Samwell built his upper eastern gallery, so that there were now two galleries on the eastern side. Woodliffe moved his stage westward so that it adjoined his tiring house, and he built a roof over the stage. A boxing ring may have been allowable in a primitive playhouse but not, it seems, in one of the great playhouses of the time. Woodliffe and Samwell must have agreed that the players needed the solid backdrop of the tiring house with its doors and arras for entrances, exits, and discoveries.

Woodliffe's new western gallery was 4' deeper than the old one, hence 7' deep. It was well above the stage. Like its predecessor, it had a roof and was for spectators. The space under it must have been boxed in and stage doors made in front. That space must have been an extension of the "certeyne Romes" and so an enlargement of the tiring house. Evidently the tiring house comprised two of the certain rooms. It was below the gallery, hence probably had nothing to do with places on the upper story of the certain rooms. In 1603 three people who should have known about these things described them often. They were Robert Browne, who led the company playing in the playhouse; John Mago, the builder who directed its building; and John Marsh, a carpenter who worked in its building. The three of them referred about nineteen times to the western gallery as "over the stage," and Mago referred to it once as "the galleryes ou*er* & about the stage." Marsh could be more exact. He spoke of it as "the galleryes ou*er* the stage," and then, to distinguish it no doubt from Samwell's galleries, which were, in a sense, also over the stage, he had his examiner add as an interlineation, "& at one end of the stage"—the back end, surely. The three men referred about twenty-three times to the tiring house in the plural, tiring houses, but Browne referred twice to "the Tyringe howses or eyther of them." Browne, finally, described the western gallery as "the galleryes over the Tyringe howses."[7]

Woodliffe did not dismantle and rebuild his stage in 1599 but moved it as it was 6' westward. This information, together with the information that his gallery was 7' deep (east to west), leads us to a fair idea of the main dimensions east to west of the playhouse both in 1598 and in 1599 and afterward. William Browne's deed of 1621 measures the central part of the yard as 66'11" from the eastern building to the western end of the property. It gives 22'5" as the distance from the eastern building west to the front of the stage in the rebuilt playhouse, and 44'6" as that east to west of the plot on which the stage and tiring house stood. How much of this last figure was stage and how much tiring house? If the "certeyne Romes," in which the tiring house mainly was, had a gallery 7' deep along the eastern side from 1599, the amount of land available for the stage and the certain rooms without the gallery was 37'6". The stage measured 39'7" north to south. The proportion of width to depth used at the Fortune was 8:5 (43' × 27'6"). If the same proportion was used at the Boar's Head, its stage was about 25' deep (east to west), and that figure seems right for another reason. It leaves 12'6" east to west for the certain rooms without their gallery, about what we should expect of an Elizabethan structure meant as an outbuilding to contain a larder, a well, and a coal storage. The tiring house of 1599 would have been about 19'6" east to west outside, but considerably less inside because of the thickness of walls.

Because several people described it, the moving of the stage 6' westward in 1599 must have no trifle. They all said that it was moved to make more room in the yard for the men who were about to work on Samwell's eastern galleries. They were trying to show that Woodliffe and Samwell had collaborated in building the playhouse and that on this occasion Woodliffe had actually assisted Samwell. But Woodliffe must have had other, more important motives for moving his stage, and Samwell and Robert Browne (whose company of players was about to move into the Boar's Head) must have agreed with him. Woodliffe had stopped the work on his western gallery at one point, "till Samwell and he had talked together" about "that story wch then was to be done."[8] By moving the stage, they must have meant not merely to assist the building of Samwell's eastern galleries but to make the western end of the playhouse into the usual Elizabethan arrangement of stage, tiring house, and upper gallery.

The roof over the stage in 1599 and after was, it seems, a considerable structure. A man who acted under it (Browne), its builder (Mago), and one of his carpenters (Marsh) all mentioned it as though it were a separate thing, comparable to the stage itself and Woodliffe's other structures. Marsh, for example, spoke of the "stage the coueringe ouer the stage the tyringe houses & the galleryes ouer the stage."[9] If Woodliffe put something substantial over his stage in 1599, he also put something substantial under it, partly, no doubt, to take the weight of the new roof. He moved the stage, it seems, onto permanent footings dug into the yard. For long after the stage had ceased to exist, parts of its outline remained as property lines, most of which defined buildings whose walls might well have rested on those same footings. That the stage was probably so firmly placed in 1599 and, unlike nearly everything else in the playhouse, was not rebuilt may suggest that even in the primitive place of 1598 Woodliffe and Samwell could not make do with a thing of loose planks laid on trestles. Moreover, that the stage could not be moved until rubbish thrown under it during its first year had been taken away suggests that it was "paled in belowe." The stage at the Fortune was so, "with good, stronge and sufficyent newe oken bourdes."

One of the effects of moving the stage westward in 1599 was to worsen the sightlines of spectators who stood in the northern and southern parts of the yard. It must have been a price worth paying to achieve the ordinary arrangement of stage, tiring house, and upper gallery. With a great deal more space available for spectators in the galleries of the rebuilt playhouse, the economics of the place could no doubt withstand the loss of spectators in those parts of the yard. The moving of the stage meant that from 1599 the playhouse was largely confined to the central part of the yard. Yet even the worst placed of spectators in the northern or southern parts, if Ogilby and Morgan's map is right, could still see the front 8'6" or so of the stage. Perhaps as the action shown in the famous drawing of the Swan could suggest, that was sometimes enough for watching an Elizabethan production.

Because the stage was not rebuilt in 1599, it was the same size then and after as it had been in 1598. It would have had, therefore, a piece of the yard 8' wide along its northern side and another along its southern side, "wedges," in the new playhouse as in the old. It occupied the central part of the Boar's Head yard in the new playhouse much as the stage of the Fortune occupied the yard of that house. The "wedges" at the Fortune were 6' wide.

Back to front, the stage at the Boar's Head extended a little more than half way across the yard. That at the Fortune extended just halfway. At the Boar's Head, 22′5″ of the yard lay in front of the stage, at the Fortune 27′6″. The stage at the Boar's Head was rectangular (according to the deed of 1621 and, probably, Ogilby and Morgan's map), and so was that at the Fortune, unlike the tapered stages shown in the *Roxana* and *Messalina* engravings. The true orientation of the Boar's Head being northeast and southwest, rather than simply east and west, the stage was actually on the southwest, where the stages at the Globe, Hope, and Rose seem to have been.

One curious thing about the stage remains. In William Browne's deed of 1621, it and the tiring house are described as "a tyreing house or [*sic*] Stage & [*sic*] twoe ten*ements* . . . lately pulled downe to be reedified and builded in a better forme." The "or" and "and" give one pause. Was Leslie Hotson right to speculate that tiring houses could be under stages?[10] And if so, what is one to make of the two tenements? Surely, however, all the remarks in the lawsuits about the tiring house (including two remarks that make it two structures) and the stage put the matter quite beyond doubt. The writer of the deed meant "and" when he wrote "or" and vice versa. He knew that two tenements, a tiring house, and a stage all belonged to one scheme but not how. By using "or" rather than "and" between "tyreing house" and "Stage," he combined those two, both long defunct, and then he put separately the two tenements, recently useful and soon to be useful again. What he wrote was sufficiently meaningful in 1621, perhaps, but would have been wrong twenty or even five years before. The deed should refer, that is, to the stage *and* tiring house *or* two tenements.

When Samwell rebuilt his part of the playhouse in 1599, he extended his galleries of the year before only 3′ rather than the 4′ that Woodliffe urged on him, so that they were now 6′ wide, and he built his upper eastern gallery. The central part of the yard came to have more substantial galleries on all four sides, single ones on the western, northern, and southern sides, and two, one above the other, on the eastern side. Samwell's eastern galleries must have been massive—their builder, Mago, called them "the great new galleryes"—and his northern and southern ones smaller. As his galleries of the year before had been, these were above the yard, held up by posts, so that people could stand under them. These galleries, therefore, did not diminish the size of the yard, anymore than his old ones had done. This was, it seems, no novel way of building galleries in 1599 or 1598.

At the bear-baiting house in Paris Garden up to 1583 there were "double" galleries all around the yard, and the whole system rested on posts. It collapsed on 13 January 1583 and was back up, presumably in the same fashion, within six months. Two contemporary descriptions of the collapse suggest the plan of the galleries. John Field wrote that "This gallery that was double, and compassed the yeard round about, was so shaken at the foundation, (y[t] it fell as it were in a moment) flat to the ground, without post or peere, that was left standing, so high as the stake wherevnto the Beare was tied"; and, some pages later, "they were most hurt and in danger, which stood vnder the Galleries on the grounde, vpon whom both the waight of Timbre and people fell." John Stow described the fallen galleries as "the old and vnderpropped scaffolds round about the beare-garden, commonlie called Paris Garden."[11]

Samwell's new galleries on the northern and southern sides of the play-house were probably connected with his lower eastern gallery, and that with his upper eastern one, so that people could pass freely from one of his galler-ies to another. For, as we shall see, one stairway seems to have led up to all his galleries. These northern and southern galleries extended along the sides of the playhouse, beside the stage, to Woodliffe's western gallery, which they abutted. Because Samwell's structures were legally and commercially distinct from Woodliffe's, spectators would not have been meant to pass from the northern and southern galleries into the western one. Francis Langley made a legal point on 26 December 1599, however, by having his carpenter, Owen Roberts, cut a door from the western gallery, which Langley had just bought from Woodliffe, into the northern or southern gallery. As Langley explained four months later, he was simply opening a doorway into his own property, Samwell's galleries being his because the posts holding them up rested in the yard, which he claimed he had also bought. There would have been about 2′ north to south between the front of each of these galleries and the northern or southern side of the stage, because the galleries were about 6′ wide and were above 8′ strips of the yard beside the stage.

Samwell also added 3′ to his eastern gallery in 1599. Though we hear several times that the gallery was old and long, of how wide it was we hear nothing. It existed, as we have seen, before the playhouse, running along nearly the whole length of the eastern building so as to give access to the rooms on the upper floor. In his drawings for this volume, Mr. Hodges makes it 5′ wide before 1598 because that is the width of the similar gallery along Titchfield Market Hall, an Elizabethan building now in the Weald and Downland Open Air Museum at Singleton in Sussex. Hence this eastern gallery of Samwell's would have been 8′ wide after being extended in 1599 (Ogilby and Morgan show the strip of the yard that probably lay under that gallery as 8′ wide). Like the northern and southern galleries, the eastern one was held up by posts resting in the yard.

Contemporaries said even less about the size of the new gallery that Sam-well built over this one in 1599. To build a gallery above another is not simple when they are against a two-story building and the lower gallery is at the level of the upper story. Samwell and his builder, Mago, had to reckon somehow with the roof, eaves, and gutters of the eastern building, all of which would have been just behind this gallery. Hollar's merely suggestive picture map of 1667 has the roof ridge of the eastern building running north to south. Since the lower gallery was held up by posts, presumably the upper one was, too. It could not have hung securely on the face of the eastern building at or near the top of the building. So probably the posts holding up the lower gallery were simply carried up another, say, 8' (Mr. Hodges's figure) and the upper gallery set on them. In that case, the upper gallery would have been as wide as the lower one, perhaps 8', a few inches more if it had a jetty. If the two galleries were that wide, they would have been, as Mago said they were, "great new galleryes" compared to the other galleries of the playhouse. Moreover, the workmen putting them up would have had only about 8'5" of the yard in which to work between the front of them and the stage placed as it was in 1598. They would have complained, and the stage might well have been moved partly to accommodate them.

Before they began rebuilding the playhouse in 1599, Woodliffe and Samwell decided that the galleries would be not only bigger but more comfortable. Samwell's galleries would have seats rather than only standings as in 1598. Surely Woodliffe's western gallery would have seats, too, and very likely had them in 1598, because similar places in other playhouses were choice. Samwell duly installed seats in at least one of his galleries. They may have been benches, for they were fixed to the gallery or galleries in which they were. On 20 May 1600 Francis Langley had his creature, Richard Bishop, charge Robert Browne with, among other things, throwing down posts and seats fixed into the playhouse, or as the charge goes in the original, "quosdam postes & sedes in domo predicta fixas."[12] The posts and seats could be involved together only if the seats were in a gallery held up by posts, as Samwell's were. Bishop was claiming to own Samwell's galleries, which Browne had bought from Samwell. Browne was probably repairing or improving his structures.

The advance in comfort that these seats represented, however, was not to be measured in light-years, if Samwell accepted Woodliffe's ideas about such things. When Woodliffe saw the playhouse of 1598 (he had been broad when it was built) and spoke of enlarging the galleries, his remarks about seats had less to do with comfort than the money he could make. If, he said, the new galleries were made 4' wider, "then would there be roome for three or foure seats more in a gallery, and for many mo people" (he meant rows of seats), and, he went on, because the galleries were to be up on posts, "yet neuer the lesse roome in the yarde." As we shall see, such seats could have been 6" or 8" deep. By modern standards, the spectator might have been more comfortable standing on than sitting in them. All the galleries at the Fortune (and hence, presumably, the Globe) had "seates," according to the builder's contract, as had at least two boxes in the lowest gallery at the Hope. So did at least one of "the vpper romes" at the Theatre. Did the builders of all these places think of comfort as Woodliffe did?

One stairway led from the yard up to Samwell's galleries. At its bottom, two or more doors opened into it—hence it was enclosed and rather broad—and there the gatherer stood to take the money of spectators who meant to see the play from Samwell's galleries. We know these things because of the events at the Boar's Head on the afternoon of 24 December 1599, when Francis Langley and helpers invaded the place before a "stage Playe" was to take place. He and his carpenter, Roberts, "set they^r hands" to "a dore at the stayres foot leading vp to the sayd Galleryes," and they "did thrust it open." Langley then had one of his people, Anthony Strayles, "stand there at the galyere dores to take the mony of those that Came in to see the sayd playes," as Samwell said in one place, "and toke away the Mony of those *persons* that were to goe vpp into the said galleryes to the said stage Playe," as he said in another. The stairway (as we shall see) was probably at the southern end of the old gallery along the eastern building, and the spectator arrived at it before reaching the entrance to the yard. There were also enclosed stairways taking the spectator up to the galleries at the Theatre, Hope, and second Globe; and at the Theatre, at least, the gatherer also stood at the foot of the stairway.[13]

Samwell's galleries were mainly timber affairs held together with a good many nails. They were roofed, it seems, and not with the thatch that had just been put over the galleries at the Globe, but with tiles. Like the galleries at other playhouses, they had some lath and presumably plaster in them. According to the younger Samwell, who kept his father's book of expenses, the galleries of 1598 and 1599 were made of "tymber nayles bords tyles lathes & other stuffe." For those of 1599, according to their builder, Mago, the timber (and presumably other things) cost about £140, the nails about £20, and labor about £100.[14]

In Elizabethan and Jacobean playhouses, galleries were very important things, so important that for a man like Francis Langley the Boar's Head consisted solely of them. As he said in 1600, "there hath bin some store of mony bestowed in building of Galleryes in the sayd Inn fytt for a playe house."[15] What people of the time meant by the word has occasionally seemed worth reflecting about, for they used some strange words as equivalents if one thinks of galleries in the modern theatrical sense. The documentation about the Boar's Head is no exception. For Samwell's structures, seven people paired the word "galleries" with "rooms," "buildings," "chambers," and that curious word, "roomths." Samwell, in February 1600, alluded first to his "Romes or Galleryes," then went on to his "galleryes or buildings," his "buildings," his "Galleryes and Romes," and finally his "Galleryes" or "buildings." All three of his witnesses said his structures were "certeine roomes or galleryes" or vice versa, then repeatedly just "galleryes." Two months later, Samwell introduced his structures as "diu*erse* Romes galleryes Chambers and other necessary Buyldings" and then referred to them as "the said new galleryes or buyldings . . . the said Buyldings . . . the said galleryes

. . . the said galleryes and Romes . . . the said galleryes and buyldinges"—all in the same passage. In 1601, Browne, Hoppdale, and the younger Samwell referred to them as "certaine newe galleries" and/or "romes," and Hoppdale added "roomths": "certen new galleryes and Romes . . . the same galleryes and romeths . . . the said galleryes and romes," all in the same sentence, and in the next sentence, "galleryes and romeths" and, twice, just "galleryes." In 1603, however, Browne and both his witnesses repeatedly called the same structures just "newe galleryes."[16]

These words suggest partitions, compartments, and the like. Doubtless the galleries had uprights at regular intervals holding up a roof or, in the case of the lower eastern gallery, another gallery, and so looked like rows of rooms and chambers, as the galleries at the Swan did. But the loose and random way in which people used such words at the Boar's Head suggests that they intended them to mean little more than constructed space from which paying spectators might watch plays.

In some conspicuous ways the Boar's Head playhouse was a peculiar place, at least to us who have been looking intently at the Swan, Globe, Fortune, and Hope. The scheme of things there, however, confirms some important aspects of our theorizing about the general playhouse of Elizabethan and Jacobean times. The tiring house and the gallery above it were quite separate from the main galleries, not only in ownership but in the structures adapted and built for them. The stage belonged to the tiring house and the gallery in ownership, but it was a quite separate piece of carpentry. It was also a very considerable structure, especially in view of the size of the other structures and spaces that made up the playhouse. The yard did not much concern the financiers, at least in the original planning for the playhouse.

The Boar's Head playhouse may have been used particularly in the winter, like other playhouses contained in inns. Robert Browne's company moved into the Boar's Head in time for the winter season of 1599–1600, and Francis Langley tried to collect money at performances there on 24 and 26 December 1599. Worcester's men agreed in the autumn of 1601 to pay Langley's exactions for the use of the playhouse until Shrovetide 1602, and Mago said they did so because they "had no other wynter house licenced for them to play in." Mago also remarked that "rushes and cressett lights in Wynter . . . some weeks came to ten or twelve shillings a weeke."[17] Moreover, Woodliffe chose Christmas 1602 as the moment to press his elegit against Browne, whom he wanted to drive out of the Boar's Head.

Now, Professor Wickham believes that playhouses in inns would not have been used especially in winter if their plays and audiences could not have moved indoors in bad weather. He suggests that such inns had large halls into which plays could move, or yards that were covered over. At the Boar's

Head, he proposes, plays could be moved into the great barn.[18] Unfortunately, there is no evidence that plays at the Boar's Head took place anywhere but at the playhouse in the yard. Nothing hints at the many contractual adjustments that would have been necessary among Woodliffe, Samwell, and the players if the whole enterprise were to move into Samwell's great barn for the winter. Nor was the inn yard covered over if Woodliffe's western gallery had its own roof in 1598 and got a new one in 1599, and if in 1599 the stage also had its own roof. Those performances at the Boar's Head on 24 and 26 December 1599 certainly took place in the yard, for Langley tried to take money from people going up into Samwell's galleries to see them.

Besides, not many people at the Boar's Head would have been without shelter in bad weather. The stage and at least some of the galleries, probably all, were roofed as, in effect, was the great share of the yard that lay under the galleries. The only uncovered places were the 2′ strips of the yard between the sides of the stage and the northern and southern galleries and the 14′5″ or so of the yard between the front of the stage and the eastern gallery. If I am right about the measurements of the yard, that is much less than half the space in it available for spectators (not counting the northern and southern parts of the yard). If I am right about the measurements of the galleries, it is less than a fifth of the space in the whole playhouse available for spectators. We have probably spent too much time worrying about the comfort of Elizabethan and Jacobean audiences. We might equate the conditions in the old public playhouses not with those in our theatres but with those in our terraces, from which thousands sometimes watch outdoor games in appalling weather.

My measurements in the Boar's Head, incidentally, yield about 1,646 square feet in the yard for spectators from 1599 onward, about 1,364 square feet in Samwell's galleries for them, and about 305 square feet in Woodliffe's gallery for them. Altogether there would have been about 3,315 square feet in the playhouse of 1599 for spectators.

When Samwell rebuilt his part of the playhouse in 1599, he spent some of his money "buylding and altering . . . the syncks and gutters wth in the sayd greate yarde." These must have been in the part of the yard where the playhouse was and must have drained into the northern part of the yard. There, as we hear in 1621, the main drain began, "the common watercourse in the said yard where vsually it hath ben accustomed to passe awaie" water from the Boar's Head. This drain flowed northward to a place just north of the Boar's Head, where "the comon sinke & setlinge of the said water is & hath ben kept & vsed for the water to fall out of the said Boares head yard."[19] Samwell's sinks and gutters suggest that the surface of the playhouse yard was more sophisticated than dirt, perhaps cobbles or bricks. They also suggest that in the playhouse of 1598 standing water in the yard was not uncommon but in the great playhouse of 1599 was not to be tolerated. Hence, again, bad weather need not stop plays. The only other playhouse known to have had a paved yard is the Fortune, where the paving was bricks.

Mago's remark that Samwell and his successors had to pay ten or twelve shillings a week in winter for rushes and cresset lights may settle a question about not only the Boar's Head but playhouses in general. What did players do for light on mid-winter afternoons when darkness began to fall and they had reached only the third or fourth act? We have heard before that they could have used cresset lights. Randle Cotgrave defined "falot" in his French-English dictionary (1611) as "A Cresset light (such as they vse in Playhouses)." We have been reluctant, however, to apply the remark to galleries, yard, or stage. One writer has recently decided that Cotgrave's cressets were used only as stage props or devices to light dark passageways. The galleries, yard, and stage, he says, had no artificial lighting, even at Christmas when darkness could be total well before the ends of plays and when plays were especially to be seen at such places as the Boar's Head. Cresset lights were iron baskets in which rope "wreathed" and "pitched" was burned for light. They were fixed on top of poles, or hung from roofs on chains, or perhaps placed on stands not much different from lamp stands. They were used to light open places like wharfs and streets.[20] Mago's pairing of cresset lights with the familiar rushes suggests that the cresset lights were for the stage, as the rushes no doubt were. When darkness fell on performances at the Boar's Head and elsewhere, someone must have gone round with a torch lighting cressets. Several blazing cressets beside or on the stage would have lighted it and much of the rest of the playhouse as well. They would also have caused a good deal of smoke that should have found its way out of the playhouse up through the roofless yard but often blackened eaves, walls, and ceilings, including the "heavens" over the stage. So, perhaps, one of the conditions came about that John Webster thought caused his *White Devil* to fail in 1612. It was "acted," he wrote, "in so dull a time of Winter, [and] presented in so open and blacke a Theater, that it wanted . . . a full and vnderstanding Auditory."

The Boar's Head was a much smaller and more intimate playhouse than some of its famous competitors. Its yard was about the same size as that of the Fortune, especially if customers could use at least a little of the northern and southern parts of the inn yard. But evidently the whole playhouse provided only about a third as much room for people as the Fortune did, mainly because Samwell's galleries had about a fifth as much square footage as the equivalent galleries at the Fortune had. This was the consequence of what a visitor accustomed to the Fortune and such places would have found mainly different about the Boar's Head. In them, the main galleries stood beside the yard, the lowest only inches above it, and there were three of them, one above the other, around, in effect, three-quarters of the yard. At the Boar's Head, the main galleries were not beside the yard but wholly above it, and there were only two on the east and one each on the north and south. If this arrangement limited the space available in the galleries, it caused two things that must have made the Boar's Head an agreeable place in which to attend a play. Much of the yard was, as we have seen, out of the weather because under galleries—at the other playhouses of which we know the whole yard was exposed to the weather. People in the galleries at the Boar's Head were much closer to the stage than people in those at the Fortune, Swan, and Globe were likely to be, and that at a time when people went into such galleries not necessarily to see but, as Francis Langley could say in the spring of 1600, "to here the playe."[21]

CHAPTER 13

The Theatrical Enterprise

The Boar's Head was the third playhouse in a golden time of playhouses, the third licensed by the Privy Council, and the home for nearly a year of one of the strongest companies, Worcester's men. They wanted to make it their permanent house in the spring of 1602, and after some notable vicissitudes for both them and the playhouse, they wanted to make it one of their two permanent houses in the spring of 1604.

The place was designed for a somewhat rougher trade than were the Globe, Fortune, and such places, if one may draw the obvious conclusion from the size of the yard relative to that of the main galleries. The yard had about as much room for people as that at the Fortune, but the main galleries had much less than the equivalent places at the Fortune. The Boar's Head prospered, at least during its first five years, if it was worth a complete rebuilding in 1599 and many surely expensive legal maneuvers from the autumn of 1599 to the summer of 1603. Francis Langley was no doubt exaggerating wildly when he said in April 1600 that Samwell had rebuilt his part of the playhouse entirely from the profits of the primitive galleries during the first year, but he was probably expanding on a truth, that the playhouse had had a very good first year. During the nineteen months between 22 August 1601 and 19 March 1603, as we have seen, the place was probably used about forty full weeks. One of the greatest companies, the Admiral's men, averaged thirty-eight full weeks a year in London during the late 1590s, and during the nineteen months in question they may have played there about sixty weeks. So the companies at the Boar's Head would have played in London about two-thirds as often as the Admiral's men did, at least in the early years of the seventeenth century.[1] Perhaps something about the place made it rather less suitable for sustained playing than the Globe or Fortune. In any event, both Worcester's and Derby's men often played in the provinces, and the Boar's Head was probably closed for a time during the winter of 1602–3 because of the elegit.

During the nineteen months, as we have also seen, the half profits, net, in the western gallery were about £1 a week and would have been twice as much but for repairs to the complex of the gallery, tiring house, and stage. Hence the full profits, net, were about £2 for that period. We have no figures for the profits in Samwell's galleries at the same time, but an incident before a play was acted on 24 December 1599 may suggest what those galleries could yield. Samwell claimed that Francis Langley's man collected £4 at the foot of the stairs leading up to Samwell's galleries. Langley did not deny the £4 but insisted that his share was only 5s. Both figures could be about right. Samwell's represented actual cash supposedly taken, and the net profit that afternoon would be less. Langley's figure represented what was left over after he had deducted everything he could, and the net profit would have been greater. Arguing that he owned Samwell's galleries, Langley would have deducted what the owner was supposed to pay to keep the place open (as we shall see, about 38s. a week in winter), then his gatherer's fee. He would have paid the players their share of the takings in the galleries, which might have been half, because that is what Henslowe's players had in his galleries and what the players at the Boar's Head had in the western gallery. Langley would, finally, deduct something for his carpenter's work that afternoon and for his personal expenses. He could easily have had only 5s. left over. Some of Langley's deductions would have been unusual, but the audience on a Christmas Eve would probably have been unusually large. So maybe the full net profit of Samwell's galleries could average 10s. a day, or £3 a week. If so, the full net profit of all the galleries would average about £5 a week, which, curiously, is exactly what the galleries at the old Theatre in Shoreditch seem to have yielded at least during the first half of their history.[2]

This episode of Christmas Eve 1599 also leads to calculations about how Samwell's customers paid their pennies and how many people his galleries could accommodate. He probably would not have known how much money Langley's man collected, but he would have known and claimed what a capacity audience paid. On a very good afternoon, therefore, it was possible to collect 960 pennies at the door to Samwell's galleries. Those galleries must have been the familiar two-penny ones of the time,[3] but their patrons could not have paid their pennies as the patrons of similar galleries at some other playhouses seem to have done: one to the players' gatherer at the entrance to the yard and the other to the gallery owner's gatherer at the entrance to the galleries. For Samwell's galleries could not have accommodated anything like 960 people. People going to the playhouse, therefore, reached the door leading up to the galleries before the entrance to the yard, and those going into the galleries paid both pennies to Samwell's gatherer at the gallery stairs. The players must have got their share of the takings there through Samwell's gatherer, as Langley's remarks about the incident also suggest. The gallery stairs must have been at the southern end of the old gallery along the upper story of the eastern building and the entrance to the playhouse yard a little north of them. More important than all this, Samwell's galleries must have accommodated 480 people. If I am right to conclude that those galleries comprised about 1,364 square feet, when they were filled to capacity each person in them occupied 2.84 square feet, or (assuming that people could not have used literally every inch) a space somewhat smaller than $1'8'' \times 1'8''$.

These calculations must be at least reasonably sound, because the space they yield for each seat at the Boar's Head is exactly that allowed in several theatrical ventures with which Inigo Jones had to do from 1605 to 1635.[4] In at least one of these (1605), gentlemen sat on seats 6″ and ladies and royal servants on seats 8″ deep—hence, no doubt, Woodliffe's remark that 4′ was space enough for three or four rows of seats. The galleries at the Fortune equivalent to Samwell's could have held at this rate of space per spectator upward of 2,500 people. Even if a person standing in the yard occupied the same room as a person sitting in the galleries, rather than less as one might imagine, the Fortune as a whole, like the Swan and Globe, could easily have held 3,000 people. The Boar's Head could equally easily have held 1,000, more if much of the northern and southern extremities of the yard were used.

The financial arrangements at the Boar's Head were designed for two owners. At the beginning they were Oliver Woodliffe and Richard Samwell, then Francis Langley and Robert Browne, then Woodliffe and Browne, then Woodliffe's widow and Browne's widow. Each party had distinct responsibilities and looked for distinct rewards. In theory, each party was protected by the real estate he owned in the inn. The players who used the playhouse also had a distinct commercial relationship with each of the owners. Woodliffe and his successors took half the profits of the western gallery, "the gatherors beinge first payed," and the players the other half. Samwell and his successors probably had a similar arrangement with the players for the other galleries. The players, presumably, had all the takings from the yard, that being the custom in other playhouses and nobody saying anything different about the Boar's Head. Woodliffe's interest was a silent one. Samwell and his successors managed the place; they dealt with players, saw to repairs and improvements, and paid many of the incidental charges of keeping it in business. Samwell saw that Woodliffe got his half profits, from which he deducted the cost of repairs and improvements to Woodliffe's theatrical real estate (the stage, tiring house, and western gallery).

A list survives of the incidental charges that Samwell and his successors paid. They paid the wages of the stage keepers, which came to 6s. a week. They paid for rushes and cresset lights, the rushes presumably used on the stage, the lights used to light the place on dark afternoons in winter, the two together costing in some weeks 10s. or 12s. More important, perhaps, and certainly more expensive, they also paid all the charges required to keep a semilegal or even illegal business functioning openly. These included the fee to the master of the revels, 15s. a week when the playhouse was used; the fee to the parish for the poor, 5s. a week; and the fees for "all sutes at Court." Whether the court was of law or the Queen is not clear, but the suits were "to vphould playinge in the said house," or "to have toleracion from tyme to tyme to vphold the house to play in," and they "came to much money." Samwell and his successors paid, too, "for all the lycences for Warrants from the M^r of the Revells," which cost £10 each.[5] Nobody said, however, that they also paid the 7s. that Henslowe paid the master of the revels for each new play produced in his playhouse. Nor did anybody say that they advanced the players money for costumes, as Henslowe did at the Rose and Fortune and Francis Langley at the Swan, and for new plays, properties, even personal matters, as Henslowe also did. At the Boar's Head, it seems, such advances were either unnecessary or, more plausibly, the responsibility of the players rather than the owners.

The players at the Boar's Head had one other amenity there, in addition to the use of yard, stage, and tiring house and a share of the takings in the galleries. It was the right to shut the gates of the inn when they pleased. As the carpenter, Hoppdale, explained it, Woodlife had agreed that the elder Richard Samwell "should have . . . a com*m*aunde of the openinge and shutting of the gates." The younger Richard Samwell explained it better but left some questions. It should be lawful for his father "& his assignees to shutt the gates of the *sa*id Inne or messuage at xj of the clocke, or at suche other tymes as the players or the *sa*id Rich*ar*d Samuell should thinke conveynient."[6] The "assignees" were no doubt the players, but why give them the right to shut the gates when they pleased yet mention eleven o'clock? Why omit saying whether eleven o'clock was at night or in the morning, and when, having shut the gates, the players should open them?

Woodliffe and Samwell must have supposed that players would not ordinarily want to shut the gates at other times. Whether eleven o'clock was A.M. or P.M. must have been obvious enough not to need expressing, as must the time when players would open the gates. If eleven o'clock was at night, Woodliffe and Samuell must have thought that players would want to protect their goods in the tiring house and onstage during the small hours and would open the gates at the beginning of business in the morning. Eleven o'clock, however, is likely to have had directly to do with the players' most obvious concern, the playing of plays, and hence to have been in the morning and on playing days. Players would have wanted to discourage visitors to the inn ready to wait a while so as to become playgoers for nothing. They would also have wanted three or four hours in which to get their show together relatively unobserved. Peter Quince led his players into the palace wood for the same purpose, "for," as he said, "if we meet in the city, we shall be dogged with company." This right to shut the gates may explain how the players at one playhouse were expected to carry out the common necessity of players to get several different plays onstage a week.

What theatrical equipment players had to work with at the Boar's Head is mostly beyond certain knowledge. The stage measured 39'7" by perhaps 25', so that it was about 84% of the size of that at the Fortune—a statistic that may be worth thinking about with another: the Boar's Head had about 33% of the room for spectators that the Fortune had. The documentation, however, alludes to nothing so meretricious as stage doors, trap doors, acting space "above," music rooms, machinery in the "heavens," and the like. For them we must turn to stage directions and textual allusions in surviving plays that we can associate with the Boar's Head. We cannot rely absolutely on what we shall find, however, because we cannot show that any surviving plays were unquestionably written for performance at the Boar's Head. Still, thirteen plays belonged to companies while they were, or could have been, playing at the Boar's Head. Of these, two plays may well have been written for performance at the Boar's Head, six more might have been, and if not written for the place, all thirteen could easily have been played there. A study of these plays should suggest what the companies at the Boar's Head were accustomed to in the way of theatrical equipment, hence provide an idea of what was there.

Many companies could have played at the Boar's Head during its eighteen years, but so far we can probably identify only three: Derby's men, from the late summer of 1599 until the late summer of 1601 and from the summer of 1602 until March 1603; Worcester's men (who became the Queen's men), from the late summer of 1601 until the summer of 1602 and from April 1604 until 1605 or 1606, a period during which they also used the Curtain; and Prince Charles's men, in the summer of 1609, possibly earlier and from time to time until the leases ran out at the Boar's Head in March 1616.

The two plays that may well have been written for performance at the Boar's Head are:

1. *A Pleasant conceited Comedie Wherein is shewed how a man may chuse a good Wife from a bad* (London, 1602), "*sundry times Acted by the Earle of* Worcesters *Seruants.*"

2. *The History of the tryall of Cheualry* (London, 1605 twice), "lately acted by the right *Honourable the Earle of Darby his* seruants"; *Stationers' Register*, 4 December 1604. All the London playhouses were closed from 19 March 1603, when Derby's men probably left the Boar's Head forever, until 9 April 1604. They could easily have had the play a couple of years before it was printed.

Apart from a bare stage, the first suggests only a trap and the second only two stage doors. In *How a man may chuse a good Wife from a bad*, a character says,

> This is the Church, this hollow is the Vault,
> Where the dead bodie of my Saint remaines,
> And this the Coffin that inshrines her bodie.

Eleven lines later the stage direction appears, *"Mistresse Arthur in the Tombe,"* a cue it seems, because three lines later still she sits upright in the tomb (sig. H2). In *The tryall of Cheualry*, three stage directions specify an entry *"at one dore"* and, immediately after each, another specifies an entry *"at the other."* A fifth stage direction reads, *"Enter at seuerall doores."* Two men open a tent with a key and find Bellamira, or as the stage direction has it, *"Discouer her sitting in a chayre asleepe."* As soon as she awakes, she seems to leave the tent for the stage proper. Could she have been just behind one of the stage doors? (Sigs. A2, A4ᵛ, D, G2ᵛ, I2ᵛ, I3ᵛ.)

Of the six plays less likely to have been written for performance at the Boar's Head, five were published from 1603 to 1607 as belonging to the Queen's men and one in 1617 as belonging to Prince Charles's men. They are as follows.

3. Thomas Heywood, *If you know not me, You know no bodie* (London, 1605); *Stationers' Register*, 5 July 1605. Heywood was a leading member of the Queen's men and wrote regularly for them.

4. Heywood, *The Second Part of, If you know not me, you know no bodie* (London, 1606); *Stationers' Register*, 14 September 1605.

5. *No-body and Some-body* (London, n.d.), *"acted by the Queens Maiesties Seruants"*; *Stationers' Register*, 12 March 1606.

6. Thomas Dekker and John Webster, *The Famous History of Sir Thomas Wyat* (London, 1607), "As it was plaied by the Queens Maiesties Seruants."

7. *The Fayre Mayde of the Exchange* (London, 1607); *Stationers' Register*, 24 April 1607; often given to Heywood, hence the Queen's men.

8. William Rowley and Thomas Middleton, *A Faire Quarrell* (London, 1617), "As it was Acted before the King *and diuers times publikely by the* Prince his Highnes Seruants."

One of these plays, *A Faire Quarrell*, requires only the bare stage. Three of the five others specify two stage doors, the two parts of *If you know not me* twice each (sigs. Dᵛ, E3ᵛ and H, K) and *The Fayre Mayde of the Ex-*

change once (sig. G4); another, *No-body and Some-body,* specifies more than one, so that people can enter *"seuerallie"* (sigs. C3, F3, G4ᵛ). The first part of *If you know not me* requires a space *"aboue"* in which three people can stand and from which they can *"descend"* (sigs. Gᵛ–G2ᵛ); *Sir Thomas Wyat* may require a similar space so that Pembroke might enter *"vpon the Walles"* at Ludgate (sig. E3). The first part of *If you know not me* requires a chair of state: an actor says of it, "Take it downe," and the clown later pulls it *"from vnder him";* the same play also requires an arras behind which King Phillip might step and speak an aside and from which he might then *"Enter"* (sigs. E–Eᵛ, F3ᵛ).⁷

As for special business not requiring permanent equipment, two of the plays specify none at all. Two have scenes in a shop: in the second part of *If you know not me,* actors *"Enter in the shop"* and open it, and in *The Fayre Mayde of the Exchange* scenes begin with the directions *"Enter Boy in a Shop cutting of square parchments"* and *"Enter Cripple in his shop, and to him enters Franke"* (sigs. D3 and E4ᵛ, H2ᵛ). The first part of *If you know not me* also requires an entry in a bed, torches, trumpets and the like, and a goat (sigs. B2, Dᵛ etc., B etc., E4ᵛ). The second part requires *"A blasing Starre"* that everybody sees and speaks about, then *"Musick, and a Banquet serued in,"* and, finally, *"A peale of Chambers"* (sigs. E2ᵛ, E4ᵛ, I3ᵛ). *No-body and Some-body* specifies trumpets and drums (sig. F4 etc.). More interestingly, it has an actor say,

> *somebody* once pickt a pocket in this Play-house yard,
> Was hoysted on the stage, and shamd about it,

alluding, it may be, to the yard of the Boar's Head (sig. Iᵛ).

Five more plays could have been performed at the Boar's Head but were evidently written for performance at other places. Four belonged to a company while it was at the Boar's Head,⁸ and the fifth could have done. They are:

9. 10. *The First and Second partes of King Edward the Fourth* (London, 1599 and again 1600), as *"diuers times . . . publiquely played by the Right Honorable the Earle of Derby his seruants"* and entered in *Stationers' Register,* 28 August 1599, when the company was just settling into the Boar's Head, as "lately acted by the Right honorable the Erle of Derbye his servanᵗˢ."

11. *The Weakest goeth to the Wall* (London, 1600), as *"sundry times plaide by the right honourable Earle of* Oxenford . . . *his seruants,"* a company that soon joined Worcester's; *Stationers' Register,* 23 October 1600.

12. Thomas Heywood, *A Woman Kilde with Kindnesse* (London, 1607), acted at the Rose between 5 February and 7 March 1603.⁹

13. John Day, William Rowley, and George Wilkins, *The Travailes Of The three English Brothers* (London, 1607), "As it is now play'd by her Majesties *Seruants*"; *Stationers' Register*, 29 June 1607, "as yt Was played at the Curten."[10]

The *Edward IV* plays specify two stage doors once and allude to more than one twice; they also call for what might have been the same thing, the gates of London on which rebels beat, and perhaps a space above from which Josseline "on the walles cries to them" (sigs. T2, M3ᵛ, O, B3, Cᵛ). *The Weakest goeth to the Wall* requires a trap and a state (sigs. A3, I), and both the other two plays seem to require three doors (sigs. F3 and H4ᵛ). Only the *Edward IV* plays call for much special business: "solemne musicke" is played "the while within," trumpets blare, a table spread for a banquet is brought in twice, apprentices prepare a goldsmith's shop with plate, "great shot from the towne" wounds Lord Scales and kills two soldiers on stage, and a man is hanged on stage (sigs. T2, D3 etc., F3ᵛ, G3ᵛ, H2, N, Y3). The *Woman Kilde with Kindnesse* requires the familiar bed: "*Enters Mistris Frankeford in her bed*" (sig. H2ᵛ).

Two things are striking about the requirements of these plays. No play requires elaborate lifting gear in the "heavens." Of the eight that could have been written for performance at the Boar's Head, no fewer than four specify that their original playhouse had two stage doors, and none specifies one, or three, or more. Additionally, the play most likely to have been written for the Boar's Head seems to require a trap, but none of the seven other plays does. One of the plays less likely to have been written for the Boar's Head requires a space "above" for three people and a descent from it, a state dropped from the "heavens," and an arras. None of the other plays that could have been written for the place requires either a state or an arras, and only one a space "above"—for one person and no descent.

On this evidence, one can say of the fixed theatrical equipment at the Boar's Head only that there were probably two stage doors and a trap and perhaps modest accommodation for action "above." The stage at the Boar's Head could have looked like that in the famous drawing of the Swan, where there were also two stage doors, a stage roof, and a gallery above and at the back for spectators.

That gallery above the stage at the Boar's Head is the most explicit evidence yet about the galleries shown above and behind the stage in all four drawings of regular Elizabethan playhouses, and it should end forever the long debate about what those galleries were used for. The gallery at the Boar's Head was on the western side of the yard, as its owner and others said repeatedly, and over the stage, as three men who knew it well said some nineteen times. One of them referred to it also as over the tiring houses, and another of them as at one end of the stage, which could only be the back. It seems to have consisted of a single upper story with nothing over it but a roof. The gallery at the Boar's Head, then, is the precise equivalent of those galleries in the drawings. As two lawsuits and several orders out of Chancery in connection with another lawsuit make quite clear, that gallery was for spectators.

If such galleries were for spectators, what is one to conclude about action "above" and "within" in a fair number of old plays? Such upper and inner stages as Dr. Cranford Adams proposed in his much-read book simply could not have existed, the upper one because spectators occupied the space, and the inner one because people above and behind the stage could not see what was going on there. We seem to have rejected the inner stage without much help from the Boar's Head, but speculation about the upper one continues. Supposing that the galleries over the stage must have been for spectators, Mr. Hodges and others proposed that actions "above" took place on easily portable scaffolding erected on the stage against the tiring house. Dr. Hotson proposed similar scaffolding at the sides of the stage. Neither proposal has caught on, but another apparently has: that actions "above" took place in the gallery over the stage, either among spectators or in space temporarily denied to them. Writers have also put musicians in those galleries, which have become "a multi-purpose upper area used by spectators, actors or musicians as circumstance permitted or occasion demanded."[11]

The events at the Boar's Head tell against this proposal. Half the profits of that gallery above the stage were due to Woodliffe and later Francis Langley, businessmen who were not only far from stage struck, but sharply at odds with the men who controlled and used the playhouse. Had Woodliffe and Samwell agreed in 1598 or 1599 that the players could turn spectators away from that gallery so as to accommodate scenes "above" and musicians, Browne and his witnesses would have said so in 1603 when they explained these agreements. They said nothing of the sort, but they did say, for example, that the people who took the spectators' money for that gallery were paid before Woodliffe's or Langley's profits were reckoned. That the players could claim space in the gallery for acting and music and so reduce Woodliffe's and Langley's profits further would have been an important matter to Browne. At the Boar's Head, no doubt, the players would have had to pay fully for every spectator they turned away, by forgoing their share and refunding Woodliffe's or Langley's. Some sort of low, portable scaffolding for their scenes "above" would have been cheaper and easier.[12]

Moreover, similar arrangements for the takings in the galleries were common in the other London playhouses, such as those Henslowe's companies used, and the Theatre, the Globe, the Swan, the Red Bull, and the Hope. None of the evidence about the money taken in these galleries has them specifically over the stage, it is true, but Edward Alleyn had a quarter of the takings of all the galleries (including, presumably that over the stage) at the Hope from March 1616, and his father-in-law, Henslowe, had half the takings of the "Galleries & tyring howse" at whatever house Lady Elizabeth's men used in 1614. The Burbages and other housekeepers had all the takings at the tiring house door of the Globe.[13] The takings of the tiring house must have been those of the gallery over the stage, and the tiring-house door must have led to that gallery. If in some of those enterprises the relationships between investors and players were better than at the Boar's Head, the principle was the same everywhere. A spectator displaced was money lost, and Henslowe, at least, counted money as carefully as Woodliffe.

Could Woodliffe and Samwell, Henslowe, the Burbages, Langley at the Swan, and others have agreed, then, that there would be space in the gallery over the stage permanently set aside for acting and music, so that the spectators' money was not an issue? Browne and his witnesses might not have thought that they had to explain such an arrangement. Then, however, valuable space would have lain fallow through the many plays for which there are no scenes "above" or only scanty ones. The waste would have pained the players as much as Woodliffe. As Professor King says (pp. 2–3), from 1599 onward three plays out of five had no scenes "above." As for the two in five that did have scenes "above," the history of the Boar's Head will not take us much farther. Where these scenes were played must constitute one of the most important problems in the study of the English stage.

The events at the Boar's Head have also to do with another problem, licensing. In July 1597, the Privy Council ordered that the London playhouses be not only closed, but destroyed. The playhouses duly closed, but none was destroyed and at least two were playing again within about three months. Then on 19 February 1598, the Privy Council ordered that there be only two companies and two playhouses (the Burbages' and Henslowe's enterprises), and that an unnamed third company be suppressed. Two months later, Woodliffe leased most of the Boar's Head to Samwell so that they might build a playhouse there, and shortly after that the playhouse went up, opened, and began a successful year. In the summer of 1599, Woodliffe and Samwell expensively rebuilt the playhouse, and a well-connected company, Derby's, moved into it and played at court that winter and the next (1599–1600, 1600–1601). The following autumn (1601), in the teeth of two recent reminders and another strenuous order from the Privy Council that only the two companies and two playhouses be allowed, an impressive company, Worcester's, replaced Derby's at the Boar's Head. Francis Langley promptly demanded more money from them for the use of the stage, tiring house, and gallery over the stage than they had agreed to pay. They decided to pay Langley because, as a close observer of affairs at the Boar's Head (John Mago) said, they "had no other wynter house licenced for them to play in." The Privy Council ordered twice again that winter that there be only the two playhouses, but Worcester's men carried on at the Boar's Head nonetheless and played at court. In the spring, finally, the Privy Council issued an order permitting a third company, Worcester's, to use a third playhouse, the Boar's Head.[14]

Professor Wickham has explained why the Privy Council's authority might not have applied to valuable existing playhouses.[15] Word from the Boar's Head, however, that while the Privy Council was repeatedly ordering that just two playhouses exist, a third could be built, rebuilt, and used successfully, and, moreover, actually licensed—that adds a new curiosity. The people at the Boar's Head seem regularly to have paid the 15s. a playing week to the master of the revels, the 5s. a week to the parish for the poor, and the other fees and charges that the master of the revels demanded of the allowed playhouses, all while the master's masters ordered that such places as the Boar's Head not exist.

The Privy Council could efficiently stop playing at the Boar's Head forty years before, in Mary's time, at all the playhouses in July 1597, and at the Swan thereafter. The authorities in Middlesex could also act effectively against playhouses. In April 1600, they demanded and got a bond of £40 from John Wolf that would be forfeit if he continued putting up another playhouse in Whitechapel—in Nightingale Lane—without the permission of the Privy Council.[16]

The Privy Council in Elizabeth's time must eventually have thought of theatrical enterprises as falling into one of three categories: (1) those that the central government for one reason or another would not allow at all, (2) those that it would allow and take fees from but not protect from local authorities, and (3) those that it would allow, take the same fees from, and protect from local authorities. Cynically, as Professor Wickham suggests, or not, from 1597 the Privy Council often gave local authorities an excuse to act against theatrical enterprises in the second category. The Privy Council must have thought that if local authorities would not or could not end them it was only reasonable that the master of the revels and the parishes should have their fees. As the people at the Boar's Head must have thought, the Privy Council probably could have extinguished such enterprises soon enough if the fees were not paid. During the last six years of the Queen's reign, the enterprises at the Boar's Head, the Curtain, the Rose, and probably other places all fell for a time into the second category. The Burbages' and Henslowe's enterprises fell into the third, as eventually did that at the Boar's Head. Langley's affairs at the Swan fell in 1597 into the first.

Though used in 1598, the Boar's Head was really one of the three public playhouses opened during the fifteen months beginning in the spring of 1599. It was built in its lasting form just after the Globe and a year before the Fortune. It was smaller and perhaps less well equipped than they. It was organized and built by novices in the theatre business, unlike the Globe and

Fortune. By comparison with them, it must have suffered in the abilities of the people who wrote for it, Heywood and possibly the earl of Derby being the only ones now known by name. It did not suffer similarly, however, in the abilities of some of the players who used it, and they seem to have thought its stage a worthy thing to have under them.

Maps

I have reproduced the maps so that the reader may compare them easily, despite their different orientations and sizes. The maps in plates 1 and 2 do not have a compass rose or any other device to show where north is. The other maps do have such devices: two of these show north as about 7° (plate 3) and 9° (plate 4) to the left (west) of a line running at right angles from top to bottom of the map; the two others (plates 5 and 6) show north as directly at the top of such a line. All the maps are of different sizes, the smallest having a scale of 6½″ and the largest of 60″ to the mile.

For my purposes, the most important map is that in plate 4, and all the other maps should be compared to it. To facilitate this comparison, I have reproduced the maps in plates 3, 5, and 6 to have the same orientation as that in plate 4 and to include about the same amount of ground. I have not used the orientation on modern maps because the map in plate 4 has the Boar's Head so close to the top of the sheet that changing the orientation would cause either part of the Boar's Head to disappear or the reproduction not to be rectangular. I have reproduced the maps in plates 1 and 2 with the original orientation because inventing a new one on these maps would be a most uncertain business. Moreover, to show all the places that could represent the Boar's Head, I have included much more of the High Street and its environs on the maps in plate 1, and somewhat more on that in plate 2, than on later maps.

Despite these differences and changes in orientation, north is roughly at the top of all the reproductions, south at the bottom, east at the right, and west at the left. The maps in plates 3–6 are discussed in chapters 9 and 10.

MAP 1: (a) The "Agas" map, c.1562, original scale about 28″ to the mile; (b) the Hogenberg map, 1572, original scale about 6½″ to the mile. The reproductions show Whitechapel High Street from St. Botolph's church to

Brick Lane and beyond, also some of the land north and south of the High Street. The street running north from "The Barres" is Brick Lane. The street running north from the back of the properties along the High Street is probably Hog Lane (later Petticoat Lane and now Middlesex Street). It should join the High Street, and the bars should be at the junction and not where Brick Lane joins the High Street.

These two maps obviously have much to do with another. They probably derive from a common original, perhaps the so-called copperplate map (c.1553–59), whose two surviving sheets do not show Whitechapel. Much of the drawing on these maps, including, probably, all of it in the High Street, was meant to show what one could expect to exist in a given place, not what actuall did. If one is to look for the Boar's Head, one should consider: (1) the lands and buildings where Hog Lane should join the High Street but does not, roughly halfway between the church and Brick Lane, the Boar's Head having been mostly behind the buildings on the eastern side of that corner, and (2) the lands and buildings on the eastern side of the corner of the High Street and Brick Lane—assuming that in mistakenly placing the bars the mapmakers also mistakenly placed what belonged with them.

MAP 2: Newcourt's map, 1658, original scale about 11″ to the mile. This and all the following reproductions show mainly the corner of the High Street and Hog Lane—the High Street running from the southwest to the northeast and Hog Lane from the High Street to the northwest. The Boar's Head lay mostly behind the buildings around the eastern side of the corner, but four buildings in the High Street also belonged to the Boar's Head. They should be those east of the four beginning with the one on the corner; the entrance to the Boar's Head should be between the third and fourth Boar's Head buildings, counting from west to east.

MAP 3: Leake's Survey (the drawing by Hollar), 1667, original scale abut 17 ½″ to the mile. The dotted line and similar marks on later maps running along Hog Lane and across the High Street indicate the City boundary. Hollar seems to have tried to represent many buildings as they actually were.

MAP 4: Ogilby and Morgan's map, 1676, original scale 52.8″ to the mile. The passage running east from Petticoat Lane on this and the next map (map 5) is what I call Needler's alley. The yard into which it runs, marked "g 18" here and identified in the *Explanation* as "Bores Head Yard," was the northern end of the great yard. The alley running south from Needler's alley is what I call Browne's alley. The seven buildings and one enclosure east of Browne's and south of Needler's alley lie in what had been the middle part of the great yard, and it is there that the playhouse had mainly been.

MAP 5: Ordnance Survey map, 1873–75, original scale 60″ to the mile. Only the southern part of what is called "Boar's Head Yard" seems to have had anything to do with the Boar's Head of the playhouse, and it was the northern end of the great yard.

MAP 6: Ordnance Survey map, 1971, original scale 50.69″ to the mile. The buildings in the High Street marked as nos. 141 to 138 stand on the site of the four buildings in the High Street that belonged to the Boar's Head in the time of the playhouse; for over two hundred years the buildings on the site were known as nos. 146–141 Whitechapel High Street. The playhouse lay where the southern part of the United Standard House and the sidewalk in front (west) of it are. The two buildings cut off by the northern edge of the reproduction are Cromlech House (partly embracing United Standard House) and the premises of the Sheepskin and Leather Discount Centre. The dotted lines running in a curve through the map from the southwest to the northeast mark the tunnel of the Metropolitan Railway. The "Subway" is for pedestrians.

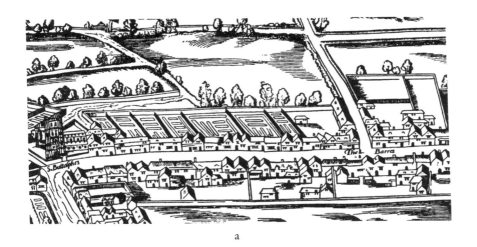

a

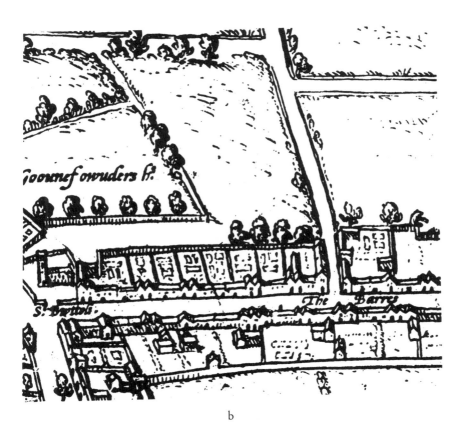

b

MAP 1: Reproduced by permission of the Guildhall Library, City of London

135

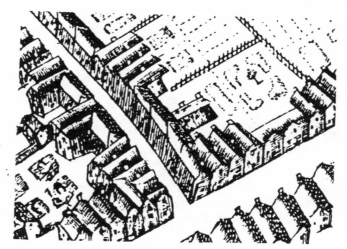

MAP 2: Reproduced by permission of the Greater London Council

MAP 3: Reproduced by permission of the Greater London Council

MAP 4: Reproduced by permission of the Greater London Council

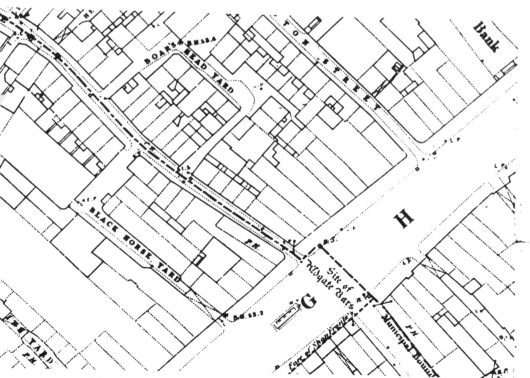

MAP 5: Reproduced by permission of the British Library

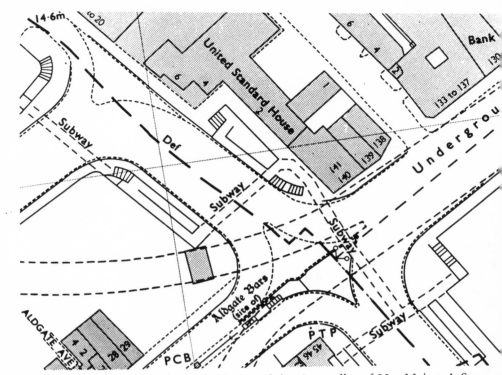

MAP 6: Reproduced by permission of the Controller of Her Majesty's Stationery Office. Crown copyright reserved.

Illustrations

Illustrations cannot stop where lawsuits, deeds, and maps do. The evidence about the Boar's Head gave Mr. Hodges (as he has written) "a not-quite-complete skeleton" upon which he had to put a good deal of "imaginary . . . flesh." His task, therefore (as he has added), was to prepare sketches, not architectural drawings. He had to decide at the outset what to make of the general style of the inn. Should it have the "ambience" of a Renaissance palace like Hatfield, or of the half-timbered grammar school at Stratford-upon-Avon where Shakespeare went to school, or of something humbler? The evidence not unreasonably suggested something humbler to him, something "utilitarian, horsey & barnyardy." He had then to decide about the ambience of the playhouses built in the inn and arrived at a scheme partly utilitarian and partly grander. He had, finally, to supply a great many structural details not found in the evidence. He had to design a system of roofs and gutters, for example, and invent the height of everything, including the stage.

The Boar's Head lies in the illustrations as, for obvious reasons, it does in virtually all the evidence and in the text, simply north and south, east and west. Because Whitechapel High Street, however, really runs from the south-west at the City boundary to the northeast, the Boar's Head really lay north-west and southeast, northeast and southwest; and the stage was on the southwest.

Below I point out those aspects of the illustrations not explained in the text.

ILLUSTRATION 1: Plan of the yard before the building of the playhouses.

The buildings in the High Street are 30′ north and south, and the eastern building is 20′ east and west, because Ogilby and Morgan's map shows them about so. The entrance to the great barn also dervies from the map. That barn adjoined the eastern building, but of where it began and ended on the east and west the evidence gives no hint. There was, it seems, a stairway at the southern end of the gallery along the eastern building, and this stairway eventually became the means by which people reached the eastern, northern, and southern galleries of the playhouse. Mr. Hodges shows an additional stairway toward the northern end of the gallery. The map shows the entrance into the Boar's Head from the High Street as much too small and awkward for the sort of traffic that would pass through the principal entrance to an inn: about 4' wide east and west at the High Street, then a right angle, then about 7' wide north and south. Mr. Hodges keeps the right angle but widens the entrance to 8' east and west and, after the right angle, to 10' north and south. He also widens and lengthens the drinking room beside the entrance to 9' east and west and 40' north and south (the map shows about 7' and 37'). As a result, his eastern building is about 3' shorter north to south than the map shows, and his Boar's Head buildings in the High Street (other than the drinking room) about 6' shorter east to west.

This scheme of things is repeated in subsequent illustrations.

ILLUSTRATION 2: Plan of the yard with the first playhouse (1598) in it.

Mr. Hodges supplies here and subsequently a scheme of pillars to hold up the northern, southern, and western galleries.

ILLUSTRATION 3: Plan of the yard with the second playhouse (1599) in it.

Nothing in the evidence suggests how people got into the western gallery, which was structurally separate from the other galleries. So Mr. Hodges guesses at two stairways, one in each corner.

ILLUSTRATION 4: Elevations from the western side of the yard, (a) before the building of the playhouses, and (b) after the building of the second playhouse (1599).

None of the evidence deals with elevations. Mr. Hodges has had, therefore, to invent a scheme of them, including roofs and chimneys. He makes the lower eastern, northern, and southern galleries 10' from the ground (to allow horses and wagons to get into and out of the northern part of the inn) and 8' high. The upper eastern gallery is also 8' high. Railings are all 3' high. The stage is 3'6" high, less than might have been customary because the owners would have wanted people standing in the northern and southern extremities of the yard to see something of the play despite the northern and southern galleries. Moreover, a higher stage would have created problems under the western gallery in the second playhouse. All the doors, windows, and posts are, of course, Mr. Hodges's.

The stairway at the southern end of the eastern building, which was, it seems, the main entry to the eastern, northern, and southern galleries, had double doors at the bottom, hence may well have been enclosed, not open as shown here.

There might well have been more degrees in the galleries of the second playhouse than shown here (b) and subsequently: altogether, four or more in the northern and southern galleries and six or more in the eastern ones.

ILLUSTRATION 5: Elevations from the south, (a) through the central part of the yard with the first playhouse (1598) in it, (b) through the central part of the yard with the second playhouse (1599) in it, and (c) from the southern part of the yard after the building of the second playhouse.

Mr. Hodges makes the ground floor of the tiring house 9' high and the western gallery 11' above the ground (a foot higher than the northern, southern, and lower eastern galleries). His roof over the stage in the second playhouse (b and c) is 24' east and west. It also covers the western gallery but, like that over the stage of the Swan in the famous drawing, not the front part of the stage. The pillars holding it up are 1' thick, and their centers are 11' behind the front of the stage. The small tower at the back of the stage roof (c) is over one of the stairways to the western gallery. Mr. Hodges encloses much of the playhouse by giving the southern gallery (and hence the northern one) an exterior wall (c).

ILLUSTRATION 6: Elevations from the eastern side of the yard, (a) before the building of the playhouses, and (b) after the building of the second playhouse (1599).

The "certeyne Romes" seem to have consisted on the ground floor of a larder, a room with a well, and a coal storage, and on the upper floor of a parlor over the larder, another over the well, and an oat loft over the coal storage. The garden gate south of the certain rooms is, of course, Mr. Hodges's, as is the wall of which it is part. The two towers on either side of the western gallery (b) house his stairways up to that gallery. He writes that he "was bothered by the need to make a gutter carrying rainwater away from the overstage roof back to a point where it could spill away to one side," and as he thought about the problem, the towers "built themselves."

The stage doors are 6'6" high, and the main one is 8' wide, the other two 3'. The western gallery is 7' high. The distance from the stage to the bottom of the tie beam of the stage roof is 16' 6", and from the eaves to the ridge, that roof is 8' high. The space in the roof from the top of the tie beam to the ridge pole is 4' high—if not enough for the machinery necessary to fly things onto and off the stage, then enough for pulleys leading to machinery in the tiring house. The stage pillars are 22'6" apart from their centers. The stage facade is a simpler version of those Mr. Hodges has postulated for both the first and second Globe (in *The Globe Restored* and *Shakespeare's Second Globe*).

ILLUSTRATION 7: A sketch of the yard before the building of the playhouses (looking northwest).

The ground floor of the certain rooms is not the same as in illustration 6-a, the assumption here being that the larder might have been bigger than the well room and the coal storage. There was a pump in the northern part of the Boar's Head, but the evidence does not say where.

The two buildings north of the certain rooms appear here as the lawsuits seem to describe them rather than as Ogilby and Morgan's map has them. North and south, the two together measure about what the map shows, but because the Poleys lived in its upper story, the southern one is bigger than the map shows and hence the northern one smaller. The Poleys' building is 18'6" here, the "ostry" 12'; the map has almost the opposite, roughly 12'6" and 18'. The Poleys' building is 32' east and west here without the shed behind it, 41' with it; the map has about 36' for the whole property. The east-west size of the ostry is not clearly shown here but seems to be about what the map has, some 19'. These two buildings had to do with the equine side of the inn trade. Like the great barn immediately north of them, they may well have been rebuilt as different kinds of structures long before the map was made.

ILLUSTRATION 8: A sketch of the yard before the building of the playhouses (looking northeast).

The gardens are behind the buildings in the High Street that did not belong to the Boar's Head.

ILLUSTRATION 9: A sketch of the yard with the first playhouse (1598) in it.

Because his stage is only 3'6" high, hence easy for spectators to climb onto, Mr. Hodges here and subsequently has put a railing around it.

ILLUSTRATION 10: A sketch of the yard with the second playhouse (1599) in it.

ILLUSTRATION 11: A sketch of the second playhouse (1599).

Here and in the next illustration, the stage facade is somewhat different from that in illustration 6-b, because the main door is narrower and the other doors wider.

ILLUSTRATION 12: A sketch of the second playhouse (1599) with a differrent scheme of roofs.

Mr. Hodges suggests here that the tiring house and western gallery had separate gabled roofs and the stage a flat, sloping one. He thinks this scheme simpler and "perhaps more likely," though it would not provide room in the stage roof for machinery or much else.

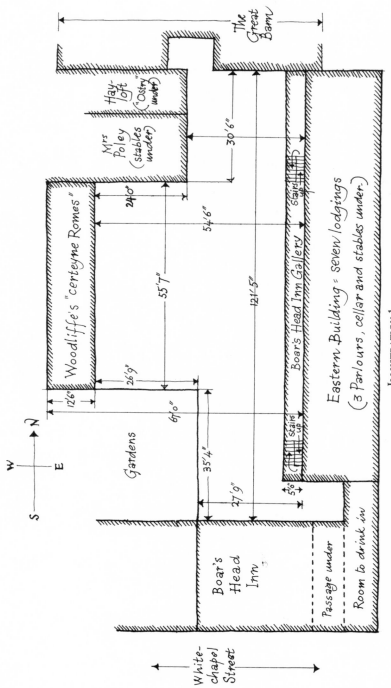

ILLUSTRATION 1

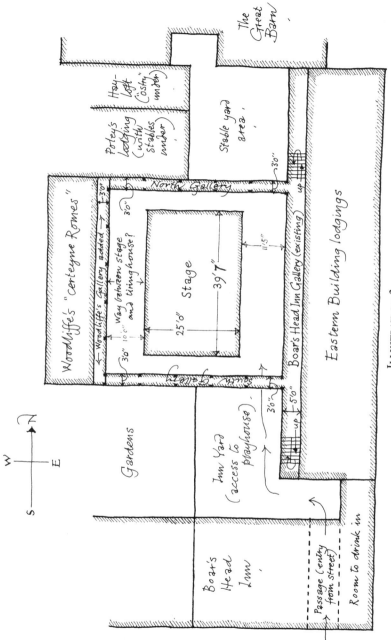

ILLUSTRATION 2

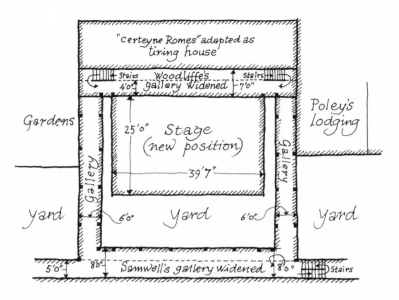

"certeyne Romes" adapted as tiring house

Stairs 4'0" Woodliffe's gallery widened Stairs 7'0"

Gardens

Poley's lodging

Gallery

25'0" Stage (new position)

39'7"

Gallery

yard

6'0" Yard 6'0"

yard

5'0" 8'0" Samwell's gallery widened 8'0" Stairs

Boar's Head lodgings

ILLUSTRATION 3

146

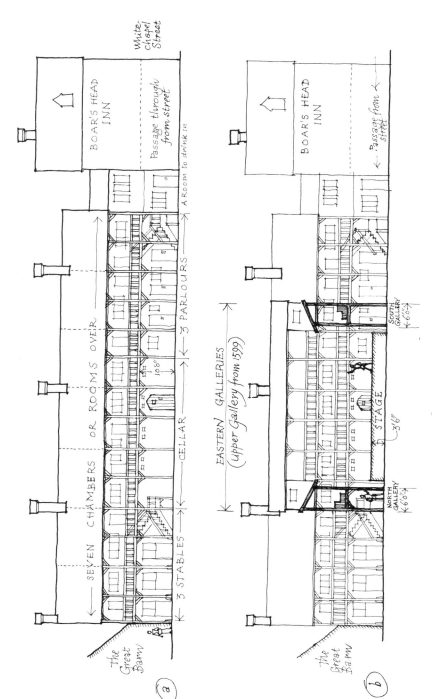

ILLUSTRATION 4

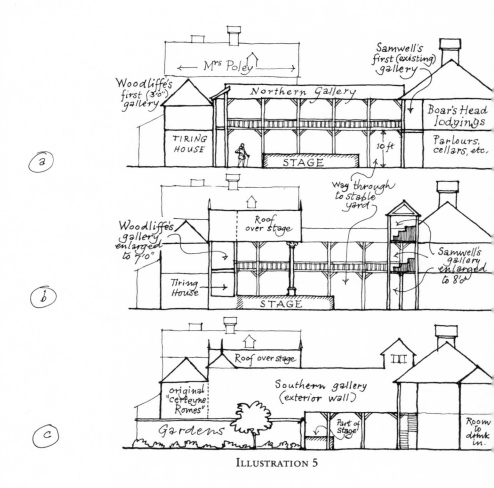

a

b

c

Mrs Poley

Woodliffe's first (3'0") gallery

Northern Gallery

Samwell's first (existing) gallery

Boar's Head lodgings

TIRING HOUSE

STAGE

Parlours, cellars, etc.

10 ft

Woodliffe's gallery enlarged to 7'0"

Roof over stage

way through to stable yard

Samwell's gallery enlarged to 8'0"

Tiring House

STAGE

Roof over stage

original "certeyne Romes"

Southern gallery (exterior wall)

Gardens

Part of stage

Room to drink in.

ILLUSTRATION 5

148

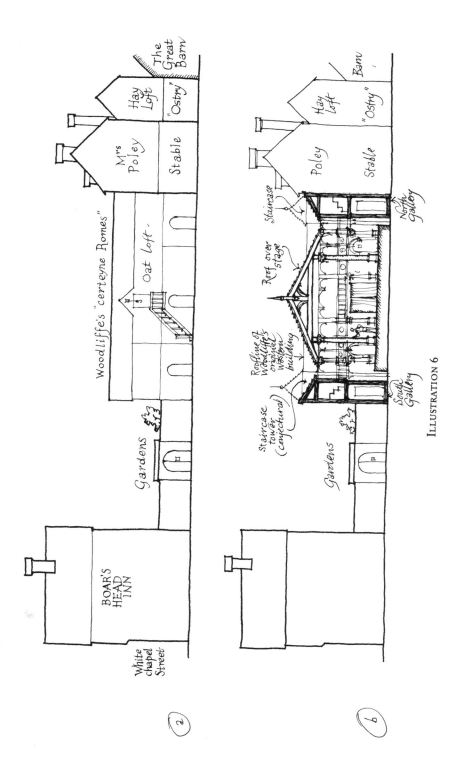

a

White chapel Street

BOAR'S HEAD INN

Gardens

Woodliffe's "certeyne Romes"

Oat loft.

Mrs Poley

Stable

Hay Loft

"Ostry"

The Great Barn

b

Gardens

Staircase tower (conjectural)

Roofline of Woodliffe's original westorn building

Roof over stage

Staircase

South Gallery

North Gallery

Poley

Stable

Hay Loft

"Ostry" Barn

ILLUSTRATION 6

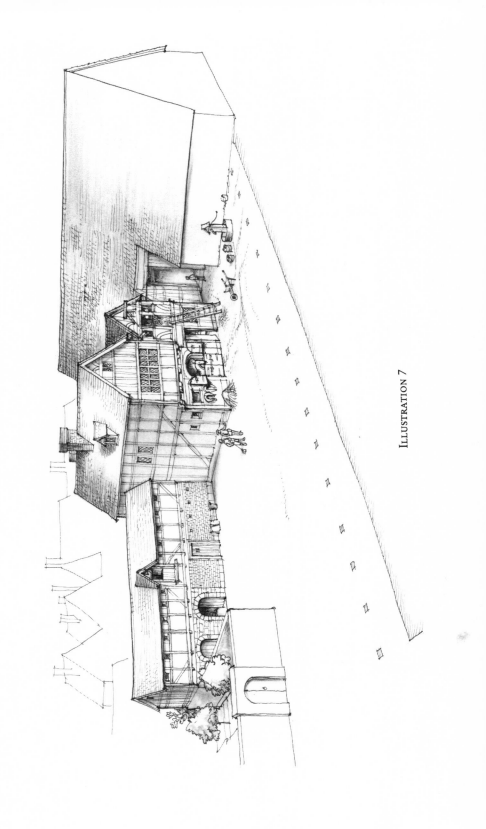

ILLUSTRATION 7

ILLUSTRATION 8

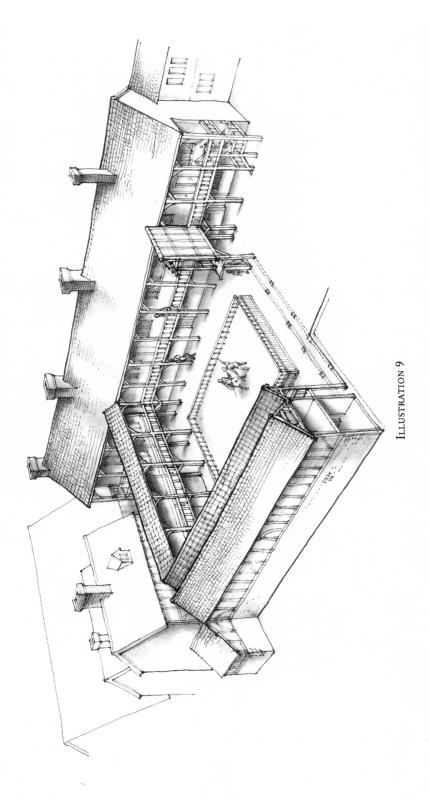

ILLUSTRATION 9

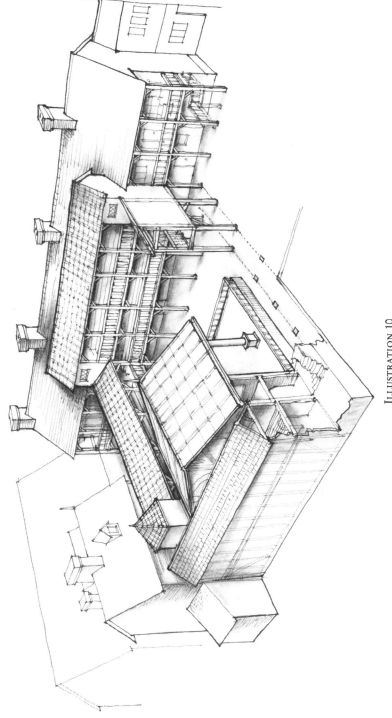

ILLUSTRATION 10

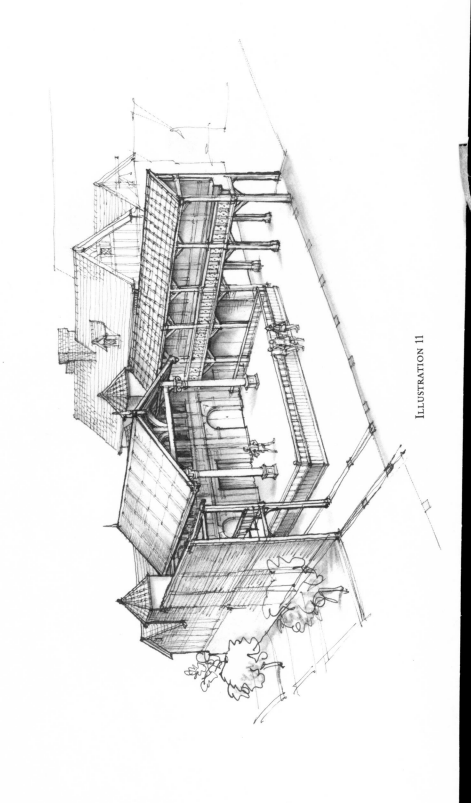

ILLUSTRATION 11

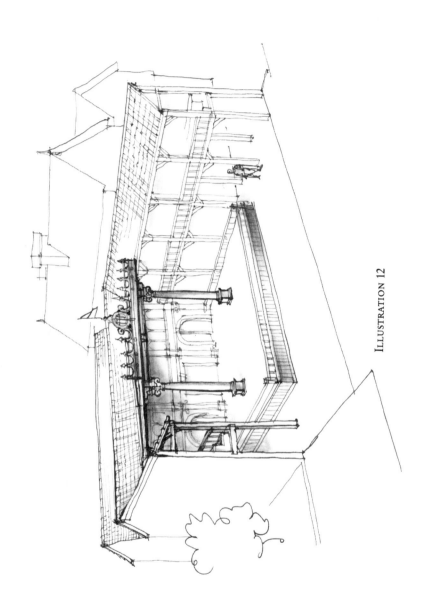

ILLUSTRATION 12

The Study of the Boar's Head

When E. K. Chambers published his *Elizabethan Stage* (1923), nobody knew much about the Boar's Head. He could report only that the Privy Council stopped a play there in 1557, that Worcester's men considered it theirs in 1602 and again in 1604, and that the Prince's men probably belonged to it in 1608. He knew, that is, only what had been printed among the papers of the Privy Council, among the calendars of state papers, domestic, and (by Murray) among the municipal records of Leicester. He knew that the Boar's Head was somewhere in Whitechapel, but not whether it was in the City or Middlesex. "The Boar's Head," as he concluded, was "a short-lived house of which practically nothing is known."

Sometime during the next thirteen years, Professor C. J. Sisson found some of the most important documents about the Boar's Head. He did not, however, publish the significant study for which he had plenty of information. He published instead a popular piece in 1936, "Mr. and Mrs. Browne of the Boar's Head," in which he used some of the most interesting things in his documents but did not analyze his information rigorously or cite his sources. He used information he had found in the following documents:

1. a Chancery deposition, C.24/290/3
2. a Chancery deposition, C.24/304/27
3. a Star Chamber bill with answers, St.Ch.5/S.74/3
4. a group of Chancery decrees and orders (which I list completely though Sisson did not use them all), C.33/101/f.573, 611, 643–43^v, 735 in the A book; and /102/f.577^v, 616, 648^v, 798^v in the B book
5. a group of Chancery decrees and orders (which I list completely though Sisson used only a few), C.33/99/f.473^v, 464^v, 526, 577^v; /101/f.207^v, 263^v, 290, 324^v, 309, 406^v, 450; /103/f.43–43^v, 346, 700^v in the A

book; and /100/f.461, 452^v, 518, 564^v; /102/f.249^v, 302, 326^v, 343–43^v, 344, 433, 470^v; /104/f.44^v, 359, 744^v in the B book.

He dealt with some of this information again in an article of 1942, "Notes on Early Stuart Stage History," again without much analysis. This time, however, he tried to identify three of the groups of documents above (nos. 2, 3, 4), but he gave the first two citations incompletely and the third wrongly. Moreover, he gave the first two as proof of assertions they do not really prove, and he got the date and the occasion wrong for the events reported in the third. He dealt with some of these things yet again in an article of 1954, "The Red Bull Company and the Importunate Widow," where he used and identified the group of documents in no. 4 above as he had done in 1942.[1]

Soon after, Dr. Leslie Hotson stumbled on the one deposition Professor Sisson had not tried to identify (no. 1), one of those he had identified incompletely (no. 3), and three other important documents Prof. Sisson had evidently not seen:

6. a Chancery deposition, C.24/278/71
7. the interrogatories and depositions for no. 3, St.Ch.5/S.13/8
8. a bill and answer in the Court of Requests, Req.2/466/pt.II [/1].

Dr. Hotson cited all these documents fully in his *Shakespeare's Wooden O* (1959), pp. 264, 269 n., etc.[2] He glanced at them briefly, but he was embarked on a quest for which they were not of much use.

That is where the Boar's Head lay when I joined the work. I meant to study the Boar's Head in two parts (which became three) and then bring the parts together in a book. I read the first part as a paper at a conference at the University of Waterloo in Ontario in the summer of 1968. Among other things, I used all the documents Dr. Hotson had identified along with the two groups of Chancery decrees and orders (nos. 4, 5), which I had found for myself. I used, that is, all the documents above except no. 2. I tried to analyze these documents closely, and I corrected Professor Sisson's confusion in no. 4. In the audience happened to be the late Professor T. J. B. Spencer, director of the Shakespeare Institute, the University of Birmingham. He remembered that he had recently seen a piece of writing by Professor Sisson at the Institute. Professor Sisson had died in 1966 and left the Institute a manuscript about the Boar's Head. In his last years, it seemed, he had essayed the work that he had not done in 1936. Professor Spencer soon found the manuscript and kindly consulted Professor Sisson's family about how the manuscript and my work might be brought together. The family decided that they should publish the manuscript separately and hence that I should not see it. At Professor Spencer's suggestion and my own inclination, I continued my work. I read the second part of my work at Waterloo in the summer of 1970, in which I adjusted some of my conclusions of 1968, announced many new documents, two of them among the most important,

9. C.54/2471/17
10. C.54/2515/11

(the deeds of 1621), and introduced Ogilby and Morgan's map of 1676 to the study of the Boar's Head. In the following summer, 1971, I read my third paper at Vancouver, dealing with the history of the Boar's Head in the sixteenth century. The first of these papers was published in 1970, the third in the autumn of 1972, and the second (much delayed in press) in 1973. I have since discussed the Boar's Head in four other papers presented to academic meetings but not published.[3]

Professor Sisson's manuscript appeared as a book edited by Dr. Stanley Wells in the spring of 1972, *The Boar's Head Theatre* (Routledge & Kegan Paul). Dr. Wells published Professor Sisson's work, as he says (p. xiii), largely as he found it. He chose to allude in his apparatus only to my first part because that was the only part in print when he did his work, though the other parts were available to him.

In this book Professor Sisson announced at last the complete citation of the one deposition that neither Dr. Hotson nor I had found, no. 2 above. He studied the documents that he had used in 1936 and again in 1942 and 1954, along with those that Dr. Hotson had announced (without saying that Dr. Hotson had announced them). He did not know that he had muddled the matters in no. 4, but he did realize that something was wrong with the citations, for he omitted them. One gathers that Professor Sisson even now did not attempt a strenuous study of his documents. He was an old and famous man in failing health trying to carry out an obligation that, by implication, he had made to his readers thirty years before (he had declared the obligation in 1954). Understandably, perhaps, he trusted too often to an instinct for the old stage, and he assumed too often that events would take the shape that abstract logic might suggest. He had a curious tendency to believe that a certain name could apply to only one person, despite great improbabilities—like the two Edmund Poleys, whom he continued to make one even after finding the burial record of one of them and evidence that the other lived on (p. 26, n.4). He also had the tendency that we all have, to dismiss or not look for evidence that could prove inconvenient to a cherished hypothesis. Sometimes his guesses hardened into facts that then supported further guesses.

Where we differ in important things, I discuss Professor Sisson's view as I come to those things in the chapters above. I discuss one such thing more fully than the others, however, in appendix 9—the identity of the two or more theatrical people named Robert Browne.

APPENDIX 2
The Building of the Playhouse, 1598 and 1599

Woodliffe and Francis Langley argued often that the great yard of the Boar's Head was theirs because Woodliffe had not specifically conveyed it to Samwell in the lease of 1598. It was not in their interest, therefore, to advertise that Woodliffe and Samwell had meant the lease mainly as a device by which they might protect themselves while jointly building a playhouse in and around that yard. So the evidence about what Woodliffe and Samwell built in the yard in 1598 and a year later appears only in the testimony of Samwell, his successor Browne, and their witnesses.

Samwell asked his witnesses in February 1600 to explain whether he had built "any Romes or Galleryes in a greate yard of the Messuage or Inne called the Bores Hedd," and "what galleryes or buildinges" he had caused "to be there made and who were the workmen and what chardge or Somes of money" he had borne and paid "for the same buildings." Two of the witnesses should have known the answers to these questions, for they were Samwell's builder of 1599, John Mago, and Mago's "chief workman," the carpenter, Walter Rodes. The third witness was Samwell's servant, Edward Willys, who had apparently watched much of the work going on.

Samwell asked next whether these three knew that Woodliffe "was Contentid that the playntiffe [Samwell] should buyld the said Galeryes and Romes and howe do you knowe the same and whether dyd the said Olyver [Woodliffe] sett forthe the Scytuacion of the same buildinges to be erected and allowe out of the said yard suffycyent ground to build and erecte the same."

Mago replied that Samwell had indeed built "certeine roomes or galleryes in the yeard of the messuage or Inne called the Bores Head," and "that there were three galleryes so made there, one on the east side of the said yard

159

another on the north side, and the thirde on the south." He went on to say how much money Samwell had spent (see chapter 3). He replied to Samwell's second question by saying that Woodliffe was quite contented that Samwell "should buylde the said galleryes and roomes," for Woodliffe actually told Mago "how farr forth" he might extend Samwell's galleries in 1599. Woodliffe said this "when" Mago and Rodes "tooke measure for the framinge of the tymber according to the proporcion of the ground wch the said Oliver [Woodliffe] appointed for the scituacion of the galleryes"—a remark that is logically inconsistent, possibly because it is incomplete (a line is illegible just before the "when" clause). Mago and Rodes would not have been taking measure for Woodliffe's "proporcion" before Woodliffe told them what it was.

Rodes was of like mind about Samwell's first question, though less precise. Samwell had built "three galleryes or roomes in the Yarde of the messuage or Inne called the Bores Head." In his answer to Samwell's second question, however, Rodes, after mentioning Woodliffe's moving the stage (see appendix 3), very usefully expanded and clarified Mago's inconsistent remark about Woodliffe's part in the rebuilding of Samwell's galleries in 1599. "And after [he meant "before"—see appendix 3] the removinge of the said stage," Woodliffe "cominge to the depont [Rodes] as he was takinge measure for a story to be made ouer the longe old gallery sayd these words or the like in effect to him, yf the case were myne as yt is Samuells I would pull downe this older gallery to the ground, and buylde yt foure foote forwarder toward the stage into ye yarde and wth a lath or some other thinge wch he then had in his hande, did poynt how farr he would wish the said longe old gallery to be buylt and qth he yf yt were buylt so farr forwarder then would there be roome for three or four seats more in a gallery, and for many mo people, and yett neuer the lesse roome in the yarde." After such speeches, Samwell "caused the said old longe gallery to be pulled downe, and to be built & placed according to his the said defendts [Woodliffe's] direccion savinge that yt was not sett out so farr into ye said yard as the said defendt did appoint yt by a foote at leaste."

Willys also agreed about Samwell's first question, though less precisely than either Mago or Rodes. Samwell had built "certeine galleryes or roomes in the great yard of the" Boar's Head. Willys was less precise about Samwell's second question, too, but he agreed with the others, and in speaking of posts, he suggested the design of Samwell's galleries in both 1598 and 1599. Willys cited the same speech of Woodliffe's that Mago had mentioned and Rodes had explained. He remembered "that when the carpenters tooke measure or were in hande to make the same galleryes the said defendt [Woodliffe] gave them direccion how wide to make the same galleryes, and how farr forth to sett the posts, in this manner viz[:] Yf the case were myne at yt is Mr Samuells, I would sett the posts and other things in this and this manner."

Then "when some of the said galleryes were fynished & done or very neare fynished the said Woodliffe dislikinge as yt should seeme that they were not so well placed & fynished as he could have devised them, sayd these or like words to this depon^t [Willys] Yf the galleryes were myne as they be yor Masters, I would have had them sett thus & thus poyntinge in what manner he would have had them made, and how farr forth he would have sett them into the yardward wch was wyder by a foote & half as he gessath then" Samwell "caused them to be made." (C.24/278/71, interrogatories 1, 2, Mago nos. 1, 2, Rodes nos. 1, 2, Willys nos. 1, 2.)

In June 1601 Browne asked two new witnesses if Samwell and Woodliffe had agreed in 1599 that Samwell "should pull downe certaine newe galleries and romes by the said Samuell before that time builded and sett vpp in the greate yarde of the saide howse or Inn called the bores hed, and should make build and sett vp the same galleries & romes in the said greate yarde larger and further into and vppon the said yarde so farr as he the said olyver Wood-leff then did measure and sett oute the same." Like Samwell's witnesses of the year before, these should have known the answers, for one was Mago's workman, William Hoppdale, a carpenter, and the other was Samwell's son, the younger Richard Samwell, who had kept his father's accounts during the building operations.

Hoppdale merely agreed with the question as it was read to him. Samwell and Woodliffe did agree that Samwell "should pull downe certen new gal-leryes and Romes wch he had formerly sett vp, in the great yarde of the sayd Inne, and should sett vp agayne the same galleryes and rometh larger out, into and vpon the sayd yarde viz: so farr as the sayd Oliver Woodlef did then measure and sett out in the presence of this dep^t [Hoppdale] and Mr Cuckow and others." Accordingly, as Hoppdale said in answer to a later question, Samwell "did pluck downe the old and erected and sett vp the new galleries larger then the former were."

The younger Samwell was the best of the witnesses. He was literate (unlike Rodes, Willys, Hoppdale, and, later, Marsh), he knew the business of the Boar's Head intimately, having seen all the documents and been present at the making of all the agreements, and he was clever and articulate enough to put all his father's and Browne's arguments. He alone, for example, dis-tinguished clearly between the building of 1598 and that of 1599. His testi-mony in answer to Browne's question is worth quoting at length. He well knew, he said, that after his father and Woodliffe had made their lease (13 April 1598), his father "did (when the said Woodleffe was at sea or abroade) erect & sett vp in the great yard of the *said* Inne certeine galleryes or roomes for people to stand in to see the playes, and that afterwards when Woodleffe came home againe, Woodleffe found fault because the *said* galleryes or roomes were made so little, wherevppon Yt was afterwards agreed by and betweene this depon^ts [the younger Samwell's] father & Woodlieffe that this deponents father should pull the said new galleryes downe againe, and should buylde or sett vp larger galleryes and further into the yarde viz [:] so farr forth into the yarde as the said Woodlieffe did measure or sett out wth a rule or lathe wch he had in his hande, wch so farr as he remembreth was some three or foure foote or more further into the said yard then the said little galleryes did stande[.] And he sayth that the same little galleryes were accordingly pulled downe, and larger galleryes sett vpp, by the appoyntment of his father." (C.24/290/3, interrogatory 3, Hoppdale nos. 3–4, 5, Samwell no. 3.)

As though to make up for the confusion of his remark of February 1600, Mago partly confirmed in July 1603 Rodes's statement that the workmen were taking measure for the gallery over the long gallery when Woodliffe first proposed that the playhouse be rebuilt. The agreement between Woodliffe and Samwell to rebuild, Mago said, "was made in the great yard of the said Inne when the great new galleryes were in buyldinge in the yard next the parlo^{rs}." The parlors were no doubt the three that all three good accounts of the lease of 1598 give as in the eastern building, on which the long gallery was (see chapter 11 and appendix 3). (C.24/304/27, no. 3.)

These statements are the useful evidence for most aspects of the building of the playhouse in the Boar's Head. There are many other allusions to that building in these documents and in the other statements by Samwell, Browne, and their witnesses (St.Ch.5/S.74/3, the bill; /S.13/8; Req.2/466/ pt.II[/1], the reply; C.24/304/27), but most are so general as merely to confirm that a playhouse was built in the Boar's Head. Some are repetitions of the statements above, made two and three years after the original statement (see chapter 7). I mention a few in the notes for chapters 3 and 12 rather than here because they concern matters that seem peripheral to the main ones. The rest concern the particular aspects of the building of the playhouse with which I deal in appendixes 3 and 5.

APPENDIX 3

Positions of the Galleries, Tiring House, and Stage

None of the litigants or deponents in the lawsuits about the Boar's Head, or anybody else, explained neatly what theatrical structures lay in and around the playhouse yard. They alluded so often and so consistently to the structures in the yard, however, that by compiling their remarks one can see the scheme of things clearly. I discuss first the evidence for each side of the yard and then that for the stage.

A. The Western Side

In April 1600, Samwell said that when Woodliffe leased much of the Boar's Head to him on 13 April 1598, the parts of the place Woodliffe kept for himself were on the western side, including a three-foot strip of yard he kept to build on. As Samwell put it, Woodliffe had the right to "buyld on the west parte of the said greate yarde nere adioynynge to certeyne Romes excepted in the said Indenture [of 13 April 1598] to the said Olyver and his wife a full yard further in length into the greate yarde aforesaid" (St.Ch.5/S.74/3, the bill). Two months earlier, Samwell had described Woodliffe's part of the Boar's Head as his "Romes by the yard" (C.24/278/71, interrogatory 4). Woodliffe himself confirmed and amplified these remarks in May 1603. The Poley lease of 1594, he explained, required him to "bestowe 100^{li} in building of the Larder the Larder parler the well parler the Cole house the oate Loaft the Tireing house & stage wthin seaven yeares or the said Lease to be forfeited," and he had entered into a bond of £300 that would also be forfeit if he did not do this building. Accordingly, in his lease with Samwell, Woodliffe had kept, as he said, the right "to enter into the said Inn at all tymes

163

convenient wth Carte & Caryage for the building of the west *parte* of the great yard of the said Inn w[ch] . . . [he] was tyed to build in seaven [years] or els the originall Lease to be forfeited." Eventually, when the lease was in danger of being forfeit because Woodliffe had not done all the building he had bonded himself to do, the Court of Chancery ordered him to do this building, rather than the Langleys, to whom he had by then leased his parts of the Boar's Head, "by reason," as Woodliffe put it, "that y[e] *said* Broune would not suffer the said Langleys to build in and vpon the west side of the said Inn as they were bounde to doe." (Req.2/466/pt.II[/1], the bill.) Woodliffe, then, had the western side of the yard for his structures.

Those structures, according to the man who built them, John Mago, were "the stage tyringe houses & the galleryes ou*er* & about the stage wth the coue*rings* ou*er* them w[ch] the *said* Woodliffe buylded" (C.24/304/27, no. 3), and as two commissioners of Chancery, Woodliffe, and Browne all agreed, they were on the west. In October 1602, the men of Chancery described Woodliffe's part of the Boar's Head as "the stage Tyring Howse and galleryes scytuat on the West syde of the great yard of the said Inne lately buylt by" Woodliffe (C.33/103/f.43–43[v] in the A book, and /104/f.44[v] in the B book where the galleries are in the singular). In their lawsuit of May 1603, Woodliffe and Browne agreed about little except that one of the arguments concerned (as Woodliffe put it twice) Woodliffe's "stage tyreing house & galleries on the west side of the great yarde of the said Inne," and especially about the profits of those galleries, which Browne described four times as "the said weste galleryes over the said Stage" (Req.2/466/pt.II[/1], the bill and reply). In February 1600, Mago indirectly named the western gallery as Woodliffe's when he remembered that Woodliffe had given orders about it when it was being rebuilt in 1599: Woodliffe had not objected to the work on any of the galleries "vntill suche tyme as the said galleryes were all fynished savinge one storye of the gallery on the west side of the said yarde, w[ch] when this depon[t] [Mago] beganne to fall in hand w[th]all and to take off the roofe, he [Woodliffe] willed this depon[t] to forbeare and go no forwarder till Samuell and he had talked together" about "that story w[ch] then was to be done" (C.24/278/71, no. 4).

Of the dozens of remarks about Woodliffe's structure, only this one of Mago's mentions a story and so suggests that the structure had more than one. All the other remarks about stories refer, as we shall see, to the structure on the eastern side of the yard. Could Woodliffe's structure have comprised, like the eastern one, two galleries, one above the other? Apparently not. Mago's phrase, "one storye of the gallery on the west side of the said yarde," is revealing, as are his next phrases: to work on the story, his workmen had to take off the roof of the structure. Although he differentiated between "storye" and "gallery," which ought to have been the same thing, Mago thought of the structure as containing one gallery, and it was at the top of the structure. People at the Boar's Head and elsewhere usually used the plural, "galleries," to mean a single gallery; so they were being consciously precise when they used, as Mago did, the singular. Two other allusions to Woodliffe's structure have the singular, both in one official copy of a Chancery order of 15 October 1602. Both allusions have the plural in the other official copy, however, and so do all the nearly forty allusions in the lawsuits of 1603. Woodliffe's structure must have contained a single upper gallery, reminiscent of the equivalent galleries shown in all four drawings of the interiors of professional playhouses of the time. Mago must have thought of the arrangements under the gallery (the stage wall and the things behind it) as constituting another story. (C.33/103/f.43–43ᵛ in the A book, /104/f.44ᵛ in the B book.)

B. The Eastern Side

Before the building of the playhouse in 1598, there was a gallery on the eastern side of the yard. It ran along the upper story of the long building that formed the eastern boundary of the Boar's Head and of the yard. It was used for access to the quarters in that upper story, and it was probably one of the things about the Boar's Head that suggested plays to the Poleys, Woodliffe, and Samwell (see chapter 11). One would expect this gallery to be long and, before the rebuilding of 1599, old. A gallery was, as it happens, so described by the builder, John Mago, and his foreman, Walter Rodes. Moreover, by a rather circuitous route one can establish that it was the eastern one.

In February 1600, Samwell tried to prove that Woodliffe had allowed him to build galleries over the yard by showing that Woodliffe had suggested and then collaborated in the rebuilding of 1599. Samwell asked Mago, Rodes, and the servant, Edward Willys, to describe the conversation in the yard in which Woodliffe suggested that the place be rebuilt, and to describe the most conspicuous example of Woodliffe's collaboration, his moving the stage at least partly to make more room for Samwell's galleries. Fortunately, when arguing that larger galleries would bring in more profit, Woodliffe used the eastern gallery as his example, and when moving the stage, he most facilitated the rebuilding of the eastern gallery. Unfortunately, the three men tended to confuse the two events because Samwell asked about them in reverse order, the stage first and the suggestion to rebuild second.

Mago quoted Woodliffe like this: if Samwell's galleries (on the north, south, and east) "were myne as they bee Samuells I would pull downe that longe gallery & bringe yt forwarder into yᵉ yarde, and wᵗʰall poynted wᵗʰ a rod wᶜʰ he then had in his hande how farr further he would sett that gallery into yᵉ yard warde, wᶜʰ to this deponᵗˢ remembrance was foure foote or thereab:." A moment or two earlier Mago had said rather confusedly that he and Rodes were taking measure "for the scituac*i*on of the galleryes" when this episode took place, and that Woodliffe then "did help this depon[t] to measure out the said ground."

Rodes was more explicit, but he mistakenly began his account of Woodliffe's remarks by saying "and after the removinge of the said stage. . . ." He meant "and before," for Woodliffe would hardly have moved the stage to accommodate the rebuilding and then suggested the rebuilding. Moreover, Mago began his own account of those remarks by saying "and before the removinge of that stage. . . ." Rodes explained what he was taking measure for when Woodliffe made his remarks: a story they were about to build over the long old gallery (I quote Rodes's words in full in appendix 2), and that is why, probably, Woodliffe used that long old gallery as his example. Rodes identified the gallery three times as the "longe old" one in his account of Woodliffe's remarks. (C.24/278/71, interrogatories 2, 3, Mago nos. 2, 3, Rodes nos. 2, 3.)

According to the evidence about the leases of 1594 and 1598 (see chapter 11), there was only one gallery that was "old" in 1599, the one on the east, and it was likely to have been long. Moreover, Mago and Rodes plainly implied that one of Samwell's three galleries was long, not two. There would hardly have been a long gallery on the north or south and not one on the other. That, again, leaves Samwell's gallery on the east as the long one. But two other lines of reasoning also suggest that the long gallery was on the east. One concerns the parlors in the eastern building and the other Woodliffe's moving of the stage.

Mago returned in July 1603 to Woodliffe's remarks that led to the rebuilding of the playhouse. This time he tried to do what his foreman, Rodes, had done in 1600, to identify the structure on which the men were beginning to work when Woodliffe made the remarks. The agreement to which those remarks led, Mago reported, "was made in the great yard of the said Inne when the great new galleryes were in buyldinge in the yard next the parlo[rs]." Mago's great new galleries must have been the rebuilt form, with its story above, of Rodes's long old gallery, and these galleries must have been the eastern ones. There were three parlors in the eastern building, one of them considerable, for, according to Moxlay (in October 1600) and Browne and Marsh (in July 1603), Woodliffe and his wife lived in it. Moxlay identified that parlor as one of the eastern ones when he quoted a conversation between Woodliffe and Samwell at the sealing of their lease on 13 April 1598. The two had agreed informally that Woodliffe (as Moxlay quoted him) "should have this parlour to my selfe till I have built on the other side of the yarde." Woodliffe, of course, built only on the western side of the yard. Samwell called Woodliffe's parlor the "hither" parlor, presumably a mistake for "higher" (his son called it the "vpper" parlor). (C.24/304/27, interrogatory

16, Mago no. 3, Marsh no. 16; /278/71, interrogatory 3, Moxlay no. 3; /290/3, Samwell no. 8.)

If Woodliffe moved his stage in 1599 so that his gallery would be where several people said it was, over the stage, and, as Marsh said and Mago implied (C.24/304/27, no. 3 for both), at one end of the stage, he must have moved it westward, for his gallery was on the western side of the yard. If he moved the stage westward, he must have moved it away from the eastern gallery. And that is what Mago, especially Rodes, and Willys seem to have said when they answered the question in February 1600 by which Samwell tried to prove that Woodliffe had helped in the rebuilding of the playhouse by moving his stage.

Mago said vaguely (for our purposes) that Woodliffe "caused to be removed a Stage wch stood in the yard of the said Inne to give the p^{lt} [Samwell] more scope or roome for the erecting or building of the said galleryes, And sayth that the same stage was removed about sixe foote from the gallery further then yt stood before." By "the gallery," he could only have meant the eastern one. For he could hardly have alluded to either of Samwell's other galleries, on the north and south, without alluding to both.

Rodes was more explicit again. Woodliffe, he said, "caused the stage wch stood in the yard to be removed and pulled inward to make more roome for the longe gallerye and the yarde." Then in answer to another question, he added, "the said stage was removed inward about fyve or six foote, as he taketh yt for ye enlargem^t of the said yard and to give the compl^t [Samwell] the more scope for the better enlarginge of his galleryes." The only way Woodliffe could make more room for the yard was to move his stage toward his side of the yard, the western. The long gallery, then, as in the other evidence, can only have been the eastern one. Rodes's use of the word "inward" takes on more meaning when one reads Willys's remarks.

Willys said that Woodliffe "caused to be removed a Stage wch stood in the said yarde to give more scope and roome as he thinketh to the p^{lt} [Samwell] for the erecting and buyldinge of the said galleryes," and he added a moment later, "the said stage was removed some three quarters of a yard or more inwards towards the house." The "house" must have been either the hostry, which was on the west, or, much more likely, the tiring house, which was also on the west. "Inwards" may have been a suitable word because of the way the great yard bulged to form the part of it I have called the central one. "Inwards" would have been toward the bulge, which was westward. (C.24/278/71, interrogatory 3, Mago no. 3, Rodes nos. 2, 3, Willys no. 3.)

Mago and his men, finally, found a good deal of rubbish under the stage, which they had to cast into the yard before they could move the stage. Then Woodliffe and Samwell had to "make cleane the *said* yard," and, perhaps significantly, they did that (according to the younger Samwell) "after, or at

suche tyme as the said easte galleryes were fynishing or fynished"
(C.24/290/3, Bagnall no. 7, Samwell no. 7).

The eastern gallery, then, ran along the eastern building. It was long and
old before the rebuilding of 1599. After the rebuilding it was part of a massive structure consisting of two galleries, one above the other. These galleries
must have been connected by a stairway, since spectators seem to have got
into both and the northern and southern galleries as well by one main stairway leading up from the yard (see chapter 12).

C. The Northern and Southern Sides

In February 1600, Mago said that Samwell had built three galleries in the
yard of the Boar's Head, "one on the east side of the said yard another on the
north side, and the thirde on the south," and Rodes agreed that Samwell had
built three galleries (C.24/278/71, no. 1). Both were speaking about the
building operations in general and not distinguishing between the original
building of 1598 and the rebuilding of 1599.

In June 1601, however, Hoppdale, the younger Samwell, and especially
Browne all implied several times that the galleries put up in 1599 were enlarged versions of others put up in 1598 (see appendixes 2 and 5), rather than
completely new structures. Mago and Rodes, therefore, had meant that Samwell had built galleries on the northern and southern sides of the yard in 1598
and rebuilt them a year later. Hoppdale and the younger Samwell were answering three questions of Browne's that partly involved the same information: did Samwell and Woodliffe agree that Samwell "should pull downe
certaine newe galleries and romes by the said Samuell before that time
builded and sett vpp in the greate yarde of the saide howse or Inn . . . and
should make build and sett vp the same galleries & romes in the said greate
yarde larger and further into and vppon the said yarde"? did Woodliffe let
Samwell have the great yard in return for Samwell's "pulling downe and . . .
newe building and setting vp againe of the said galleries and romes as
aforesaid"? and how much did Samwell and Browne spend "in the pulling
downe new building and setting vp againe of the said galleries and Romes in
the said great yarde"?

In their answers, Hoppdale and the younger Samwell implied the same
information about the galleries, but, in general, less clearly than Browne had
done in his questions. Hoppdale answered the first question by repeating the
language of the question, and the younger Samwell said that his father and
Woodliffe had agreed that his "father should pull the said new galleryes
downe againe, and should buylde or sett vp larger galleryes and further into
the yarde." For the second question, Hoppdale spoke "of the pluckinge

downe of the sayd galleryes and romes, and of settinge vp agayne of the
new," and the younger Samwell of "the pulling downe of the said little galleryes" and of pulling "downe the same &" setting "vp larger galleryes."
Hoppdale answered the third question by saying that the elder Samwell "did
pluck down the old and erected and sett vp the new galleries larger then the
former were." The younger Samwell answered the question by speaking of
his father's "settinge vp the said little galleryes, and afterwards . . . takinge
the same downe againe & setting vp the larger as aforesaid." (C.24/290/3,
interrogatores 3, 4, 5, Hoppdale nos. 3–4, 5, Samwell nos. 3, 4, 5.)

That Mago and Rodes used the words "long" and "great" to differentiate
Samwell's eastern structure must imply that his northern and southern ones
were smaller. Woodliffe's remark, quoted by many people, that all Samwell's
galleries could be built farther out into the yard without diminishing the size
of the yard indicates that like the lower eastern one, the northern and southern galleries were above the yard on posts. (See above and appendix 2.)

At Christmas 1599, Francis Langley (as he said on 17 April 1600) had his
carpenter, Owen Roberts, "cutt downe certeyne quarters and bords in the
wall of the newe gallerye buylt in the said great Court for to make a dore
waye from this defts [Langley's] house into the said gallerye." Quarters are
$2'' \times 4''$ studs. Thirteen days later, Langley said that Roberts "Cutt downe
certen quarters in the end of the said Galleryes wth such tooles as Carpenters
do vse in such case and made a dore waye into the sayd Galleryes." Samwell
and Langley agreed that the gallery was one of those Samwell had built.
Langley was trying to assert that the gallery was his because its posts rested
in the yard, which he claimed he had just bought from Woodliffe. The only
"house" he could have owned in the Boar's Head was Woodliffe's premises
along the western side of the yard, which Langley had just bought. If, therefore, Langley's doorway opened from his "house" into the end of one of
Samwell's galleries, it must have opened from Woodlife's premises on the
western side of the yard into the end of either the northern or southern
gallery. The matter is most important, especially if the northern and southern galleries were companion pieces, as no doubt they were. For it shows
that those galleries ran along the northern and southern sides of the middle
yard, along the sides of the stage and above the heads of the groundlings, up
to the western buildings. (St.Ch.5/S.74/3, the reply of Langley and Roberts;
/S.13/8, interrogatory 10, Langley and Roberts nos. 10.) The northern and
southern galleries must also have joined the lower eastern one (see chapter
12).

As, finally, Rodes noted in February 1600, it was while he, Mago, "& the
rest of the workmen were in hande wth a gallery wch standeth on the north
side of the said yarde" that Woodliffe moved his stage in 1599 (C.24/278/71,
no. 2).

D. The Stage

Our knowledge about the moving of the stage comes from a question Samwell asked in February 1600 and the four answers to it, one by Mago, two by Rodes, and one by Willys. The question reads, "Dyd the sayd Olyver Woodliffe remove a Certen Stage in the yard of the said Inne to thende to geive more Rome to the plaintiff [Samwell] thereby to erecte and build the said Galleryes . . . and how muche was the same Stage Removed?" I have quoted the answers in my remarks above about the eastern side of the yard. That the stage was moved is confirmed in the question and six answers about the rubbish that Mago and his men found under the stage when they set about moving it, but neither question nor answers say more than that the stage was in fact moved. All these remarks about moving the stage were to show generally that Woodliffe had cooperated in building the playhouse and specifically that he had allowed Samwell to use the yard for the enlarged galleries of 1599. Samwell implied, therefore, and Mago, Rodes, and Willys plainly said that Woodliffe moved the stage to give Samwell "more Rome" (Samwell) or "more scope" and/or "roome" (Mago, Rodes, Willys) for his galleries, especially those on the east. Can one move a stage any way but westward so as to give more room or scope for galleries on the east? (C.24/278/71, interrogatories 3, 5, Mago no. 5, Rodes no. 5, Willys no. 5; /290/3, Bagnall no. 7, Samwell no. 7, Harryson no. 7.)

Mago thought that he and his men had moved the stage about six feet, and Rodes thought five or six. Willys (Samwell's servant), however, thought that they had moved it some three-quarters of a yard or more. Surely one must side here with the men who actually moved the stage and so conclude that six feet cannot be far wrong.

APPENDIX 4

Arrangements among Owners and Players for Managing the Playhouse

Like the building of the playhouse (appendix 2), its management was not a thing Woodliffe and Langley hastened to explain in their lawsuits. The reason was the same. Their principal case required them to insist that the only interests in the Boar's Head were those spelled out in writing in the Woodliffe-Samwell lease. Conveniently for them, the management of the playhouse was as much a matter of oral understandings as its building. Management required collaboration between the owners and hence suggested that Samwell and Browne had interests in the playhouse not mentioned in the lease. So for a long time Woodliffe and Langley based their arguments on the lease and denied any other understandings. Samwell and Browne also rested their case for a time on the lease (though a much looser reading of it than Woodliffe and Langley had in mind), and then on Woodliffe's collaboration in the rebuilding of 1599. Perhaps Samwell and Browne were intimidated by the reluctance of the courts to deal with purely theatrical matters (see chapter 6). It was, in any event, not until late in the history of the lawsuits that anybody turned deliberately to the management of the playhouse. Ironically, it was Woodliffe and Langley who first did so, because by that time Browne owed them money according to the arrangements Woodliffe and Samwell had settled upon. Browne then decided that those arrangements were a useful way of establishing that Woodliffe and Samwell had meant to share the playhouse. In his last legal venture he explained them carefully and got two witnesses to agree with him.

Browne's witnesses hinted as early as June 1601 that there were fixed arrangements for managing the place from the start, at least between the owners. Young Samwell suggested that his father was in charge of the playhouse and Woodliffe a silent partner by remarking that Woodliffe was abroad when the playhouse was first built and during its first year of business. He, seconded by Hoppdale, made the same suggestion by remarking that his father had the right "to shutt the gates of the said Inne or messuage at xi of the clocke, or at suche other tymes as the players or the said Richard Samuell should thinke conveynient." (C.24/290/3, nos. 3, 4.)

It was Browne's refusal from 22 August 1601 onward to pay the half profits of Woodliffe's western gallery to either Woodliffe or his successor, Francis Langley, that caused those two to introduce the arrangement between the owners into the legal argument. Coincidentally, the episode is another suggestion that Samwell and his successor, Browne, managed the place while Woodliffe and his successor merely took part of the income. In the midst of his lawsuit against the Langleys in Chancery, Woodliffe paused to advise the court on 15 January 1602 that "one Browne whoe ys tenant of parte of the howse or Inne in questyon taketh the proffytt of the whole house & payeth nothinge ether to" the Langleys or Woodliffe "for the same." Woodliffe broached the matter again in Chancery on 6 and 10 February and 21 April 1602 in an effort to get Browne to pay him some of the profits. Finally, on 15 October 1602, when Woodliffe and the Langleys agreed for a moment that Woodliffe would get back his "stage Tyring Howse and galleryes scytuat on the West syde of the great yard of the said Inne," Woodliffe pointed out that Browne paid nothing for "the said Stage Tyringhouse and gallaryes for the w[ch] the said Browne paid before better then iiii[li] a weeke." Browne by this time had confessed to Chancery that he had to pay for the use of those structures, but he had insisted that he should pay it "to him that shall prevale" in the lawsuit between Woodliffe and the Langleys. (C.33/101/f.207[v], 290, 324[v], 406[v] in the A book, /102/f.249[v], 326[v], 343–43[v], 433 in the B book; /103/f.43–43[v] in the A book, /104/f.44[v] in the B book; see also chapter 6.)

Woodliffe next took the arrangements between the owners into his lawsuit against Browne in the Court of Requests in May 1603. He added nothing to the remarks of 1602, however, except to say that the money Browne had paid per playing week was more than £5, rather than the more than £4 of 1602, and to calculate that more than £5 a playing week from 22 August 1601 to, presumably, the closing on 19 March 1603 came "to better then 200[li] . . . due for the stage tyreing house & galleries" (see chapter 7). In his reply, Browne revealed at last the crucial part of these arrangements. Samwell, and after him Browne, should use "the said Stage Tyreinge houses & gallaryes over the stage dueringe all such tyme and Terme of yeares as the said Richard Samuell had the other parte of the p[r]mysses" from Woodliffe. In return, Samwell and Browne should pay Woodliffe "the one half of the profytts Cominge arisinge and to be taken out of the said weste galleryes over the said Stage at such tyme and tymes as there should be any playes or Comodyes acted and played vpon the Stage aforesaid." (Req.2/466/pt.II[/1], the bill and reply.)

When Browne sued Woodliffe for the last time two months later, in July 1603, he made the arrangements for conducting the playhouse an important part of his case. He asked two witnesses, the builder, Mago, and Mago's carpenter, Marsh, two questions that amount to a full statement of those arrangements. Both witnesses agreed with all the particulars, but both, especially Mago, added details and sometimes expressed Browne's point more clearly than he did. Browne took it for granted that he, and Samwell before him, were to manage the place. They should use Woodliffe's "stage, the Coveringe over the stage the Tyringe howses and the galleryes over the stage in the said howse Called the Bores head dueringe such terme of Yeares as" they held the bulk of the place according to their lease of 13 April 1598 (until Christmas 1615). In return they should:

1. pay Woodliff "half the profytts of the same galleryes over the stage Cleerlye dischardged the gatherors beinge first payed" (Mago and Marsh added, "and the players the other half"),
2. "paye the Chardges for all the lycences for Warrants from the M^r of the Revells, And did not the said Warrants cost Tenn poundes a Warraunte?"
3. pay (or, rather, "dischardge the said Wodlyffe of") "all weeklye payementes to the said M^r of the Revells," which, as Mago added, "was affirmed to be xv^s a weeke when they played,"
4. pay "for the Weekely payement to the poore" of the parish, which according to Mago, "was said to be v^s a weeke,"
5. pay "the wages of the stage keepers," which, according to Mago again, "was said to be vi^s a weeke,"
6. pay for "all Rushes and Cressetts lights," or as Mago put it, "rushes and cressett lights in Wynter wch some weeks came to ten or twelve shillings a weeke, as they said,"
7. pay for "all Chardges of suytes conc^{r}ninge the vpholdinge and maynteyning of the playeinge there," or as Mago and Marsh put it, "all sutes at Court to vphould playinge in the said house," and as Mago added, "wch came to much money." Later in the same document, Browne said that the suits were "to have toleracion from tyme to tyme to vphold the house to play in." (C.24/304/27, nos. 3 and interrogatory 16.)

Browne wanted it to appear that Woodliffe and Samwell had agreed to these conditions in the same conversation in which they agreed to rebuild the playhouse. In that way, Browne could argue that Samwell had in a sense bought these conditions by rebuilding his galleries. Browne had been arguing since 1601 that Samwell had bought the use of the yard in just that way and at just that time. So now Browne asked Mago and Marsh where and when Samwell and Woodliffe had agreed to the conditions for the use of the stage, tiring house, and western gallery, and those two did their best with fading memories. Mago said that the agreement "was made in the great yard of the said Inne when the great new galleryes were in buyldinge in the yard next the parlo^{rs}"—when, that is, the men were at work on Samwell's eastern gallery in 1599. Marsh said that the agreement was made when Samwell's galleries "were in buyldinge," or, rather, rebuilding, in 1599. Woodliffe and Samwell had agreed to rebuild the playhouse as they talked in the great yard when the carpenters were taking measure for Samwell's upper gallery on the eastern side. (/nos. 3.)

Browne, therefore, said nothing in 1603, and asked his witnesses nothing, about the conditions under which Samwell used the stage, tiring house, and western gallery during the first year of the playhouse, 1598–99, while Wood- liffe was abroad. But the conditions then must have been similar to those rehearsed in the great yard in the summer of 1599.

One condition of 1598 Browne and his witnesses did mention in 1603 because its history suggests that Samwell bought the conditions of 1599. Before he went abroad, Woodliffe and Samwell agreed that each would pay for the repairs to his parts of the playhouse, and Samwell would see that they were carried out. By the summer of 1599, Samwell had spent, according to Browne, "about Twelve pounds" in repairing "the stage and Tyringe howses." Mago and Marsh made the sum "about twelve or xiiii^{li}," and Mago added, "or more . . . wch this depon^t knoweth for that he did worke in the same works at that tyme." For some reason, Samwell forgave Woodliffe the money as part of the agreement to rebuild the playhouse, hence Browne's interest in the matter in 1603.(/interrogatory 4, Mago no. 4, Marsh no. 3.)

Woodliffe and Samwell agreed again in the summer of 1599 that each would pay for the repairs to his structures—Woodliffe's structures provided for in the words "Cleerlye dischardged" of item 1—and that Samwell would see the work done. In 1603, Browne asked his witnesses what he had spent repairing Woodliffe's structures, and Mago replied, "thirtie or fortie pounds or more," and Marsh, "fortie pounds at least, wch this depon^t knoweth to be true for that he was a workman in that worke" (/nos. 13). No doubt, Browne subtracted the money from that he owed Woodliffe in the spring of 1603 (see chapter 7).

Browne, Mago, and Marsh all said that Woodliffe was content with these conditions for the use of his stage, tiring house, and western gallery. They also said that he and Langley accepted the half profits of the western gallery as they were offered to them. (/nos. 3, 13.) Explained as they were by Browne, who managed the playhouse, owned much of it, and led a company of players, and by the builder who built the place and kept it in repair, and by one of his carpenters, these conditions are as good a thing of their kind as we have for any Elizabethan playhouse.

APPENDIX 5

The Dates of the Building
of the Playhouse

The playhouse could first have been built in the great yard only after Woodliffe's and Samwell's lease of 13 April 1598, and in June 1601 the younger
Samwell said that it was. His father, he said, erected it "after the said lease to
him made by Woodleffe & his wyfe . . . (when the said Woodleffe was at sea
or abroade)" (C.24/290/3, no. 3). Offering no evidence, Sisson wrote in 1936
(p. 102) and 1954 (n. 16) that the playhouse was first built in 1595 and, apparently having doubts, in 1972 (p. 37) that it was built "in part between 1595
and 1598."

The rebuilding of 1599 must have followed Samwell's and Woodliffe's
agreement to enlarge the place, and, apparently, it followed immediately. Six
statements mention when either the agreement or the rebuilding took place,
and all six specify the summer of 1599. Four of them, including two by
Samwell, point to July, but three of the four are partly wrong:

1. On 2 February 1600, Mago's foreman, Rodes, said Samwell "did this
   last summer buylde three galleryes or roomes in the Yarde of the"
   Boar's Head (C.24/278/71, no. 1).
2. On 11 April 1600, Samwell meant to say that at least the rebuilding had
   taken place in July 1599. An obvious part of his remark, however, was
   at first omitted. In supplying it, Samwell also supplied words probably
   intended to mean that the agreement, too, belonged to July, 1599, but
   gave the regnal year as forty (1598) rather than forty-one. He took
   possession of the Boar's Head, he noted, after Woodliffe and his wife
   had agreed to the lease, "and after," as the document originally went
   on, "by the good lykeinge Consente allowance and agreem^t of the said
   Olyver and Susan and vppon theyre graunte to" Samwell "then made
   to enioy the said did in July last past or thereabouts buylde in the said

greate yard for the necessary vse of" Samwell "diuerse Romes galleryes Chambers and other necessary Buyldings." Samwell then had two interlineations made. The first, which follows "and after," refers to the agreement: "abouts Julie in the fortyth yere of your Ma^ts reigne It was agreed betweene" Samwell "& the said Olyver & Susan that." The second, which follows "enioy the said," supplies the obvious omission: "great yarde duringe all thestate of the said Olyver & Susan by force [of] their leas yor said subiect" (St.Ch.5/S.74/3, the bill).

3. On 22 April 1600, Samwell suggested that the rebuilding took place after 24 June 1599. He had spent his money, he said, "vppon newe Buildinges in the said messuage or Inne sythence mydsomer last past for and towardes the erectinge and settinge vpp of the Galleryes" (St.Ch.5/S.13/8, interrogatory 2).

4. Bagnall said on 10 June 1601 that the rebuilding took place "about twoo yeeres paste" (C.24/290/3, no. 7).

5. Hoppdale said on 11 June 1601 that the agreement between Samwell and Woodliffe took place "about St James tyde," 1599—that is, 25 July. Unfortunately, before that remark he said that the lease was granted at Easter in the same year, so getting the lease a year late. He did not pretend to know first-hand about the lease, however, but did know first-hand about the agreement and rebuilding, for he was present at the one and a workman in the other (C.24/290/3, no. 4).

6. On 11 June 1601, young Samwell said that the agreement took place between Midsummer and St. Bartholomew's Day 1599, which would put it on 24 July. Unfortunately, he added "about the tyme that the great trayning was at Myle end greene, in the tyme the earle of Essex was in Ireland" (C.24/290/3, no. 4). Presumably, he meant the great training of citizens, householders, and "subsidie men" at Mile End that began on 27 August, three days *after* St. Bartholomew's Day, and went on until 4 September. Essex left for Ireland late in March and returned late in September. Young Samwell's memory of the great training could easily have failed him, however, for from 1 August until early September, thousands of men from London and the shires trained on various "grounds about the City," and there were many comings and goings of armed men in the streets (Stow, *Annales* [London, 1605], pp. 1309–10).

APPENDIX 6

The Date of Robert Browne's Acquiring Part of the Boar's Head

A surprising puzzle in the documentation about the Boar's Head is the date of Robert Browne's acquiring his part of the place. According to the younger Samwell, who was present at both, there was a "bargaine making betwixt his father &" Browne and then a sealing of "a conveyance in wryting vnder" his father's "hand & seale" by which his father "did . . . assigne and sett ouer vnto" Browne all his father's part of the Boar's Head (C.24/290/3, no. 6). Evidently, the elder Samwell assigned the old lease rather than drew up a new one. Such details as when leases were made, or when they changed hands, were usually given as matters of course. But nobody gave the date, or even a direct approximation of the date, of this assignment. The Samwells and Browne declined to give one even on the two occasions when it was distinctly to their advantage to do so (see 4 and 5 below).

There may have been legal reasons for not revealing the date. Moreover, who held the lease and its assignment, and why he held them, could have been complicated matters (see chapter 4). Note:

1. In the lawsuit of April 1600 in the Star Chamber, neither Samwell nor anybody else mentioned Browne. Samwell, however, said on the eleventh that he no longer had his lease (he could not recite its details "for wante of havinge the said Indenture"), but that he had had possession of the place when Woodliffe and Francis Langley made their lease, which he thought "abouts Christmas last part" (St.Ch.5/S.74/3, the bill).

2. Though in the first version of his lawsuit (autumn 1600) Bishop did not, in the second (April 1601) he did claim that Browne had joined Wolleston as 15 December 1599 in passing part of the yard to him— hence that Browne had possession by then. Bishop's claim probably

represents what Langley thought, but neither Langley nor others put much faith in that claim. (K.B.27/1364/m.259; /1367/m199ᵛ.)

3. In asking a question about the lease in June 1601, Browne said he had got it "shortlie after" Samwell could not repay him. In answering that question, young Samwell agreed that his father had conveyed the place to Browne, but did not say when. In answering another question, however, young Samwell said that Woodliffe had kept the upper parlor from old Samwell for a year and a half and still had it. Young Samwell was saying that his father had had the lease for a year and a half, that is, until mid-October 1599, because (as Moxlay said in October 1600) Woodliffe had got the parlor at the sealing of his lease with old Samwell on 13 April 1598. Young Samwell knew these things to be true because (as he said) he was present both at the original sealing of the lease and at his father's assigning it to Browne. (C.24/290/3, interrogatory 6, Samwell nos. 2, 6, 8; /278/71, Moxlay no. 3.)

4. In May 1603, Woodliffe professed to know only that Browne had got possession of Samwell's properties "by indirect meanes" after the sealing of Woodliffe's lease with Langley (7 November 1599). Browne should have given the details of his lease in reply, but said only that he "lawfully and by good Conveyance hath" his parts of the Boar's Head. (Req.2/466/pt.II[/1], bill and reply.)

5. In July 1603, Browne asked his witnesses (Mago and Marsh) to verify that Samwell had formally ("by wrytinge vnder his hand and Seale") assigned his parts of the Boar's Head to him, "And where and when was the same graunte or Assignement made thereof." After both witnesses agreed that Samwell had formally assigned his parts of the place to Browne, however, Mago went on to the next question and Marsh added, "but more he Cannot depose." (C.24/304/27, nos. 5.)

6. In the same document, Browne, Mago, and Marsh said that Samwell effactually had possession of Woodliffe's stage, tiring house, and western gallery (as Mago put it) "both before at and after the tyme" of Woodliffe's lease with Langley, 7 November 1599. Surely Samwell would still have had control of his lease on the rest of the Boar's Head if he still controlled Woodliffe's properties. Browne then said that at the time of the elegit (Christmas 1602) he had had Woodliffe's properties "for two yeares before." (/interrogatories 7, 8, Mago no. 7, Marsh no. 7.)

APPENDIX 7

The Accuracy of Ogilby and Morgan's Map

Ogilby and Morgan's map ought to be quite reliable. People who knew the London of the 1670s very well scrutinized it carefully and approved. The Court of Aldermen supported its making from the start (in 1673), had a specially chosen committee vet it regularly as it progressed, and was satisfied enough with the finished work in October 1676 to vote Morgan £100 and ask that he give every alderman a copy. But what kind of accuracy did such people expect? Several attempts have been made to find out, and others are underway.[1] The method has been to compare apparently reliable information about a few properties with what the map shows of the same properties. This information has come from plans made within a few years of the map, from excavations, and even from a description in a lease of as far back as 1545. The properties are on sheets 12, 13, 18, 19, and 20 of the map. The conclusion so far seems to be that the map is likely to be right about streets and the number of shape of properties along streets. It can be less reliable about things troublesome or impossible to measure, like properties behind street fronts. For such places, it can show merely what its authors could reasonably guess was there. It can show "diagramatic" results even for places easily measured: the right number of properties in a given area but related to one another in some convenient rather than the correct way. No one seems to have looked into the sheet on which the Boar's Head is (15) or tried to find how reliable the map might be about measurements.

Can we use the map to confirm and augment the information about the Boar's Head in the lawsuits and deeds? The map seems to square with the lawsuits and deeds nicely, even down to measurements, but in order to assess its reliability in this exercise, we should probably look elsewhere for data to hold against it. Luckily, the parts of the Boar's Head in which we are interested were accessible to Ogilby and Morgan's surveyors if they entered the place, as Needler's alley would have prompted them to do. Unluckily, no suitable information has come to light about the properties in and around the Boar's Head at the time of the map, or, indeed, from the 1620s to the nineteenth century. Even the parish church near the Boar's Head, St. Botolph's, Aldgate, was pulled down and rebuilt. Many of the streets and alleys, however, survived until the first detailed Ordnance Survey maps of the area (most survive still), though perhaps encroached, or widened, or even moved. Some property lines also survived in the great yard of the Boar's Head and along Whitechapel High Street, also in and around Gun Square, but subject, too, to 250 years of adjustment. Ogilby and Morgan's scale (1:1,200) is close enough to those of the Ordnance Survey maps (formerly 1:1,056, now 1:1,250) that one can lay a transparency of Ogilby and Morgan's map over even the most recent Ordnance Survey map of the area and see striking similarities. It might, therefore, prove instructive to hold some of the details on Ogilby and Morgan's map against equivalent details on the earliest Ordnance Survey map.

The nature of maps in general, especially one 300 years old, does not make the task easier. Cartographers and engravers cannot draw lines with complete accuracy, nor can the printing press print or we measure them so. Moreover, maps do not lie still. Paper shrinks and expands (mainly shrinks) as the seasons go by, and it does so differently depending where and how the map is stored. For such reasons, the Ordnance Survey calculates that its large-scale maps may be accurate only down to three feet.[2] The two modern reproductions of Ogilby and Morgan's map illustrate the problem. Each was meant to be an exact copy of its parent, yet my copy of the Boar's Head sheet of 1894 is strikingly bigger than its parent, and my copy of that of 1976 is slightly smaller than its parent. Ogilby and Morgan's scale bar, which is on sheet 17, illustrates the problem, too. It is supposed to be 5″ long and so to measure 500′ of actual ground. But on none of the copies of the map I have seen does it reach the full 5″, and the difference between the biggest and the smallest is about $\frac{3}{32}$″. According to the specified scale, the biggest scale bar measures a bit less than 494′11″ (-1.02%) and the smallest a bit less than 486′3″ (-2.76%). Furthermore, on all the scale bars the inches are not quite consistent with one another, and all are smaller than those on modern rulers. I calculate that the mean inch on all these scale bars is about 2% smaller than the modern one.

The printing of the sheets of the map was done, of course, like that of the sheets of books, one going through the press and then another. The printing of a copy of the Boar's Head sheet necessarily has no connection with the printing of a copy of any other. A glance at the map under glass on the wall at Guildhall will show what happened. Its sheets are assembled so that the whole map is spread before one. Some of the sheets are heavily inked, some lightly; the details on some edges match those on adjoining edges well, and those on other edges match the adjoining ones less well. Moreover, most surviving copies of the map are probably pasted onto cloth or heavy paper to preserve them. Distortion must occur in the thorough wetting involved here and later in having the sheets bound to materials that shrink and expand differently from the way the sheets would by themselves.

I have seen eight copies of the map: two in the Crace collection at the British Museum (II, 61, 62), another at the British Museum (MAPS C.7.b.4), two at Guildhall (the wall copy and the strong-room copy), one belonging to the Honourable Artillery Company at Artillery House, one belonging to the Society of Antiquaries at Burlington House, and one (which I call G.L.C.) at Clerkenwell.[3] Each Boar's Head sheet among these copies of the map is different. Measured diagonally across the center between points about a foot apart (the eastern corner of the alley opposite Spectacle Alley in Fenchurch Street and the western corner of Red Lion Yard in Whitechapel High Street), the biggest of these sheets is nearly ³⁄₁₆″ bigger than the smallest, or 17′4″ according to the scale. A copy of the map, like the strong-room one, can have a big Boar's Head sheet and a scale-bar one in the middle of the range. A given sheet, it seems, can be relatively small in one part and relatively large in another. The best of the eight copies is G.L.C., which is the parent of the reproduction of 1976. Sheet for sheet, it is the best preserved, and it even seems the most consistent in printing. It alone has not been distorted in being pasted onto backing; each sheet is pasted only along the top onto the leaves of a large book. Its Boar's Head and scale-bar sheets are both rather small, just under the mean size of all those sheets, if the measurement across the center of the one and the length of the scale-bar on the other are an indication.

The Ordnance Survey first surveyed the vicinity of the Boar's Head for a large-scale map in 1848 and published the resulting map in 1850. It is, however, a "skeleton" one, showing only streets. The Ordnance Survey filled in this map in a survey of 1873, the new map published in 1875.[4] Both are to the scale 1:1,056. The map of 1873–75 is the first of the area after Ogilby and Morgan drawn with anything like the same scope and detail.

I have assumed that G.L.C. best represents now what was on the plate from which the Boar's Head sheet of Ogilby and Morgan's map was printed, and I have used it for all my measurements. My way of dealing with the small inches on all copies of the map has been to use the modern inch, to assume that the small inches are the result of shrinkage, and hence to add 2% to all my results. I have used the copy of the Ordnance Survey map at the British Museum. To minimize changes between 1676 and 1873 at street corners, I have squared the rounded ones in 1873 by carrying out the lines of buildings, and I have measured from the middle of the one street to the middle of the next. I have measured in a straight line across property fronts to simplify measurement.

Added to the inaccuracies to be expected in the work of surveyors, engravers, and printers, as well as in the contracting and expanding of paper, must be those in measuring. Even with a magnifying glass, one can hardly be really accurate much beyond $\frac{1}{64}$" in the placement of two points, especially on Ogilby and Morgan's map, where lines are less evenly engraved and inked than on the Ordnance Survey map. That fraction is negligible when one is measuring points an inch ($\pm 1.6\%$) or more apart but not points $\frac{1}{8}$" or so apart ($\pm 12.5\%$), as some are in and around the Boar's Head. The figures that follow, therefore, can only be approximations.

The main streets on the north side of Whitechapel High Street in both 1676 and 1873 were Houndsditch running north and south, Whitechapel High Street itself running east and west, and Middlesex Street running north and south. The streets and alleys leading off these streets were, along Houndsditch, Gravel Lane, Gun Square (Yard in 1676), and Church Row; along Whitechapel High Street, Three Nuns Yard, Bull Inn, and Black (White in 1676) Horse Yard; and along Middlesex Street (Petticoat Lane in 1676) is what I call Needler's alley. The distances between them are as follows:

	O & M	O.S.	% by Which O & M Differ
Gravel Lane to Gun Square	58' 8"	56' 6"	+ 3.83%
Gun Square to Church Row	114'10"	114' 4"	+ 0.44%
Church Row to Whitechapel High Street	227' 3"	225'11"	+ 0.59%
Houndsditch to Three Nuns Yard	152' 7"	162'10"	− 6.29%
Three Nuns Yard to Bull Inn	187' 2"	181' 2"	+ 3.31%
Bull Inn to Black Horse Yard	132' 1"	135'10"	− 2.76%
Black Horse Yard to Middlesex Street	104' 5"	86' 7"	+20.60%
Whitechapel High Street to Needler's alley	124'11"	116' 1"	+ 7.61%
Totals	1,101'11"	1,079' 3"	+ 2.10%

Four streets survived leading off the south side of Whitechapel High Street: The Minories, Harrow Alley, Irish Court (Swan Alley in 1676), and Halfmoon Passage. The distances between them are as follows:

The Minories to Harrow Alley	272' 3"	276' 2"	− 1.42%
Harrow Alley to Irish Court	330' 1"	309' 5"	+ 6.68%
Irish Court to Halfmoon Passage	227' 8"	218' 3"	+ 4.32%
Totals	830' 0"	803'10"	+ 3.26%

More to the purpose are measurements between property lines in and near the Boar's Head. The nine properties Ogilby and Morgan show along White-chapel High Street from Middlesex Street to Boar's Head Alley (Goulston St. in 1873) are also nine in the recorded payments of the county land tax, which begin in 1733, and in all the detailed maps until 1882. Starting at Middlesex Street they are (west to east) nos. 148–140 Whitechapel High Street. Their dimensions north and south obviously changed over the years, but most of those along the High Street may not have done so. I combine nos. 141 and 142 because the Ordnance Survey does, and I omit no. 140 because it must have been demolished when Goulston St. was built in the 1680s and rebuilt as a much narrower structure (Ogilby and Morgan gave it as 21'8", the Ordnance Survey as 16'3", +33.33%). The dimensions along White-chapel High Street are:

No. 148	18' 6"	12' 6"	+48.00%
No. 147	14' 6"	14'11"	− 2.79%
No. 146	18' 1"	14'11"	+21.23%
No. 145	13' 3"	15' 3"	−13.11%
No. 144	13' 8"	12'10"	+ 6.49%
No. 143	14' 1"	13'10"	+ 1.81%
No. 141–42	24' 1"	29' 1"	−17.19%
Totals	116' 2"	113' 4"	+ 2.50%

All these measurements are along important streets. How do Ogilby and Morgan fare if one measures across the map following no street? I measured from the south corner of Gun Square and Houndsditch to the eastern line of no. 145 at the High Street:

751' 4"   758' 1"   − 0.89%

This eastern line of no. 145 is critical in finding and confirming much about the Boar's Head. How have Ogilby and Morgan measured it north and south?

The High Street to Needler's alley	116' 5"	118' 2"	− 1.48%

and a detailed plan of no. 145 of 1860 shows about 118' 6". How have they placed it relative to the eastern boundary of the Boar's Head (the eastern line of no. 141)?

At the High Street (nos. 141–44)	51'10"	55' 9"	− 7.03%
At Needler's alley	53' 5"	54' 5"	− 1.80%

and how relative to Middlesex Street?

At the High Street (nos. 145–48)	64' 3"	57' 6"	+11.74%
At Needler's alley	68' 8"	71' 9"	− 4.30%

Gun Square may also be worth looking at because alone among the yards, courts, and alleys near the Boar's Head it kept something of its shape until 1873, indeed until the Second World War. The four properties on the north side of the entrance in 1676 are two in 1873, and the five on the south side in 1676 are also two in 1873, but the overall lines seem the same. The property in the southwest corner of the yard also seems to have stayed within its lines. The measurements are as follows:

Houndsditch to the eastern side of the yard along the north side of the entrance	134' 6"	144'10	− 7.13%
Yard north and south after the entrance	41' 9"	38' 1"	+ 9.63%
Yard north and south at eastern end	63' 5"	71' 0"	−10.68%
Properties on the north side of the entrance			
North side	42' 7"	42' 3"	+ 0.79%
South side	42' 7"	44' 4"	− 3.95%
West side	28' 1"	29' 5"	− 4.53%
East side	28'11"	32' 3"	−10.34%
Properties on the South side of the entrance			
North side	44' 2"	46' 9"	− 5.53%
South side	47' 0"	46' 9"	+ 0.53%
West side	30'11"	32' 7"	− 5.12%
East side	30'11"	32' 3"	− 4.13%
Property in the southwest corner			
North side	18' 1"	18' 4"	− 1.36%
South side	18' 1"	18' 4"	− 1.36%
West side	27' 1"	26' 8"	+ 1.56%
East side	27' 4"	27' 0"	+ 1.23%

Most of these differences could easily result from inaccuracies in the measuring of either map or both and much more easily from the building and rebuilding of two centuries. The differences in the sizes of nos. 146 and 145 Whitechapel High Street represent only 3' of ground and less than $\frac{1}{32}$" on a ruler in the first case and 2' and much less than $\frac{1}{32}$" in the other. The size of no. 148 and the distance from Black Horse Yard to Middlesex Street may be more troublesome. They represent much more space on both the ground and rulers. Ogilby and Morgan differ from the Ordnance Survey by only +3% or so in the distance from Houndsditch to the eastern boundary of the Boar's Head. That comes to about 25' of ground, however, largely accounted for by Ogilby and Morgan's making Middlesex Street and the places on either side of it much bigger than the Ordnance Survey.

The Boar's Head sheet of Ogilby and Morgan's map must be worth consulting about the general shape of things, and maybe it is reasonable to hope that it could often be right to 6% or 7% or better in measurements. It may show a serious mistake where Middlesex Street joins the High Street, and it may deal with the properties east of there in a "diagramatic" way. Even if it does both things, however, it is probably accurate enough for our purposes about the properties along the High Street that once belonged to the Boar's Head (nos. 141–44), for it shows them only some 4' smaller east and west along the High Street than the Ordnance Survey does. Hence it would show equally well the eastern line of no. 145 (which is also the western line of no. 144) at the High Street relative to the eastern boundary of the Boar's Head (which is the eastern line of no. 141).

Ogilby and Morgan's surveyors must have gone into Gun Square to take measurements, and in view of their placing of the eastern line of no. 145, they must have gone into the Boar's Head, too. Ogilby and Morgan show the line at its northern end (Needler's alley) almost exactly as the Ordnance Survey does—relative to the High Street in the south, the boundary of the Boar's Head in the east, and Middlesex Street in the west. Nor, it seems, were they very wrong about it at its southern end (the High Street) relative to the eastern boundary of the Boar's Head. Their map is worth consulting, therefore, about not only the number and shape but also the sizes of properties in the parts of the Boar's Head where, among other things, much of the playhouse had been. If Ogilby and Morgan were as successful about this line as comparison with the Ordnance Survey suggests, they can hardly have been very wrong in measuring properties on and near it. They would have been, that is, within the limits we find when we hold them against details in the lawsuits and deeds about the Boar's Head. The line was the western boundary of the southern part of the Boar's Head, lay roughly across the middle of the central part and the stage, and, extended northward, is the present line of the shops along the eastern side of Middlesex Street. We can use it to trace the playhouse from map to map.

APPENDIX 8

Deeds

Five deeds involved in Sir John Poley's dispersing the Boar's Head after Lady Day 1616 survive completely or partly. I transcribe here the parts of these deeds that describe the property.

1. The deed of 29 December 1621, by which Thomas Needler bought part of the Boar's Head. A contemporary copy of the deed survives complete on the Close Roll (C.54/2471/17), and the part describing the property also survives word for word in ten deeds of the eighteenth century (G.L.C., M.L.R.1721/IV/131–32; 1723/V/433; 1728/IV/263; /IV/270; /VI/297; 1730/IV/33–34; 1732/V/448–49; 1741/II/145; 1749/III/44–45; 1754/III/408; see also 1721/V/139). The deed says that the contract between Poley and Lord Wentworth enfranchising the Boar's Head should be attached, but none of these versions has it (see no. 5 below). Needler bought:

All those foure tenements scituate in the parishe of St Mary Matfellon alias Whitechaple in the County of Midd Wherein now one Elizabeth Browne widow Robert Stamford John fflorey & one Robert Lockdale now dwell with certeine other buildings sometymes called a stable & the chamber over it to the same adioyning & a place of ground adioyning being parcell of the buildings & yard of the Boares head as they doe lye in the said parish against the garden late in thoccupacion of one John Needler towards the north & conteyne in length from the end of the great barne parcell of the said Boares head vnto the outside of the corner post of the same range of buildings forty five foote & five ynches of assize & on the south side from the outside of the crosse buildings by the mayne post & the yard in right range against the Court yard measured out thirty nyne foote in length & thirty foure foote in breadth south to the post of the said great barne forty seaven foote six ynches against the Court yard & in breadth at both ends east & west thirty eight foote of assize.

Needler also acquired, among other privileges, "ingresse egresse & regresse from the said tenements & buildings . . . at all tyme & tymes hereafter
with carte & carriage to passe & repasse from the said tenements & buildings
by the said Court or common yard of the said Boares head by & through a
passage way of eight foote in widenesse to be made leading from the said
Court yard west into the common way or streete called hoggelane." Or, as
the deed says later, Needler, his heirs, and assigns were "to haue & enioy free
& quiett passage & repassage ingresse egresse & regresse into & through the
said way vnto or from the bargained premisses into & from hogge lane
aforesaid at all tymes hereafter."

2. A deed, c.1621, by which Thomas Needler acquired a rectangular piece
of ground in the Boar's Head, 23'6" × 22'9". Contemporary copies apparently do not survive, but the description of the property in them does survive in four deeds of the eighteenth century (G.L.C., M.L.R.1721/IV/131–
32; 1730/IV/33–34; 1732/V/448–49; 1757/IV/83–84). One can be sure that
this description belongs to c.1621 because the three people named in it are
also named in the two deeds of 1621 (nos. 1 and 5). The four versions are not
much different, except for occasional mistakes and attempts to modernize. I
transcribe the version of 1721, supplying in brackets a line omitted from it
and from that of 1757 but included in both the others. The opening words
signify that the property being described is different from that of no. 1. The
"peice of ground hereinafter mencioned" is described in no. 3. Needler
bought:

All that other peice or parcell of ground containing in length North and
South as well by the Eastside as on the Westside thereof Twenty Three foot
and a halfe of Assize little more or less and in bredth East and West as well
by the Southend thereof and of the Northend thereof Twenty Two foot
Nine Inches of like Assize little more or less abutting towards the East
upon the ffreehold land now or late of [Thomas Needler West upon the
ffreehold Land now or Late of] John Wood North upon that part of a peice
of ground formerly lett by lease from Thomas Needler to John Needler
for Two Hundred and ffive years and South for the most part upon another peice of ground hereinafter mencioned and for a little part of the
South west corner upon part of the lands late of Samuel Rowley.

3. A deed, c.1621, by which Thomas Needler acquired a quadrangular
piece of ground in the Boar's Head, 20'11" × 20'3" × 19' × 17'. This deed
survives as no. 2 does, and the surviving part follows immediately that of no.
2 in all four eighteenth-century deeds. It reads:

And also of and in One other peice or parcell of ground containing by
the North part Twenty foot Eleven Inches of Assize little more or less and

by the South part thereof Twenty ffoot and Three Inches and by the North [i.e., west] part thereof Nineteen foot and by the East part thereof Seventeen foot of Assize little more or less abutting towards the East upon the freehold late of Thomas Needler West upon the land sometime of the said Samuel Rowley North part on the peices of ground aforesaid and part upon the land heretofore of the said Thomas Needler.

4. A deed, c.1621, by which Thomas Needler acquired a piece of ground not in the Boar's Head but lying along its northern boundary. Needler leased the property to John Needler in 1625 for 205 years. Contemporary copies of the deed do not survive, but the description of the property in them does survive in four deeds of the eighteenth century (G.L.C., M.L.R.1728/ IV/263; /270; 1741/II/145; 1757/IV/83–84). One can be sure that this description belongs to c.1621 because the people named in it are also named in the deeds of 1621 (nos. 1 and 5). I transcribe the first version of 1728 with three corrections from 1741 and 1757: a confusing "not" dropped (silently) from an allusion to the alley of 8′, and two words added (in brackets). The second version of 1728 is a simplification omitting the abuttals. The last clause, beginning "Except . . . So much," belongs to a later time (Adrian Denise died in 1721 or so). Needler acquired:

> all that peice or parcell of Ground or Garden Plott . . . adjoyning unto a Part of the North Side of the Great Messuage or Tenement and of the buildings thereunto belonging Called the Boarshead in the parish of St Mary Matfellon . . . also near unto the East Side of the South End of Hogg Lane in the parish aforesaid Containing in breadth East and West by the North End thereof fforty Seven ffoot of Assize be it more or Less which North End abutteth upon a way or passage of three foot in breadth belonging to the said Thomas Needler and was Sometime parcell of the North part of the said peice or parcell of Ground or Garden Plott . . . But was then severed from the same . . . for a way or passage for the said Thomas Needler . . . to go and come to and from the Ground of the said Thomas Needler and to and from Hogg Lane aforesaid [in] and by a way of Eight foot in breadth at the Least North and South Leading to and from Hogg Lane aforesaid Reserved out of the North End of a peice of Ground of one John Wood Yeoman and the said peice or parcell of Ground or Garden Plott . . . Containeth in breadth East and West by the South End thereof fforty four foot and Two Inches of Assize . . . which South End abutteth upon part of the Buildings of and Belonging to the said Great Messuage or Tenement called the Boars Head Containing in Length North and South as well on the East Side thereof which side abutteth upon the Ground of the said Thomas Needler as on the West Side thereof which West Side abutteth upon the Ground there of the said John Wood Sixty one foot and three Inches of Assize . . . together with free Liberty of Ingress Egress and Regress into and from the said peice or parcell of

Ground and Garden plott . . . through the Way of Eight foot Broad at the East [i.e., least] North and South as is afore mentioned Leading to and from the street called Hogg Lane aforesaid . . . Except . . . So much of the said Ground or Garden Plott . . . as . . . was then Laid or Inclosed to the ffreehold Ground houses or Estate Late of the said Adrian Denist [*sic*] in Boars head yard by the Brick wall then thereon Standing being about four foot in breadth and sixty foot in Length on the East Side of the Ground or Garden Plott.

The alley of 8′ would have been well north of the Boar's Head and not the alley of the same width mentioned in Needler's major deed (no. 1) and Browne's deed (no. 5).

5. The deed of 27 December 1621, by which William Browne bought part of the Boar's Head. One of the original copies of the deed survives at the Folger (Z.c.22(23)) and attached is a copy of Poley's contract with Lord Wentworth of 23 June 1618 enfranchising the Boar's Head; I am indebted to Professor Ingram for notice of these documents. A complete copy of the deed, but without the contract attached, also survives on the Close Roll (C.54/2515/11). The two versions are nearly identical, differing significantly only twice in the description of the property: where the Close Roll reads "Walford," the Folger has "Palford," and after "reedified," the Folger omits "and." The two versions even share the mistake after the first mention of the Boar's Head, "as the[y]." I transcribe the version on the Close Roll. Browne bought:

All those severall roomes & dwelling places parcell of a capitall messuage or tene*m*ente comonly called or knowne by the name of the Boares head as the[y] now be or late were in the seu*er*all possessions of Elizabeth Mitchell widowe John younge John Price Willi*a*m Bowyer Thomas Gawen Nicholas Jones together with one roome called a chamber roome builded over the tene*m*ente wherein the said Elizabeth Mitchell now dwelleth now or late in the possession of Roger Meggs together alsoe with one roome late in the occupac*i*on of one ffrancis Pleyvie together alsoe with soe much of the said Boares head yard in measure as by measure & platt were lately sett out & measured from the south side of the roome in the occupac*i*on of the said Elizabeth Mitchell right downe into the said Boares head yard to a stake there sett vpp & conteyneth by estimac*i*on fiftie & three foote of assize and in bredth from the said stake vnto the yard or garden of the said Willi*a*m Browne at the north end from the east vnto the west twenty twoe foote & five ynches together alsoe with soe much of the said Boares head ground As lately was builded & knowne for a tyreing house or Stage & twoe tene*m*ents late in the severall occupac*i*ons of humphrey Plevy & John Walford and haue ben lately pulled downe to be reedified and builded in a better forme as the same by measure doe contayne at the north end next the tenemente wherein Thomas Milles butcher now dwelleth in breadth from the pale belonging to the Coppyhold tenements of Samuell Rowley west to the corner of the said tenements wherein the said Thomas Milles now dwelleth thirty six foote & a halfe of assize & in breadth at the south end next the garden of the said William Browne the like assize of thirty six foote & a halfe & doe contayne on the east & west side thereof thirty nyne foote & seaven ynches.

Three clauses in this deed have to do with alleys. The first clause defines an alley that Browne was to build on land he was not to own: "Except & alwaies reserued out of this bargaine & sale one passage way of the breadth of eight foote & from the ground the altitude of nyne foote to be made laid out & mayneteined passageable by the said William Browne & his assignes in & through the said parcell of ground where the stage was builte right discending from the way alonge out of hogge lane to be made of equall breadth into the said Boares head yard with free passage for the said Sir John Poley his executors & assignes and all other inhabitants in the said Boares head yard with free passage there into or out from the said Boares head yard by the said passage into hogge lane aforesaid at all times hereafter." The second clause gives Browne the right to use the alley described in Needler's major deed (no. 1) and alluded to in the clause above. Browne, his heirs, and assigns were "to haue & enioy free & quiett passage & repassage ingresse egresse and regresse into and through the said way vnto & from the bargained premisses into & from hogge lane afore said at all tymes hereafter." The third clause gives Poley and his agents the right to use the alley that Browne was to build. Browne was "to permytt & suffer the said Sir John Poley & all other his assignes tenants & vndertenants to haue quiett & free passage in the said passage way with all convenient carriage by carte or otherwise & to mayneteyne the same passageable in such latitude & altitude as is aforemencioned & excepted at all tymes hereafter for the vse & benefitt of the said Sir John Poley his heires & assignes or other Tenants & Inhabitants in the buildings now or late parcell of the said Boares head which shall haue their passage way thereby assigned . . . by the said Sir John Poley."

APPENDIX 9
Robert Browne

The name Robert Browne crops up often in the records of the theatre business in Elizabethan and Jacobean times. Because all the references available to Chambers could apply to one man, he supposed that they did. Chambers's man, therefore,

1. was a member of Worcester's company, 1583–89,
2. acted on the continent often from 1590 to 1607 and from 1618 to 1620,
3. had a wife and family who died of the plague in Shoreditch in August 1593,
4. had a son, Robert, baptized at St. Saviour's on 19 October 1595 and a daughter, Elizabeth, baptized there on 2 December 1599,
5. was the leader of Derby's men in performances at court during the winters of 1599–1600 and 1600–1601,
6. was a member of the Queen's Revels syndicate in 1610, and
7. wrote from Clerkenwell in 1607 recommending the wife of "an old servant" of his, Mr. Rose, an actor in Prince Henry's men, to Edward Alleyn for a place as a gatherer in that company.

Chambers also knew that an actor called "Browne of the Boares head" had died in 1603. He did not know this actor's Christian name, however, and so did not try to distinguish him from the Robert Browne alive after that or to connect his Robert Browne with the Boar's Head.[1]

Then in the legal documents about the Boar's Head, Professor Sisson found that Browne of the Boar's Head was also a Robert Browne. Obviously there were at least two theatrical Robert Brownes at the turn of the century. Sisson decided that the Robert Browne at the Boar's Head should have been a famous actor-manager, and he progressively developed such a figure in his pieces of 1936 (pp. 99–102, 107), 1942 (pp. 26, 33–34); 1954 (pp. 60, 61, 63, 64

n. 31), and 1972. He applied to him the appropriate bits of evidence bearing the name Robert Browne, together with speculations acknowledged at the outset for what they are. As the years went by, however, he tended to let speculations become facts to which he joined new speculations, and throughout to wrench the real evidence into convenient shapes.

By 1972, Sisson's Robert Browne led Worcester's men in 1583, when Edward Alleyn was an apprentice among them, and for many years after (pp. xviii, xix, 7–8, 21, 44, 59). It was he who often toured the Low Countries and Germany from 1590 onward, leading Worcester's men there (pp. xix, 42). It was his wife and family who died in Shoreditch of the plague in 1593; he soon brought a Susan to Worcester's men as his second wife and had a son, Robert, in 1595 (pp. 7–8). He involved himself in the building of the playhouse in the Boar's Head "from the beginning," in fact designed it, so that Worcester's men could have a London home, and they moved in during the autumn of 1599 (pp. 42–43, 44, 45, 49, 56, 61). He and they sued each other in 1600, and presently they disloyally left him to go to the Rose (pp. 50–51, 69, 74) but allowed him to remain a sharer (pp. 59, 73). About the other things bearing the name Robert Browne, like the leadership of Derby's men and the doings after 1603 (including the foreign tours up to 1607 and from 1618 to 1620), Sisson had nothing to say in 1972.[2] He did hint, however, that the boy born in 1595 was responsible for at least some of the things after 1603 (p. 42).

Much of this scheme is wrong and almost all the rest is doubtful. Nothing in the evidence suggests that a Robert Browne ever led Worcester's men; indeed nothing reliably says that a Robert Browne even belonged to the company after the 1580s. Nothing suggests that Worcester's men ever toured abroad, led by Robert Browne or anybody else, and during many of the very years when Sisson would have them abroad, a company of the name (ignored by Sisson) was appearing often in provincial English towns and cities. Sisson had his man at the Boar's Head from its start by ignoring the first year of the playhouse, 1598–99; nothing suggests that Browne was interested in it until the rebuilding of the summer of 1599. Sisson's account of the events from 1599 to 1603 is almost wholly bedeviled by his faulty treatment of five documents. He got the dates wrong of the four documents belonging to the lawsuit in Chancery between Worcester's men and Browne: he has the documents dating from 1601 rather than 1602 and the events they concern (the stay of Worcester's men at the Boar's Head) beginning in 1599 rather than 1601.[3] He made a passage in a document of 30 May 1603 support his thesis about Robert Browne and Worcester's men by, as we shall see, largely defying its words.

Originally (in 1936 and 1942), Professor Sisson did not think that the Robert Browne who had a son and daughter baptized at St. Saviour's in 1595 and 1599 could have been the man of both the Boar's Head and the foreign tours. To have the husband abroad while the wife was bearing children in London was to dishonor the wife. By 1972, however, he had got round this objection, but he did not say how. He should have found the same objection when concluding that the man who was at the Boar's Head from 1599 to 1603 was the Robert Browne of the foreign tours of those years. For when the one should have been busy in the playhouse in Whitechapel (for example, at Christmas 1599) and in the London law courts (for example, in the spring of 1603), the other was busy abroad. The Boar's Head man was also busy at home in other ways during those years, for his wife bore children baptized in Whitechapel in December 1600, April 1602, February 1603, and January 1604. This last child would have been conceived in the spring of 1603, when the man of the foreign tours was at Frankfurt, Cologne, Brussels, and Lille.[4]

If, finally, one must apply any of the information about Robert Browne dating after 1603 to the boy born in 1595, then one must wink at some very strange things. From 1603 to 1607, for example, an important English actor abroad was aged eight to twelve. In 1610, one of the veteran actors in the Queen's Revels syndicate was aged fourteen. The man was aged sixteen whose old servant, the actor Rose, had a wife who wanted a gatherer's place in Alleyn's company. Actually, at least in 1634, the real son, Robert, of the man at the Boar's Head was not an actor at all but a haberdasher.[5]

Recently, Professor Willem Schrickx has pressed the same material into a very different mold. In an essay about English actors on the continent, he separates the Robert Browne of the foreign tours from the man at the Boar's Head and gives much of the information bearing the name to the man of the foreign tours. His most important assertions for our purposes are that the Browne of the foreign tours led Derby's men at court in the winters of 1599–1600 and 1600–1601 and that, by implication, the company had nothing to do with the Boar's Head. Browne of the Boar's Head, it seems, was an obscure figure: one of Worcester's men who took a lease on the Boar's Head in about 1599—a place evidently not much used for acting—and died poor in 1603.

Much of this scheme does not accord very well with the evidence, either. The continental Browne led a company of English actors at Strasbourg for more than a month in the winter of 1599–1600: on 22 December, he (as "Robertus Braun der Englische Commoediant sambt noch 12 personen") asked and got permission for his company to play there a fortnight beginning on 27 December, and on 11 January the company (as "Engellandische Commoedianten") got permission to play there another fortnight, until 25 January. They were back the next winter when on 13 December 1600 they asked again for permission to play, called this time "Engellandische Commoedianten, die vor einem Jar auch hie gewesen." Yet if Browne was also the leader of Derby's men, he had to be in London both winters to play with that company at court, on 5 February 1600 and on 1 and 6 January 1601. He had to be there, too, presumably, to collect the payments made to him for the performances, authorized on 18 February 1600 and 31 March 1601.

Schrickx dismisses these difficulties as Chambers did. So that he could play with his English company at court, one reads, Browne left his continental company for home soon after 22 December 1599, and he did not leave home to rejoin the continental company until late in the next winter. That is why, one also reads, the clerks in Strasbourg referred to the continental company as English comedians in January and December 1600 rather than as Browne and colleagues. Chambers, however, unlike Schrickx, could not know that there were at least two Robert Brownes who were important in the theatrical companies of the time, hence that a much more likely explanation exists of how a Robert Browne could lead one company on the continent and another in London during the same two winters. Besides, the continental Browne could not have collected the payment made in the spring of 1601 because he was in Frankfurt then.

Schrickx shows that when at home the continental Browne was a member of the Lord Admiral's company. How then could he lead Derby's men? Schrickx offers an unhelpful suggestion. During the winters of 1599–1600 and 1600–1601, he writes, Browne "revived in some way the earlier amalgamation between the Admiral's and the Lord Strange's men by temporarily becoming one of Derby's men." The Admiral's and Lord Strange's men played together from perhaps 1588 until 1594, and Lord Strange's men became Derby's in 1593 when Lord Strange became earl of Derby. He died little more than six months later, however, in 1594, whereupon the former Lord Strange's men soon found a new sponsor, the Lord Chamberlain, and so became the Lord Chamberlain's men. The new earl of Derby (who had never been a Lord Strange) then sponsored his own company from 1594, also called Derby's men, who played for many years quite distinctly from the Lord Chamberlain's men.

Schrickx believes that Browne of the Boar's Head belonged to Worcester's men because of the Privy Council order of 31 March 1602 allowing Worcester's men to use the Boar's Head. He ignores, however, the documents showing that Browne and his company were distinct from Worcester's: those explaining that Browne leased his playhouse to Worcester's in 1601 and then wrangled with them in the law courts until they left it in 1602; and one actually stating, as we shall see, that Browne and his fellows were not Worcester's. Schrickx seems to believe that the Boar's Head was not used much for plays because, as he writes, apart from legal records, only two documents allude to the place as a theatre—the Privy Council order of March 1602 and a draft patent probably of 1604 allowing the Queen's men to play there and at the Curtain. To brush aside legal records is to deny not only most of what we know about the Boar's Head but most of what we know about the whole theatre industry in Shakespeare's time and, indeed, Shakespeare himself. The legal records about the Boar's Head are of many kinds and dates and set out many points of view. They refer hundreds of times to the playhouse in the Boar's Head, and many of these references are to its actual use as a theatre. We cannot afford to ignore them. Besides, several nonlegal records allude to the playhouse in the Boar's Head other than the Privy Council order and draft patent: for example, the reminiscence of the marquess of Newcastle of about 1660.[6]

If, then, neither the Robert Browne who led Derby's men nor the Robert Browne who owned much of the Boar's Head can have been the Robert Browne who led a troupe of actors on the continent, can the Derby's man and the Boar's Head man be the same? And can Derby's men, therefore, have used the Boar's Head? The answer to both questions, I think, is clearly yes.

The Robert Browne at the Boar's Head was a player, he led a company of players, and his company was not Worcester's. A remark of 1602 and several of 1603 indicate that he was a player: in February 1603, for example, Robert Browne, "Stage Player," was ordered to repair the public highway outside his premises in Whitechapel, and in October 1603, Edward Alleyn's wife told her husband that a fellow actor, Browne of the Boar's Head, had died.[7] Many remarks in the lawsuits probably imply that he led a company of players, but two from a lawsuit of 1603 state that he did. Woodliffe described his antagonists at the Boar's Head on 20 May as "Roberte Broune a common stage player" and "Broune & his fellow stage players." In his reply, Browne not only described himself as the leader of a company of players but said that his company was distinct from Worcester's men. The Langleys had extracted additional payments from Worcester's men for the use of the Boar's Head during the winter of 1601–2. After Worcester's men left for the Rose in the summer of 1602, Woodliffe tried to do as much to the new company at the Boar's Head. Browne explained on 30 May 1603: "aboutes two yeares past or thereabouts," Richard Langley "vnlawfully entered into the said Stage Tyringe howse and galleryes and offered to disturbe the said Playes and Comodyes to be acted on the said Stage. . . and for feare thereof Extorted from the players there diuerse sommes of money to permytt the said Comedyes there quietly to be acted and doen by the said players w^{th}out disturbance of the said Richard Langley against all Right equitie and Conscyence wch the Comp^{lt} [Woodliffe] would by lyke wronnge now exacte and gett from this defend^{te} [Browne] and his ffellowes yf he by any vndue Course might procure the same."[8]

No evidence directly connects the Robert Browne who led Derby's men with the Robert Browne who led a company at the Boar's Head, hence Derby's with the Boar's Head. Enough suggests the connection, however, that we have small cause to resist it, especially in view of the difficulties we must have trying to make the Robert Browne of the foreign tours the leader of Derby's men. The chronology of court performances by Derby's men exactly matches that of Browne's activities at the Boar's Head, and the chronology of their appearances in the provinces matches his absences from the Boar's Head. Moreover, the chronology of court and provincial appearances by Worcester's men distinguishes them from both Browne and Derby's men.

During Browne's first winter at the Boar's Head, 1599–1600, a company played there on 24 and 26 December, Worcester's men were at Coventry on 3 January, and a company called Derby's men played at court (5 February) for the first time since 1582. During Browne's second winter at the Boar's Head, 1600–1601, Derby's men played at court for the second and third times (1, 6 January) since 1582. When Worcester's men were at the Boar's Head during the next winter, however, it was they, not Derby's, who went to court (3 January). Derby's men are recorded in the provinces regularly from 1594, when the sixth earl of Derby acquired his title, and Worcester's men equally regularly from 1589, when the fourth earl of Worcester acquired that title. Derby's men cease to be recorded there in the autumn of 1599, when Browne moved into the Boar's Head, but Worcester's men continue. Derby's men are again recorded in the provinces, however, after Browne leased the Boar's Head to Worcester's men in the autumn of 1601. Derby's men are also recorded there for many years after the closing of the London playhouses in the spring of 1603 and Browne's death later in the year.[9] When Browne's widow married Thomas Greene, an actor newly made one of Worcester's (now the Queen's) men, he suddenly became one of that company's leading people, and the patent was drafted allowing the company to play again at the Boar's Head as well as the Curtain. Besides, if Browne of the Boar's Head was not Browne of Derby's men, a company played at the Boar's Head of which we know nothing, and Derby's must have used a playhouse in London of which we also know nothing.

We know for certain about a marriage of Robert Browne of the Boar's Head. His wife during his years in Whitechapel was named Susan. As Professor Sisson found, she was born in 1577 or 1578, probably had something to do with Worcester's men in 1593 (when she was fifteen or sixteen years old), and certainly belonged to the theatrical community from the mid-1590s onward.[10] She could more reasonably have been the daughter of one of Worcester's men than, as Sisson believed, the second wife in 1593 of a Robert Browne whom he would have leading the company in the 1590s.[11] She and Robert Browne of the Boar's Head had five children whom her next husband mentioned in his will. Four of the five were baptized at St. Mary Matfellon in Whitechapel as the children of Robert Browne:

> Susan, on 23 December 1600
> William, on 25 April 1602

Elizabeth, on 13 February 1603
Anne (born posthumously), on 22 January 1604.

The other was Robert. In view of the dates on which the four children were baptized, Robert should have been the eldest child, and he should have been born in the winter of 1599–1600. His parents should have been married early in 1599, when Susan was about twenty-one years old.[12]

We can still apply little of the information in Chambers about "Robert Browne" to the man at the Boar's Head and none to his son, Robert. While the Boar's Head man probably had a social connection with Worcester's men through his wife, Susan, his first provable professional one occurred when he leased his playhouse to them in 1601. There were obviously at least two and could easily have been three or more Robert Brownes who had to do with the companies and playhouses of the time. It will never be easy to decide which snippet of information bearing the name belongs with which other snippets. It is clear, however, that the Robert Browne at the Boar's Head was married to a lady well known in the world of theatres, Susan Browne Greene Baskervile. It seems clear, moreover, that he was the Robert Browne who led Derby's men and not the Robert Browne who led a company of English actors on the continent.

Notes

Chapter 1. To 1561

1. See C.66/641/6/m.23; C.82/566/1; and the payments to 1541: (1522) E.405/92/m.30, 10; (1522–23) /93/m.11, 13(2); (1523–24) /94/m.5(2), 8(2); (1524–25) /95/m.1ᵛ, 16, 13(2); (1525–26) /96/m.15, 1, 20(2), 20ᵛ; (1526–27) /97/m.17(2), 1, 24, 27, 19ᵛ; (1527–28) /98/m.1ᵛ, 2, 11, 14(2), 14ᵛ; (1528–29) /99/m.14(2), 7, 17, 11(2); (1529–30) /100/m.20(2), 1, 12ᵛ(2), 5; (1530–31) /101/m.14ᵛ, 17ᵛ(2), 1, 15, 5; (1531–32) /102/m.14ᵛ, 8ᵛ, 7ᵛ, 6ᵛ, 17ᵛ, 11ᵛ; (1532–33) /103/m.15, 14(2), 14ᵛ, 1ᵛ, 17(2), 5ᵛ; (1533–34) /104/m.15, 1ᵛ, 15ᵛ, 13ᵛ, 10ᵛ, 6; (1534–35) /105/m.12ᵛ(2), 1, 16, 17, 7; (1535–36) /106/m.18(2), 2ᵛ, 20(2), 8; (1536–37) /107/m.11(2), 3ᵛ, 5ᵛ(3); (1537–38) /108/m.17ᵛ(2), 30, 10ᵛ(2), 22ᵛ; (1538–39) /109/m.27(2), 7ᵛ, 1(2), 15; (1539–40) /110/m.24(2), 15, 8(2), 3ᵛ; (1540–41) /111/m.34, 30, 33ᵛ, 1ᵛ(2).

2. E.179/141/116/m.7–8; he is called John Dransfeld, and his name is in the lower two-thirds of the list.

3. S.P.60/2/f.61; the letter goes on, "I wold be right glade to haue some worde of yoᵘ amendment for as nowe I haue no speciall frynde to trust vnto but you." It is dated 8 November 1534.

4. E.179/141/122/m.2; his name is tenth of seventeen. The tax was only for those who had at least £20. The highest figure in Whitechapel was £50.

5. S.P.60/7/f.104–5. The letter is dated 24 August. In October 1536, a Thomas Transfeld was paid for providing carts, harness, and other necessaries (S.P.65/1/p.1).

6. S.P.1/124/f.118, 155; E.36/120/f.133–36. Even though he gave part of his first sermon before the Lord Mayor and his aldermen and declared that he would give it at length before the Privy Council, Harrydaunce does not seem to have come to much grief: he gave his goods as worth £3 in the 1520s and £6 in the 1540s (E.179/141/113/m.4; /116/m.7–8; /154/m.19; /140/m.5ᵛ).

7. E.179/141/131/m.5. Of twenty-six persons, omitting the "strangers," one had as much as Transfeild and one had more (£48 13s. 4d.). In the list for Whitechapel, only the amount of tax appears, but notations in the lists for other parishes suggest that the rate was 6d. in the pound; Transfeild paid 15s. One of the chief collectors for Ossulston Hundred (in which Whitechapel was) was Sir John Alen.

8. C.66/704/15/m.34. A James Swegar *alias* Reynolds, who was apparently called Mr. Reynolds, had married an Alice Stansfelde and had cousins Robert and Nicholas Grove. He died a rather wealthy man in 1551. A widow of the family (another Alice Stansfelde), who died in 1554, lived a few yards from the Boar's Head in Aldgate Street in the City and owned an inn next door to where she lived. In the list for the subsidy he collected, Transfeild's name was first written "Stansfeld"; then someone stroked out the "S" and inserted an "r" after the "t." Moreover, at Easter 1526 he was paid for one of his gunnerships as "Stransfeld" (Guildhall, MS.9171/12/f.94–96, 81–82; /15/f.224ᵛ–25ᵛ, 285; MS.9051/2/f.125–26; P.R.O., PROB.11/34/36).

9. C.1/1055/17 (which is only partly legible and that under ultraviolet). The document is dated by being addressed to Audley, who was Lord Chancellor 1538–44. The Transfeilds raised Reynolds's rent "abouts iii yeres past," and he had lived in the house "xix yeres or thereabout." Transfeild held his lease from Nicholas Day.

10. The payments from 1541 to 1561 are (1541–42) E.405/112/m.3ᵛ; (1542–43) /113/m.50ᵛ,24; (1543–44) /114.m.39ᵛ, 16; (1544–45) roll missing; (1545–46) /115/m.17ᵛ, 54; (1546–47) /116.m.10, 24; (1547–51) rolls missing; (1551–52) /117/no entries for Transfeild; (1552–53) /118/m.16, 35; (1553–54) /119/m.46, 29; (1554–55) /120/m.29ᵛ, 85; (1555–56) /121/m.99ᵛ, 47; (1556–57) /122/m.41, 107; (1557–58) /123/m.96ᵛ, 33ᵛ; (1558–59) /124/m.19ᵛ, 51ᵛ; (1559–60) /125/m.25, 72; (1560–61) /126/m.15ᵛ, 68. A list of gunners of 1560 includes Transfeild (S.P.12/15/21).

11. *Letters and Papers, Foreign and Domestic, Henry VIII, 1540–41,* no. 496; E.179/141/136. Upward of twenty people lent £4, the smallest amount acceptable.

12. *The Hamilton Papers,* ed. Joseph Bain (Edinburgh, 1890), 1: 171, 262–63.

13. E.179/141/146/m.6 (Transfeild is 2d; nobody whose account is legible had more); /138/m.2ᵛ (he is 3d in a list mostly illegible); /140/m.5ᵛ (he is 5th; two others had as much and one had more, £100); /160/m.11 (he is 2d; two others had as much and one had more, £50); /154/m.19 (he is 4th; three others had as much and one, a stranger, had more, £100); E.179/142/167/m.10ᵛ–11 (he is 1st; three others had as much and one had more, £100); /186/m.1 (he is 2d; nobody had as much); /179/m.2ᵛ (he is 2d from the end; six had more, five others as much).

14. The Tower gunners could be asked to serve on ships as well as in garrisons and armies away from London (S.P.12/8/15). Transfeild, of course, could have done such service for months at a time and still have collected his payments in London. Other than those I mention above, the times when Transfeild did not collect at least one of his payments and so could have been serving away from London for a longer period were Easter 1529, Michaelmas 1530, and Michaelmas 1543.

15. See Robinson's payment in advance at Easter, 1541: E.405/111/m.33ᵛ. The clerks of the Exchequer could have mistakenly omitted Transfeild's name at Michaelmas 1551 or confused his name with someone else's.

16. Transfeild probably had not often assigned payments for ready cash. Only one payment, that at Michaelmas 1530, seems so assigned. It was collected by John Porter, a mercer of London who made a business of collecting other men's payments (E.405/101/m.1(4), 5(3); /100/m.10, 12(5), 20ᵛ, etc.). At the same time, Simon Webbe collected the payment Transfeild and Sandford should have shared; Webbe occasionally collected other men's payments. Otherwise, when he did not collect them himself, Transfeild assigned payments to his wife, or colleagues like Parker and Cornelius Johnson, master ordnance maker in the Tower (Mich. 1532), or superiors like Morris and Skeffington. John Aldrege, whom I cannot identify, collected his payment at Michaelmas 1543.

17. Corporation of London, Husting Roll 248/114. Assheton left many men small bequests and in nearly all cases mentioned their wives. He mentioned none for Transfeild.

18. Sisson (p. 21) wrote that the attempt to use the Boar's Head as a playhouse in 1557 "links it unexpectedly with the More circle." He offered three main reasons: (1) the steward of the manor of Stepney at the time was William Roper, Sir Thomas More's son-in-law and biographer; (2) Roper's successor as steward (Hugh Stukeley) was in turn succeeded by Edmund Poley, who owned the Boar's Head; and (3) the manor had belonged until he was attainted in 1551 to Giles Heron, another of More's sons-in-law. The first reason is not very convincing because Roper's wife, Margaret More, had died in 1544, and his name appears nowhere in the affairs of either Transfeild or the Boar's Head. The other two reasons are wrong. The Edmund Poley who became steward was not the man at the Boar's Head but his nephew (see chapter 2). Heron did not own the manor of Stepney, only a house and lands in that of Hackney. Sisson had misunderstood the English version of a patent in the *Calendar of the Patent Rolls of Edw. VI,* 4:50, and had not seen the original, C.66/836/m.8, or its warrant, C.82/940/4, or the patent by which the crown, having just received them from the Bishop of London, passed the manors of Stepney and Hackney to Wentworth, C.66/833/m.4, or John Stow's explanation in his *Survey of London* (London, 1603), pp. 489–90. For Roper's stewardship, see Sisson's documents: C.24/55/63 [pt. II, 9th from the bottom], both of Roper's depositions; and /56/35 [24th in the box], Roper.

19. For the relationship between John, Edmund, and Richard Poley, see the wills of Edmund Poley, Sr., d. 1549 (who had sons, John, Edmund, Henry, Richard, and Thomas), and Jane Transfeild Poley (whose husband, Edmund, was certainly the son of Edmund, Sr.): PROB.11/32/31; /98/47. A John Polley, servant to the Lord Wentworth, was paid 46s. 8d. in April 1547 for "bringing of a priest out of Suff[olk] and his retorne backe" (E.315/439/f.14ᵛ) and occasionally joined Lord Wentworth in legal transactions, for example, C.66/836/m.40 (April 1551).

20. His name appears in a list of Tower gunners of January 1526; he was last paid at Easter 1539: *Letters and Papers, Foreign and Domestic, Henry VIII, 1524–26*, pp. 869–70; E.405/109/m.9.

21. *Acts of the Privy Council, 1554–56*, p. 73; *1556–58*, pp. 102, 119; P.C.2/6/pp. 590, 615; Corporation of London, Journal 17, f.42ᵛ, and Letter Book S, f.143; E. K. Chambers, *The Elizabethan Stage* (Oxford, 1923), 4:270. Earlier in the proclamation, the undesirables are "all manner of ydle vagabonds valyaunt beggars and maysterles men and such like havinge no occupacionne or mysterie." The Privy Council had urged the City to make such a proclamation three years before. The act specifies "all Fencers Bearewardes Comon Players in Enterludes & Minstrels, not belonging to any Baron of this Realme or towardes any other honorable Personage of greater Degree."

22. P.C.2/7/pp. 695, 696.

23. The original will (part of which is perished) is Guildhall MS.9172/4; the register copy (which is complete) is MS.9171/15. After small bequests, he left "The residue of all my goods movable and vnmovable whatsoever they be my funeralls, Debtes, and legacies fullie contented and paid . . . vnto the seyd Jane Transfeild my wife whome I make my sole Executrixe of this my presente Testamente and laste will." For Borne, see Middlesex R.O., MR/LV/1[f.5-5ᵛ, 17ᵛ], lists of those licensed in 1553 to keep alehouses and victualling houses in Whitechapel and Stepney. Evidently, inns were neither, for no innholder appears. The records of the Innholders Co. do not begin until well into the 17th century: Guildhall, MSS.6647–64.

24. The roll has been lost showing payments due on Michaelmas 1561, one of which Transfeild would have collected, and on Easter 1562, one of which he would not. He does not appear in the rolls for 1562–63, 1563–64, or 1564–65: E.405/127–29.

25. Poley got the license on 12 January, and the wedding took place on the 14th: *Allegations for Marriage Licences Issued by the Bishop of London, 1520-1610* (London: Harleian Soc., 1887), p. 23; registers, I, f.2ᵛ.

26. Either way, because the property was a copyhold, this transaction and any others concerning the property would not normally have been entered in the central courts of record nor mentioned in the will. They would have been entered on the court roll of Stepney, only fragments of which survive from before 1654.

27. J. Q. Adams correctly identified the site of the Boar's Head, but Chambers rejected the identification: Chambers, 2:443–45; *Shakespearean Playhouses* (Boston, 1917), p. 17.

28. See the papers in K.B.8, especially those printed in the *Third Report of the Deputy Keeper of the Public Records* (London, 1843), appx. 2:245–47, 255, 263, 267–68; *C.S.P., Dom., 1547–80*, p. 83. See also P.C.2/6/pp. 523, 550.

29.. B.M., Add. MS 5476, f. 197ᵛ; P.C.2/6/p.455; *Acts of the Privy Council, 1542–47*, p. 407, and *1556–58*, pp. 19, 124.

30. J. O. Halliwell-Phillipps, *Outlines of the Life of Shakespeare* (London, 1882), pp. 348, 352.

31. The letter licensing the Boar's Head did not mention its location but did mention the Oxford-Worcester company, which on other evidence was using the Boar's Head in Whitechapel then: Corporation of London, Remembrancia, II, 189; Chambers, 4:335; and chapter 5 below.

32. The lord mayor interfered more often in Southwark, where the Globe, Swan, Rose, and Hope eventually were, but though in Surrey and the diocese of Winchester, that place from 1550 was the twenty-sixth ward of the City. See Thomas Rymer, *Foedera* (London, 1816), 1:11; Stow, *Survey of London*, p. 503; Philip E. Mather, *A Compendium of Sheriff Law* (London, 1894), p. 3; V.C.H., *Middlesex*, 2:18, 55; S. and B. Webb, *The Parish and the County* (London, 1963), p. 288 n. 1.

Chapter 2. 1561–1597

1. The Poleys held the lease of Woodlands from William Glasscock, who had got it from John Wyberde in 1540. Poley renewed the lease in the 1570s, and his widow left it to her heir, their son, John, describing it as particularly hers. Transfeild's daughter, Frances, married a man named Wybard. See *Letters and Papers, Foreign and Domestic, Henry VIII, 1540–41*, pp. 143, 172; PROB.11/62/5; /98/47; C.24/225/58[pt. II/1], Moyses, nos. 7, 8; G.L.C., M.L.R.1724/ IV/360.

2. Both the second Lord Wentworth and Jane Poley of the Boar's Head called him nephew, and he called Edmund Poley of the Boar's Head uncle: *C.S.P., Dom., 1581–90*, pp. 21, 74; C.3/190/8; C.24/201/17, Poley; PROB.11/122/107; /98/47; /75/32; /32/31 (for Poley's two sisters).

3. He was apparently of age when his father made his will in 1548: PROB.11/32/31.

4. John Poley of Badley had a godson, John, in 1587 (PROB.11/75/32). In her will (1601), Jane Poley mentioned four living children: Frances, Anne, John, and Elizabeth (PROB.11/98/47). Isabel was baptized as "Bolley" and buried, like Raphe, as "Pooly." Edward married Isabel Lee in 1594 but is not mentioned in Jane Poley's will, nor are three other men of the name in Whitechapel: Reuben (m. 1598), Richard (m. 1601), and William (d. 1615). See the parish registers, I, f. 4ᵛ, 6ᵛ, 8ᵛ, 9ᵛ, 13(2), 20ᵛ, 29ᵛ, 36ᵛ, 41, 44ᵛ, 48, 75.

5. C.24/157/45, 46. Squire joined Poley in the bond to Bedingfield, but Poley seems to have made himself responsible for paying the money. Because Bedingfield wanted to sue the Tower Court for his inconvenience without offending the lieutenant of the Tower and so perhaps losing his house in the Liberty, he used the name of his friend, Robert Harrison, as the one who would receive Poley's money, repay Tyson, and "father the said challendge" to the court.

6. C.24/290/3, no. 7; PROB.11/98/47.

7. Guildhall, MS.9168/14/f.232ᵛ; MS.9065ᵏ/f.167ᵛ.

8. An "Englishman of credit"named Henry Poley was living in Spain in 1595 (H.M.C., *Salisbury*, 5:357). He was unlikely to be the Henry Poley of the Boar's Head, who was seen in or around London sometime between 1587 and 1591, who was in Whitechapel for the negotiations in 1594 with Woodliffe about the Boar's Head, and who died there in March 1596, being buried at St. Mary Matfelon on the twenty-seventh (C.24/225/58[pt.II/1], Leversage, no. 1; registers, I, f. 36). The Henry of the Boar's head had an uncle, Henry, who if he was alive in 1595 (he was apparently younger than his brother, Edmund: PROB.11/32/31) was more likely to be an Englishman of credit. But there were plenty of Poleys alive then, and because one of the squires of Badley had borne it, Henry was probably a common name in the family.

9. The value of Woodlands is not clear, but in her will she said that a little house there was worth £2 a year.

10. C.3/227/19; C.24/225/58[pt.II/1]. One of the lessees was a clothworker, Henry Browne. His surname crops up often in the history of the Boar's Head.

11. Req.2/466/pt.II[/1], the bill.

12. C. W. Wallace, *The First London Theatre* (Lincoln, Nebr., 1913), pp. 3, 4; and my "A Handlist of Documents about the Theatre in Shoreditch" and "Aspects of the Design and Use of the First Public Playhouse," in *The First Public Playhouse* (Montreal, 1979).

13. Registers, I, f. 36.

14. A third military Sir John Poley was an older man who had been knighted by Howard of Effingham in 1588 and was dead by 1607. The younger Sir John Poley who was not of the Boar's Head eventually married a wealthy widow, Abigail, who survived him (her maiden name was Wikes; her first husband was John Worsley and her second Richard Luther). See *C.S.P., Dom., 1595–97*, pp. 197, 280(2); H.M.C., *Salisbury*, 6:360, 361, 523, 558, 559; C.24/331 (Pooley v. Beecher); C.2/Chas.I/L.59/54;/T.48/67.

15. E.179/142/239; /234/m.3ᵛ; /254; registers I, f. 46.

16. The name appears only once in the "Freedoms" book of the Company, 1526–1614, spelled "Woodclief" in the entry, "Woodlief" in the index. His master was Edward Slatier. In his marriage license (1594) he gave himself as yeoman and in his admon. act (1603) his widow gave him as of the Diocese of London rather than as citizen of London, a title many freemen acquired. In

Robert Browne's lawsuit against him in Easter term 1603, Woodliffe is "nu*per* de london haber-dasher alias . . . civis et haberdasher london," but in his own bill of the same term meant to stop Browne's lawsuit, Woodliffe is "Cittizen & haberdasher of London" (C.P.40/1701/m.1109; Req.2/466/pt.II[/1]). See George Unwin, *The Guilds and Companies of London* (London, 1966), pp. 224–31.

17. Req.2/199/17; K.B.27/1280/m.48; /1289/m.43; St.Ch.5/D.36/9. I misread parts of this last suit in my "Boar's Head Again," in *The Elizabethan Theatre III*, ed. David Galloway (Toronto, 1973).

18. The bond she had to post on 18 July to get the administration of his goods was £77 5s. 1d., the second highest of the month in the London Commissary Court (Guildhall, MS.9168/14/f.240ᵛ). The marriage license is in *Allegations for Marriage Licences Issued by the Bishop of London, 1520–1610*, p. 212. Woodliffe gave himself as of Barking in Essex and her as of Eastham in Essex. He did not give her husband's Christian name.

19. K.B.27/1332/m.889.

20. In the early lawsuits (1600–1601) all the litigants regularly gave the lease as in both names (C.24/278/781; /290/3; St.Ch.5/S.74/3; /S.13/8), but in the later ones (1603) the litigants, in-cluding Woodliffe himself, sometimes used just his name (Reg.2/466/pt.II[/1]; C.24/304/27).

21. Oliver and Susan were certainly living in the "vpper" or "hither" (probably higher) par-lor on the east side of the great yard of the Boar's Head in 1598 and after: C.24/278/71, inter-rogatory 3 for Moxlay, and Moxlay no. 3; /290/3, Samwell no. 8; C.P.40/1655/m.724ᵛ; registers, I, f. 34ᵛ, 39ᵛ.

22. C.24/258/pt.II/6, interrogatory 6, Vickars no. 6; Req.2/285/35; C.24/258/pt.I/50.

Chapter 3. 1597–Autumn 1599

1. Chambers, 2:379–83. The four and the dates at which they are first mentioned as playing places are the Cross keys (1579) and the Bell (1576) in Gracious Street, the Bull (1575) in Bishopsgate, and the Bell Savage (1576) in Ludgate Hill. Chambers also gave the Red Lion, but it is mentioned only once as having to do with plays, in 1567 (see also Janet S. Loengard, "An Elizabethan Lawsuit," *Shakespeare Quarterly* 34, no. 3 [Autumn 1983]).

2. Richard Bagnall, indeed, thought the stage new a year later: Woodliffe hired him during the rebuilding of 1599, "at suche tyme," as Bagnall put it in June 1601, "as there were new galleryes & a new stage made in the messuage or Inne called the Boreshead" (C.24/290/3, no. 7, and below in this chapter). Sisson, however, believed that permanent theatrical structures ex-isted at the Boar's Head when Woodliffe arrived there in 1594 (pp. 8, 35–36).

3. Corporation of London, Remembrancia, II, 171, 283. The letter of 1597 adds "as in all other places in and abowt the Citie" and that of 1607 a similar phrase.

4. See Chambers, 4:321–23, 326–27; Glynne Wickham, *Early English Stages* (London, 1972), 2, pt. 2:9–29.

5. For the Theatre, see Wallace, p. 221, and my "Handlist of Documents about the Theatre in Shoreditch," in *The First Public Playhouse*, pp. 126ff.; for the playhouse in Newington Butts, see William Ingram, "The Playhouse at Newington Butts: A New Proposal," *Shakespeare Quarterly* 21, no. 4 (Autumn 1970). Though unlicensed, the Swan seems to have continued housing plays for a time; see Professor Ingram's life of Francis Langley, *A London Life in the Brazen Age* (Cambridge, Mass., 1978), chaps. 11 and 13, and his "The Closing of the Theaters, in 1597: A Dissenting View," *Modern Philology* (November 1971): 105–15.

6. To his list of May 1603 of the parts of the Boar's Head that he had leased to Samwell on 13 April 1598, Woodliffe added the remark, "all wᶜʰ were then in the occupacíon of the said Richard Samuell thelder" (Req.2/466/pt.II[/1], the bill). The remark convinced Sisson that Sam-well was innkeeper of the Boar's Head, "Clearly" as far back as Edmund Poley's time there, in the 1580s, and that Samwell's son carried on as innkeeper well into the 17th century, after Woodliffe's time (see esp. pp. 36, 37, 70–71, 74). Because, however, the lease was to run from the previous Christmas, as Samwell, not Woodliffe, said (St.Ch.5/S.74/3, the bill, and C.24/290/3, interrogatory 2), it seems more reasonable to suggest that Woodliffe and Samwell had come to an informal agreement during the winter of 1597–98 about the lease, as a result of which San·well had moved into the inn at Christmas pending the negotiation of a formal lease in the spring.

7. Samwell first gave the date as the twentieth (St.Ch.5/S.74/3, the bill) but gave it as the thirteenth at his next legal opportunity (C.24/278/71, interrogatory 2 for Moxlay), the date the younger Samwell, Woodliffe, and Browne also gave (C.24/290/3, interrogatory 2, Samwell no. 2; Req.2/466/pt.II[/1], the bill). For the sealing of the contract, see the remarks of the notary's apprentice, Nicholas Moxlay, on 22 October 1600 (C.24/278/71, no. 3).

8. The written terms of the Woodliffe-Samwell lease, which were not in dispute, were mentioned often in the lawsuits and explained at length by Samwell (St.Ch.5/S.74/3, the bill), Browne and Samwell's son (C.24/290/3, interrogatory 2 and no. 2), and Woodliffe (Req.2/466/pt.II[/1], the bill). Samwell described the agreement about the upper parlor in his interrogatories of October 1600 for the apprentice notary, Nicholas Moxlay, as did Moxlay in his replies (C.24/278/71) and the younger Samwell in his deposition of June 1601 (/290/3, no. 8). In July 1603, Marsh remembered that Woodliffe had dwelt "in a parlor parcell of the p^{r}misses wch he had lett to Samwell after the lease and demise made to Samwell" (/304/27, no. 16).

9. Gatherers at the Red Bull in 1613 earned 1s. 6d. each a week (Chambers, 2:446).

10. For the terms under which the two men built and managed the playhouse, see appendix 4.

11. For the galleries and stage, see chapter 12 and appendix 3.

12. In April 1600, Langley said that Samwell had rebuilt his galleries entirely with the profits of the year before—a preposterous assertion but one suggesting that the galleries were conspicuously successful (St.Ch.5/S.13/8, no. 2).

13. For evidence about the building of the playhouse in 1598 and rebuilding in 1599, see appendix 2.

14. Jordan's name appears in only two of the lawsuits about the Boar's Head. On 14 November 1600, Samwell abandoned a lawsuit against Browne and "Israell Jordayne" (C.33/99/f.127^v in the A book, /100/f.122^v in the B book; see chapter 4). On 20 May 1603, Woodliffe described him as "Israiell Jordane of London Scrivener belonging vnto ye said Broune & his fellow stage players . . . by whome the said Broune is directed & advysed in all his indirect dealeings & vnlawefull Courses" (Req.2/466/pt.II[/1], the bill). Jordan's name, spelled "Jordaine" in Woodliffe's other references to him, appears in this latter lawsuit because he had lent Browne money that Browne had lent Woodliffe in 1601 and about which Browne eventually sued Woodliffe (see chapters 5 and 7). In his reply to Woodliffe, Browne agreed that Jordan had lent the money and called him "Isarell Jordayne" and "Isarell Jurden." Sisson (p. 73) guessed that Jordan "was the scribe and book-keeper of Worcester's men, and perhaps their treasurer" (Sisson mistakenly thought Browne's company and Worcester's men the same company). Sisson had not seen the allusion to Jordan in 1600, and apparently he dismissed the usual meaning of "scrivener" at the time as moneylender or broker, even though both Woodliffe and Browne reported Jordan as lending money. Samwell would not have sued Jordan as well as Browne in 1600 if Jordan had not had some financial stake in Browne's enterprise at the Boar's Head. For Robert Browne and his company, see appendix 9.

15. Hatfield House, Cecil Papers 186.24 (included here by the kind permission of the marquess of Salisbury); S.P.12/271/no. 34 (in another version of the newsletter sent on the same day to Humfredo Galdelli and Guiseppi Tusinga in Venice, Fenner put it, "Our Earle of Darby is busye in penning comedyes for the commonn players": /no.35); Chambers, 2:127. The earl also financed the reopening in 1599 of the playhouse at St. Paul's, where a company of children played: H.M.C., *DeL'Isle and Dudley*, 2:415.

16. For when the construction took place, see appendix 5. Mago (as he regularly signed himself) said he was fifty-two years old on 2 February 1600 (C.24/278/71, no. 1) and fifty-six on 25 July 1603 (/304/27, no. 1). The name is spelled "Maygoe" at the top of Samwell's interrogatories of February 1600 (/278/71) and "mayegoe" in Langley's deposition of April 1600 (St.Ch.5/S.13/8, no. 3). Perhaps he died in the autumn of 1610, for on 6 October Elizabeth, the widow of John Mago of St. Botolph's without Aldgate, got custody of her late husband's goods (Guildhall,MS. 9050/4/f.387^v, for which I am indebted to Professor Ingram). His name last appears in the records of his company in 1607 (*Records of the Worshipful Company of Carpenters*, 3:206; 4:216; 7:276).

17. Rodes said that he and the others were working on the northern gallery when Woodliffe had the stage moved, and he, Mago, and Willys said that Woodliffe had the stage moved to facilitate the the work on the eastern galleries. Mago said that he began rebuilding Woodliffe's

gallery (by taking off the roof) after all the other galleries had been done. See C.24/278/71, Rodes nos. 2, 3, Mago nos. 3, 4, Willys no. 3; appendix 3.

18. Trying to show that Woodliffe had given Samwell the use of the yard, Samwell, Browne, and their witnesses said in February 1600 and June 1601 that the rubbish had come from under Woodliffe's stage. Mago, however, conceded that some of the rubbish did not come from under the stage, that only the "most part whereof was throwne from vnder ye stage." See C.24/278/71, interrogatory 5, Mago no. 5, Rodes no. 5, Willys no. 5; /290/3, Bagnall no. 7, Samwell no. 7, Harryson no. 7.

19. Samwell's remarks are in his bill of April 1600 (St.Ch.5/S.74/3). His son, Browne, Rodes, and Hoppdale all agreed with him about what his project cost, his son making the point most clearly in June 1601, "That the tymber nayles stuffe & workmanshipp wch was imployed & spent in settinge vp the said little galleryes, and afterwards in takinge the same downe againe & setting vp the larger . . . coste his father . . . three hundred pounds or thereab:." Willys said in February 1600 that he had heard his master, Samwell, say that the rebuilding cost £280 "one way & other . . . or thereabouts." By July 1603, however, the facts had grown hazy: Mago put Samwell's cost at "allmost 2 or 3 hundred pounds," and Marsh, another carpenter, said "at leaste" instead of "allmost." See C.24/278/71, Mago no. 1, Rodes no. 1, Willys no. 1; /290/3, interrogatory 5, Hoppdale no. 5, Samwell no. 5; /304/27, Mago no. 6, Marsh no. 6; Req.2/466/pt.II[/1], the reply.

20. C.24/290/3, interrogatories 5, 6, Hoppdale no. 5, Samwell no. 6; /278/71, Mago no. 1; /304/27, Mago no. 7, Marsh no. 7; appendix 6 (for the date of Samwell's withdrawal). Hoppdale, one of the carpenters, said he received wages from both Samwell and Browne and saw both "lay out mony for tymber and other things that have gone to the sayd buildinge."

21. Curiously, in commenting on Browne's figures for the loan and the payment for the lease (which I use above), young Samwell put the loan at £200 and the payment at £160 (C.24/290/3, interrogatory 6, Samwell no. 6). The Samwells seem to have been living at the Boar's Head during the events retailed in St.Ch.5/S.74/3, the last of which happened on 4 April 1600 (the bill). See chapter 4.

22. For the Brownes, see appendix 9. On 11 June 1601, the younger Samwell gave his age as twenty-three (C.24/290/3, no.1).

Chapter 4. Autumn 1599–1600

1. Between 1594 and 1600, Henslowe's players used the Rose an average of forty weeks a year (see Henslowe's lists in the *Diary*, pp. 20–37, 47–48, 54–60, 70–72, 94–95, 120–21), and in the nineteen months from 22 August 1601 to 19 March 1603 the players at the Boar's Head seem to have used the place forty weeks (see chapter 7).

2. Req.2/34/73; St.Ch.5/A.33/37; [W. W. Braines,] "Holywell Priory and the Site of the Theatre, Shoreditch," *Indications of Houses of Historical Interest in London* (London: L.C.C., 1930), 5:1–28. In May 1596, Thomas Screven, steward to the earl of Rutland, laid claim in the earl's name to a piece of void ground in the former Holywell Priory leased by the Burbages from Giles Allen. Langley leased part of this void ground from one of Screven's creatures on 23 April 1601 (after the Burbages had abandoned Holywell Priory) and soon set about trying to prove that his title was good. See my "Handlist," Cat. B.

3. See the documents that I mention in my first article about the Boar's Head (appendix B), in my second (n. 15), and St. Ch.5/A.25/27; /A.8/4; and E.159/417/Trin.41 Eliz./m.51/nos. 41, 42. Professor Ingram has recently treated all these matters and many more in his life of Langley, *A London Life in the Brazen Age*. For my articles see appendix 1 here.

4. C.33/99/f.464^v in the A book, /100/f.452^v in the B book; /100/f.564^v in the B book (the A book, /99/f.577^v, has only a brief summary); Req.2/466/pt.II[/1], the bill; St.Ch.5/S.74/3, replies of Langley and Roberts and of the Woodliffes; /S.13/8, Langley; C.P.40/1655/m.724^v.

5. See appendix 6.

6. Req.2/466/pt.II[/1], the bill.

7. H.M.C., *Middleton*, p. 463; Leics. R.O., BR III/2/68/m.2^v; see also appendix 9.

8. Samwell said in April 1600 that Woodliffe claimed the yard "aboutes mychellmas last past," meaning, probably, the term but possibly the saint's day (St.Ch.5/S.74/3, the bill).

9. It was also called the Marshall's Court and the Palace Court, because it was in the domain of the knight marshall and steward of the queen's household. Originally it had concerned itself only with the monarch's servants, but, like other courts, it had been unofficially expanding its jurisdiction for years. Its powers were curbed in the ninth year of James I, when it was officially allowed to deal mainly with debts under £5 arising within twelve miles of the palace, excluding the City. The court's records do not exist for the time of Langley's suits.

10. One of Langley's strong-arm men in Shoreditch was a John Jobson.

11. The evidence for Samwell's struggle with Langley during the winter of 1599–1600 and spring following is in Samwell's suit in the Star Chamber, the bill and replies (St.Ch.5/S.74/3) and the interrogatories and depositions (filed separately: /S.13/8).

12. Registers, I, 43ᵛ.

13. The affair is recounted in St.Ch.5/S.74/3, Samwell's bill and Langley's and Roberts's reply; and /S.13/8, Samwell's interrogatories and Langley's and Roberts' depositions (nos. 10). See also appendix 3.

14. On 18 February, the Privy Council ordered them paid for a performance before the queen on the night of Shrove Tuesday (5 February), but the clerk who entered the order in the declared accoudnts wrote Shrove Sunday (3 February) instead (P.C.2/25/p.41; E.351/543/m.57). The two entries must refer to only one performance, as Chambers wrote in one place (4:166), and not, as he wrote in another, to two (2:127). The queen was at Richmond on both days. See also Mary Steele, *Plays & Masques at Court During the Reigns of Elizabeth, James and Charles* (New Haven, 1926), p. 119.

15. Samwell's interrogatories and depositions are C.24/278/71. I have not been able to find the bill and replies. Rodes and Willys gave their ages as thirty-six and twenty-five. Rodes is given as eighteen years old at the beginning of his apprenticeship, Easter, 1582 (*Records of the Worshipful Company of Carpenters*, 6:154, 285).

16. There is no entry in E.159 of an estreat of fine for any of the litigants.

17. K.B.27/1364/m.259.

18. E.179/142/234/m.3ᵛ, 4ᵛ. The highest sum given was £30, and only eight people gave sums higher than Jane Poley's.

19. C.24/278/71.

20. C.33/99/f.127 in the A book, /100/f.122ᵛ in the B book. Samwell had taken out a subpoena that compelled Browne and Jordan to reply, but eventually he decided not to present a bill to which they could reply.

21. He was "lately decessed" on 10 June, 1601 (C.24/290/3, Saunders no. 7).

Chapter 5. 1601

1. Steele, pp. 121–22; Leslie Hotson, *The First Night of Twelfth Night* (London, 1954), chap. 1.

2. C.P.40/1655/m.724ᵛ, dated merely Hilary 1601.

3. K.B.27/1367/m.199ᵛ, dated merely Easter 1601.

4. The lawsuit first appears on 8 May, when the court gave the defendants a week to reply (in the A book, C.33/99/f.473ᵛ, in the B book, /100/f.461). The bill and replies apparently do not survive, but the interrogatories and depositions do (C.24/290/3—for the verbal lease, see interrogatory 4, Hoppdale no. 3–4, Samwell no. 4). The verbal lease may have appeared first in a confusing, interlineated passage in Samwell's bill in the Star Chamber of April 1600 (quoted in appendix 5, section 2). It certainly appeared when, in replying to that bill, the Woodliffes denied such a lease.

5. The main documents in the case apparently do not survive, but numerous statements about it do among the decrees and orders, including a summary of the bill on 6 May (in the A book, C.33/99/f.464ᵛ, in the B book, /100/f.452ᵛ).

6. Req.2/466/pt.II[/1], the bill; C.33/99/f.526 in the A book, /100/f.518 in the B book.

7. The account in the records of the King's Bench has Bishop coming before a jury on a date that is left blank, then notes that he did not make his recognizances, and then trails off. Mago said in July 1603 that one harassing lawsuit did come "to tryall . . . and in that accion the attorney against the *said* Robert Browne became nonsute before the verdict was given"; Marsh,

however, "neue*r* knew nor heard that any of those acc*i*ons were brought to tryall" (C.24/304/27, nos. 9).

8. C.33/100/f.564ᵛ in the B book (where the text is much longer), /99/f.577ᵛ in the A book.

9. Matthew Carew matriculated at Trinity College, Cambridge, in 1548 and took the B.A. in 1550–51. He was a Middle Templar before 1551. George Carew was Middle Templar in 1577. See John Hutchinson, *A Catalogue of Notable Middle Templars* (London, 1902), p. 43; John and J. A. Venn, *Alumni Cantabrigiensis* (Cambridge, 1922), pt. 1, 1:291; *D.N.B.*; *The Poems of Thomas Carew*, ed. Rhodes Dunlap (Oxford, 1957), pp. xiii–xiv; my "Handlist," C-4, C-14–15; W. J. Jones, *The Elizabethan Court of Chancery* (Oxford, 1967), pp. 198 n. 4, 436, etc.

10. C.24/290/3, nos. 8, 5. Nothing more is heard of the lawsuit among decrees and orders or elsewhere, and Browne launched essentially the same lawsuit two years later. The two ladies were present "wᵗʰin short tyme after" the sealing of the lease in April 1598, when Elizabeth, a servant of Mrs. Poley's, finding that the pump in the yard was not working, complained to Woodliffe's wife, who sent her to Samwell saying that the yard was now his. Young Samwell gave himself as a chandler of Whitechapel; in 1606, he or another of the name and age gave himself as a yeoman of Whitechapel and signed himself in a very different hand from that of the four signatures here, though perhaps only a very refined version of it (C.24/327/61). Sisson (p. 41) assumed that the second man was the same as the first.

11. C.33/101/f.207ᵛ in the A book, /102/f.249ᵛ in the B book; /103/f.43–43ᵛ in the A book, /104/f.44ᵛ in the B book; Req.2/466/pt.II[/1], the bill.

12. R.E.E.D., *Coventry*, p. 360, *Norwich*, pp. 119, 120; *Records of Plays and Players in Kent 1450–1642*, ed. Giles Dawson (London: Malone Society, 1965) (Collections, 7), p. 64; J. T. Murray, *English Dramatic Companies* (London, 1910), 1:295.

13. Sisson believed (pp. xx, 46, 56, 59 and "The Red Bull Company and the Importunate Widow," *Shakespeare Survey* 7 [1954]: 60) that Browne took the bonds from Worcester's men so as to bind them to play solely at the Boar's Head. Sisson was thinking, perhaps, of the bonds Langley had taken from Pembroke's men in 1597 to bind that company to play solely at the Swan. The evidence about Browne's bonds, however, describes them only as between "players for shares due in their playes." The shares must have been a form of rent for the Boar's Head, and Browne's taking bonds for payment was not unreasonable. For Browne's wife, see appendix 9.

14. Req.2/466/pt.II[/1], the reply; C.24/304/27, interrogatory 14, Mago nos. 8, 14, Marsh no. 14. In the former document (dated 30 May 1603), Browne said it was Richard Langley who "aboutes two yeares past or thereabouts vnlawfully entered into the said Stage Tyringe howse and galleryes and offered to disturbe the said Playes and Comodyes to be acted on the said Stage . . and for feare thereof Extorted from the players there diue*r*se som*m*es of money to permytt the said Comedyes there quietly to be acted and doen by the said players wᵗʰout disturbance of the said Richard Langley against all Right equitie and Conscyence." In the latter document (dated 25 July 1603), however, though Browne again specified Richard Langley in his question, both eye witnesses, Mago and Marsh, said in their answers that it was Francis Langley who had intruded and compelled the players to pay him. Browne and Mago agreed that the amount the players had had to pay was £3 a week "ffrom Michaelmas or therabouts vntill Shroftide then next following." Marsh said he was twenty-seven years old; in the autumn of 1601, he had evidently just finished an apprenticeship with Mago (*Records of the Worshipful Company of Carpenters* 7:27, 105).

15. So far as I have been able to find, the struggle between Browne and Worcester's men is recorded only in the decrees and orders of their lawsuit in Chancery: C.33/101/f.573, 611, 643–43ᵛ, 735 (in the A book); and /102/f.577ᵛ, 616, 648ᵛ, 798ᵛ (in the B book). All date from May and June 1602. The only date given in them for these first events is that Browne's reply belonged to Michaelmas term 1601. Sisson repeatedly misdated these decrees and orders and so got the dates of the events that they report wrong by one and two years; he also cited them wrongly or omitted citing them (pp. 51, 59, 69: "Notes on Early Stuart Stage History," *Modern Language Review* 32 [1942]: 27, 33; "The Red Bull Company and the Importunate Widow," pp. 60–61). Staverton is the only lawyer mentioned as representing Worcester's men (on 8 June 1602). He represented the Langleys against Woodliffe on 28 January 1603 but could have represented them earlier, since no lawyer is mentioned between May 1601 (when Clench represented them), and then.

16. In his lease, Browne was required to let Woodliffe and his wife, but not Langley, use the yard in carrying out the building specified in the Poley lease (Req.2/466/pt.II[/1], the bill).

17. Browker's wife, Jane, was the daughter of Thomas Cure, from whom Langley had bought the Paris Garden (where he built the Swan). Browker had guaranteed some of Langley's bonds for that purchase, and he was now buying the place from Langley (C.2/Jas.I/L.13/62; C.3/279/18; C.24/305/1; C.P.25(2)/173/Easter 43 Eliz./1; /Easter 44 Eliz./17; /Mich. 44 & 45 Eliz./13). For a sudy of why Browker underwrote this and other ventures of Langley in 1601 and just before, see Professor Ingram's life of Langley, *A London Life in the Brazen Age*, chap. 16.

18. So I construct the complicated business in C.2/Jas.I/L.13/62, the bill (3 February 1603) and Browker's reply (13 May 1603). In the bill, Langley's widow said Browker had "certaine Conveyance Leases & other deeds in yᵉ name of yᵉ said Hugh Browker . . . yᵉ said deeds were taken in his name to his owne vse & for his securitie of Certaine debts as if he had paid all yᵉ mony due for yᵉ said purchase [of Paris Garden] & yᵗ yᵉ said ffrauncis Langley were yet in Arrerage vnto him wᶜʰ are very hard Courses." Browker replied, "touchinge anye Conveyances or bondes made to this defendant in trust for the sayed ffrauncis Langley this defendant knoweth not of anye other then one obligacion made to this defendant by one Ollyver [Woodliffe in] the somme of Eight pounds or thereabouts and one Indenture purportinge that the sayed ffrauncis Langley did demise vnto the sayed Woodliffe Certaine Rometh parte of A messuage Called the Bores Head in White Chappell parishe for the tearme of Certaine yeares [a word or two perished] deliuered by the sayed Woodliffe to this defendants Custodye to be kepte to the vse of the sayed ffrauncis Langley in Consideracion of twelue pounds payed by this defendant to the sayed Woodliffe by the appointment of the sayed ffrauncis Langley for the Redempcion of the sayed [two to four words perished]." Later in the document he added, "And the . . . obligacion made by Woodliffe and Indenture to Woodliffe he is and alwayes hath bene readye to deliuer to the sayed Complaynant [Langley's widow]." See also hints in C.33/101/f.207ᵛ in the A book, /102/f.249ᵛ in the B book; and Woodliffe's remarks in Req.2/466/pt.II[/1], the bill.

19. Req.2/466/pt.II[/1], the bill and reply; C.33/101/f.207ᵛ in the A book, /102/f.249ᵛ in the B book; C.P.40/1701/m.1109.

20. Req.2/466/pt.II[/1], the bill.

Chapter 6. 1602

1. Steele, p. 123 and chap. 7 below. Worcester's men could have played at Barnstaple and Coventry (twice) during the period: R.E.E.D., *Coventry*, pp. 358, 360, and in the North Devon Athenaeum at Barnstaple, Book 3972, f.162ᵛ (for notice of which I am indebted to Professor John Wasson).

2. C.33/101/f.207ᵛ, 263ᵛ, 290, 324ᵛ, 309, 406ᵛ in the A book, /102/f.249ᵛ, 302, 326ᵛ, 343–43ᵛ, 344, 433 in the B book. Consistent with Langley's new argument of the previous autumn, Woodliffe spoke in these orders only of the profits of the playhouse, or "certen" profits, rather than of the half profits of the western gallery.

3. Corporation of London, Remembrancia, II, 188, 187, 189; Chambers, 4:329–35; G. E. Bentley, *The Jacobean and Caroline Stage* (Oxford, 1968), 6:123.

4. C.33/101/f.406ᵛ, 450 in the A book, /102/f.433, 470ᵛ in the B book.

5. C.P.40/1655/m.724ᵛ. The account of this first stage of the elegit ends by saying that Richard Langley is pardoned and quit of the debt, a remark that cannot be literally true, among other reasons because an account of the long subsequent history of the elegit follows immediately. Besides, the sum here is £207, rather than the £107 that appears just above in the account of the judgment.

6. Chancery made a similar declaration about plays and players on 23 June 1626, when it threw out the case of some former Queen's men against Susan Browne (then Baskervile): C.33/149/f.844ᵛ in the A book, /150/f.953ᵛ in the B book; Chambers, 2:238.

7. Ingram, *A London Life in the Brazen Age*, pp. 280–81. See also C.2/Jas.I/L.13/62; C.3/279/18; C.33/103/f.700ᵛ in the A book, /104/f.744ᵛ in the B book. Richard Langley must have filed a bill of revivor to keep the Chancery lawsuit against Woodliffe going after Francis's

death, but no hint of it seems to survive, except that the two remaining notices of the case are in Richard's name only.

8. Chambers, 2:225–26; *Henslowe's Diary,* pp. 213f. It is clear that a company was at the Boar's Head during the autumn and winter 1602–3, for in May 1603 Woodliffe claimed and Browne admitted that money was earned in the western gallery from Michaelmas 1602 to the closing of the playhouses in March 1603. Browne implied it was his own company that was currently there: when complaining about the Langleys' extorting £3 a week from the "the players" (no doubt Worcester's) at the Boar's Head at Michaelmas 1601, he concluded, "wch the Compl^t [Woodliffe] would by lyke wronnge nowe exacte and gett from this defend^te [Browne] and his ffellowes" (Req.2/466/pt.II[/1], bill and reply).

9. Browne must have satisfied Woodliffe somehow early in May, perhaps by making the requisite oath and promising the requisite accounting, for Woodliffe did not pursue him in Chancery then. Browne eventually paid, as he said, "the Moytie of the profytts of the said galleryes ou*er* the Stage due vntill Michaelmas," 1602, and immediately after that (15 October) Woodliffe did pursue him in Chancery for insufficient payment. On this occasion, Woodliffe's lawyer said that Browne had made the oath because of the order of 21 April and in it "confessed that he ys to render an accompt to the p^t [Richard Langley] or deft [Woodliffe] of the proffitts made thereof to him that shall pr*e*vale in suyte." See Req.2/466/pt.II[/1], bill and reply; C.33/103/f.43–43^v in the A book, /104/f.44^v in the B book; and below.

10. The order of the court spelling out the new arrangement merely reads that Langley would reassign the lease to Woodliffe and that the two sides would "deliu*er* each to other all bonds bills and sp[ec]ialtyes conc*er*nynge" the Boar's Head (C.33/103/f.43–43^v in the A book, /104/f.44^v in the B book). In May 1603, well after the Langleys had disappeared from the Boar's Head, Woodliffe said that "Vpon order of" Chancery, he "was to have the said messuage reassigned to him againe and to deliu*er* vnto the said Langleys their three seu*er*al bonds" (Req.2/466/pt.II[/1], the bill). But note in chapter 7 the Chancery order of 28 January 1603 and the subsequent history of Woodliffe's elegit.

11. C.P.40/1655/m.724^v.

12. C.24/304/27, interrogatories 8, 9, 12, 15.

Chapter 7. 1603

1. C.P.40/1655/m.724^v; C.33/103/f.346 in the A book, /104/f.359 in the B book.

2. C.2 Jas.I/L.13/62, his reply; see chapter 5, n. 18.

3. Woodliffe's remark in May 1603 that Browne "hath by force entred in & vpon the stage tyreing house & galleries on the west side of the great yarde . . . ," which he "hath & doth detaine & keepe by force" must suggest that Browne was using those properties without paying suitably for them up to the closing in March and meant to go on using them when the play-houses should reopen. So must Browne's remark in reply, that Woodliffe wanted to get from Browne and his men now as much as the Langleys had got from Worcester's men—money that Woodliffe "would by lyke wronnge nowe exacte and gett from this defend^te and his ffellowes." See Req.2/466/pt.II[/1], bill and reply.

4. K.B.29/242/m.54^v, 55, 55^v. By April 1604, Browne's part of the work had been done. The word used for Browne's dimensions is "virgata." He has ten of them by one. The word can mean either "yard" or "virgate," that is, a rod. Usually it meant yard when used for such things as cloth, but rod when used for land. By a statute of 35 Eliz., a rod was 16 ½'. The pieces of highway other men were charged on the same day to repair were 30 *virgata* by 1, and 6 *virgata* by 1. If the word means rod, those dimensions would seem much too big for any man's prop-erty along Whitechapel. If it means yard, they could be about right for footpaths, and Browne's would be that beside the buildings of the Boar's Head fronting Whitechapel. The company at the Red Bull had to repair the footpath outside their house several times from 1616 to 1622. See *N.E.D.,* "Yard," sb.^2, 8–10; Eric Partridge, *Origins* (London, 1966), "Verge," 2, "Yard," 2; Bentley, 1:169n; 2:366, 367–68.

5. Req.2/466/pt.II[/1], the reply.

6. C.P.40/1701/m.1109.

7. The bill and reply are Req.2/466/pt.II[/1], and the two orders are Req.1/21/f.169, 172.

8. C.33/103/f.43–43ᵛ in the A book, /104/f.44ᵛ in the B book.

9. C.24/304/27, nos. 13, 14. To his denial that he owned Woodliffe "the som*m*e of ffyve poundes a weeke for the Stage Tyringe howse and galleryes . . . ever sythence the Two and Twentyeth daye of Auguste," 1601, Browne added two remarks: first, that Richard Langley "aboutes two yeares past or thereabouts vnlawfully entered into the said Stage Tyringe howse and galleryes and offered to disturbe the said Playes and Comodyes to be acted on the said Stage . . . and for feare thereof Extorted from the players there diu*er*se som*m*es of money," and second that Woodliffe "would by lyke wronnge now exacte and gett" the same sums "from this defend^te and his ffellowes."

10. Only Browne's interrogatories for Mago and Marsh and their answers seem to survive: C.24/304/27. In the heading to the interrogatories, the lawsuit is said to be against not only Woodliffe and Langley, but one Henry Sibdall, whose name appears in no other document concerning the Boar's Head. Browne said (interrogatory 9) that Sibdall and Langley shared the cost of the elegit.

11. C.33/103/f.700ᵛ in the A book, /104/f.744ᵛ in the B book. The record of the lawsuit in Common Pleas that produced the elegit trails off at this point with a blank for the date when the elegit was now to expire and no further remark (C.P.40/1655/m.724ᵛ).

12. Nos. 11, 13, 16. Browne avoided saying that he had paid the rent as he said Samwell had paid it, "at the dayes of payements," though Mago said he had paid it so.

13. Registers, I, 51ᵛ.

14. They were in Coventry sometime between the autumn of 1602 and that of 1603 and again in the year following (R.E.E.D., *Coventry*, pp. 362, 364).

15. Registers, I, 53, 48; Guildhall, MS.9168/15/f.246 (Woodliffe's bond was 57s.4d.); C.2/ Jas.I/V.4/42.

16. Registers, I, 54; *Henslowe's Diary*, p. 297; PROB. 6/6/f.183.

17. C.24/304/27, Mago no. 13, Marsh nos. 6, 13.

18. See appendix 9. Susan married Thomas Bond; Anne died unmarried in April 1621; Robert became a haberdasher; William married, it seems, the widow of a man named Massam, then Anne, the widow of Edward Neale. Only a few months after marrying Anne Neale, William died, between 23 October and 10 November 1634, giving himself in his will as of Clerkenwell, gentleman. Because he had named his mother rather than his wife as executrix, the interests of mother and widow in his and Edward Neale's estates collided. So the two women sued one another vigorously from 1635 to 1637, Anne using the name of her next husband, John Rodes, and Susan calling herself "Greene ali*a*s Baskervile." Rodes may have been one of the theatrical people of the name, like the one whose wife, Anne, died in 1644 or (and?) the one who had to do with Susan Greene in 1648. See Edwin Nungezer, *A Dictionary of Actors* (Ithaca, N.Y., 1929), pp. 60–62; Chambers, 2:237–38; Bentley, 2:391–92, 544–46, 636–37; *Registers of St. James Clerkenwell* (London: Harleian Soc., 1891), 4:152. For the lawsuit, a great many notices of which survive, see esp. Req.1/207/f. 98ᵛ, 119ᵛ; /66/9 July [f.218]; /159/f.66ᵛ).

Chapter 8. 1604–1615

1. He once played a baboon. He also played, it seems, the clown, Bubble, in John Cooke's play whose printed title was meant to be a memorial to him, *Greene's Tu quoque* (London, 1614), for Bubble repeatedly says, "Tu quoque." A woodcut appears on the title pages of all three early editions of the play in which a figure says, "Tu quoque, To you Sir"—a likeness of Greene? Among the drolls based on old plays in Francis Kirkman's *The Wits* (London, 1662) is "The Bubble" based on Cooke's; and in the famous picture before the book of a stage filled with characters from these plays is a figure in a dunce cap just coming through the curtains to join them, saying, "Tue quo que"—a reminiscence of Greene? See Chambers, 4:254–55; 3:269.

2. S.P.14/2/100; Chambers, 2:229–30, 208–9.

3. C.66/1827/29; Chambers, 2:231, 187–88. These two and later versions of the patent added a clause protecting the rights of the master of the revels.

4. G.L.C., DL/C/360/129; *Registers of St. James Clerkenwell*, 1:55; 4:120. *Greene's Tu quoque*, sigs. A2, A2ᵛ. There are three more epigrams in Richard Brathwaite's *Remains after Death* (London, 1618), sig. G5ᵛ.

5. C.24/500/9, interrogatories 21, 22, Basse no. 22; C.33/149/f.844ᵛ in the A book, /150/ f.953ᵛ in the B book; *Registers of St. James Clerkenwell*, 4:279. Most of the information about Susan Baskervile and some of that about Greene appears in her complicated lawsuit against the Queen's men, 1617–26 (F. G. Fleay, *Chronicle History of the London Stage* [London, 1890], pp. 270–97; Chambers, 2:236–40; Bentley, 1:158–60; Sisson, "Notes on Early Stuart Stage History," pp. 30–36, and "The Red Bull Company and the Importunate Widow," p. 59 and passim). Some money she lent the Queen's men was delivered to them by William Jorden, a relative, one might guess, of the Israel Jordan who figured largely in the affairs of her husband, Browne (C.24/500/9, interrogatories 27, 28, Perkins no. 13; /103, interrogatory 10, Keble no. 6). She twice signed a deposition of 17 April 1618 by drawing her initials (C.24/446/pt.I/156, reproduced by Sisson in "The Red Bull Company . . .").

6. Corporation of London, Remembrancia, II, 283; Chambers, 4:339.

7. Murray (1:239; 2:310) and Chambers (2:190, 242) date the payment as 1608. It is, however, the second of two undated payments between payments dated 6 June and 21 August in an apparently chronological list of payments (about half dated, beginning in October and ending in September) belonging to an account from Michaelmas 1608 to Michaelmas 1609. Moreover, an earlier payment (12 April) has to do with the "aid" being collected in 1609 ostensibly toward the knighting of Prince Henry. See at the Leics. R.O., BR III/2/75/f.98–100; also *C.S.P., Dom., 1603–10*, pp. 494–570 passim.

8. Sisson (pp. 76–77) went even further, but his reasoning seems bizarre. In the parish registers, he found that a John Garland was married in Whitechapel in 1576 and a Thomas Garland in 1578. In Chambers (2:241) he noted that John Garland of Lennox's men lived at Old Ford in 1605, like Whitechapel a part of the manor of Stepney (but at the opposite end of the manor, several miles from the playhouse). He then found a John Garland in a list of copyholders in Stepney in 1618 (actually 1617). Admitting that it "is not conclusive," he thought this evidence might lead us reasonably to believe "that Garland took over the lease of the Boar's Head from Susan and Greene, until its expiry in 1616" (it expired, actually, at Christmas 1615). He did not note in Chambers that Garland was "owld Garlland" in 1606 and last appeared in the affairs of Prince Charles's men in 1610, after which William Rowley became leader. Nor did he say that the copyholder of 1617 is given as of Bow, not Old Ford or Whitechapel, which are listed separately: *The Free Customes, Benefits and Priviledges of the Copyhold Tennants, of the Mannors of Stepny and Hackny* (London, 1617), p. 59 (B.M., G.3712[1]).

9. Chambers, 2:238–40, 242, 244–45, 448, 472–73; Bentley, 1:202–13. Robert Pallant's name is sometimes given as Richard (Chambers, 2:230–31; C.66/1827/29).

10. Chambers, 2:374.

Chapter 9. 1616–1676

1. C.2/Chas.I/P.90/54; C.142/546/481/118. His eldest child alive in 1637, Elizabeth (baptized 20 January 1614), gave the earlier date of his death, his Inquisition Post Mortem the other. One of his daughters, Dorothy (baptized 5 October 1615), died in 1636. His wife was dead by 1651 (C.54/3597/m.38–41).

2. Guildhall, MS.8478/esp. f.68–68ᵛ; *The Free Customes, Benefits and Priviledges of the Copyhold Tennants, of the Mannors of Stepny and Hackny*, pp. 8–10, which the printer licensed on 14 April and dated 4 December (p. 67). Poley also levied a fine for the enfranchisement: C.P.25(2)/324/Hil.19 Jas.I/10.

3. The deeds of 1621 mention no stables, save "certeine other buildings sometymes [i.e., formerly] called a stable & the chamber over it" in Needler's deed.

4. The evidence for Rowley's piece of the yard is in Browne's deed. A Samuel Rowley probably owned other properties in or near the Boar's Head (appendix 8, nos. 2, 3) and with Nicholas Hallam sold a messuage and curtilage in Whitechapel in 1624 to Thomas and William Meggs and ten other men (C.P.25[2]/324/Trin.22 Jas.I/17)—not the copyhold in the Boar's Head unless it had been enfranchised, because according to both the old (item 47) and new (item 49) customs the manor did not allow copyholds to be sold by fines, as this place was. A Samuel Rowley and Hallam subscribed to the new customs in 1617. It is tempting to guess that the Samuel Rowley of the Boar's Head was the veteran actor and playwright in Henslowe's enter-

prises, who lived and owned property in Whitechapel and was alive in 1621 (he was buried at St. Mary Matfellon on 20 October 1624). He might have been interested in the yard originally as a way of having a share in the profits of the playhouse. None of the property he mentioned in his will (23 July 1624), however, was in or near the Boar's Head. See Alan Somerset, "New Facts Concerning Samuel Rowley," *Review of English Studies* 17, no. 67 (1966): 293–97.

5. Sisson (pp. 25, 27) read the old customs (1587) as providing that copyholders could make leases of up to thirty-one years without license or fine (i.e., fee), and he built a case about the events of 1594 on that reading. Those customs, however, provide distinctly that the free period was only three years, and, indeed, that anybody who made a longer lease without license and fine would lose his copyhold. It was the new customs of 1617 that allowed leases of up to thirty-one years and four months without license or fine. A list of subscribers appears at the end of the new customs as printed in 1617, and a list of those who subscribed later appears at the end of later editions. Poley never subscribed. See the old customs: *Hereafter ensueth the auncient seuerall customes, of the seuerall Mannors of Stebunhuth, and Hackney* (STC 23252, undated, but a note written inside the back leaf of the copy at the Folger suggests 1591 rather than the usual conjecture of 1610), items 37, 46; and the new customs: *The Free Customes, Benefits and Priviledges of the Copyhold Tennants, of the Mannors of Stepny and Hackny*, pp. 10–11, 57–62, item 38. I am indebted to Professor Ingram for information about the copy at the Folger.

6. In 1723 the eastern side of the Boar's Head is described in a deed of a house in Goulston Street as the "Walls of the Old houses in Boares head Yard" (G.L.C., M.L.R.1723/I/65).

7. See appendix 8 for all the deeds. A copy of the contract with Lord Wentworth is attached to the copy of Browne's deed at the Folger: Z.c.22(23). To make certain that Poley could sell the properties as freeholds, Needler and Browne seem to have had him levy a fine for the enfranchisement of the Boar's Head: C.P.25(2)/324/Hil.19 Jas.I/10. Needler called himself "Nedle *alias* Needler" in his deed, but he and his family called themselves only "Needler" afterward.

8. Neither a lawsuit about his estate (C.2/Chas.I/P.90/54) nor his Inquisition Post Mortem (C.142/546/481/118) mentions property in Whitechapel. The sale of 1632 could have been of Woodlands (C.P.25[2]/457/Hil.7 Chas.I/19).

9. See his deed in appendix 8 and an analysis of it in chapter 11.

10. Guildhall, MS.9172/42, 20 June 1634 (when his widow proved the will). This William Browne may have come from Westward in Cumberland, where some of his relatives lived. He was surely not the William Browne, son of the actor Robert Browne, who was probably born in the Boar's Head, though William Browne also died in 1634. The actor's son was only thirty-two years old in 1634 and left his own will (see chapter 7).

11. C.P.25(2)/457/Easter 13 Chas.I/3,19. Abraham had, among other properties in Whitechapel, two freehold messuages in Whitechapel High Street that he left to his daughter, Sara, when he died in 1643 (PROB.11/191/35). She married Thomas Adie and left the two messuages to her son, Benjamin Adie, who mortgaged them in 1721 (G.L.C., M.L.R.1721/II/219).

12. See appendix 8.

13. C.54/2947/24; /2964/4; C.7/250/33, bill and reply; /545/25; C.24/840/pt.II/9. Presumably it was another Nicholas Parker, lawyer in Common Pleas, who represented Robert Browne in his lawsuit of 1603 against Woodliffe for the bond of £16, and represented Grace Darrell in another lawsuit of that year against Francis Langley's widow for one of Francis's debts (C.P.40/1701/m.1109; /1693/m.1514ᵛ).

14. Ogilby and Morgan give two Boar's Head Alleys, one immediately east of the Boar's Head and the other just inside the entrance of the Boar's Head on Whitechapel High Street. Perhaps one or two other passages in or around the Boar's Head, unnamed in Ogilby and Morgan, could also have been called Boar's Head Alley. When Needler's parts of the Boar's Head were sold in 1865 and 1879, they were accompanied by an adjacent line of six houses in Goulston Street (nos. 17, 19, 21, 23, 25, 27). Because the Boar's Head Alley east of the Boar's Head became part of Goulston Street in the 1680s, it is tempting to guess that the six houses of 1865–79 stood on the site of the eight of 1632–59. Two things, however, must give one pause. The transactions involving Needler's properties before 1829 do not mention houses in Goulston Street; and the houses of 1632–59 were, according to both the Needlers and Parkers, owned, like the Boar's Head, in free and common socage, but those of 1865–79 were owned on a 1,000–year lease granted in 1610 by Sir Thomas Bodley for property adjacent to the Boar's Head on the east. The six houses of 1865–79 probably joined Needler's part of the Boar's Head when William

Cordell bought them in about 1800 and then bought Needler's property in 1802. See: C.7/250/33, bill and reply; G.L.C., M.L.R.1802/VII/551; 1829/V/776; 1865/III/218; Guildhall, MS.6015/59/p.14; /61/p.16; etc. And for Bodley's lease see C.8/452/41, reply of the Etheredges; Middlesex R.O., M.D.R.1726/I/107.

15. Ida Darlington and James Howgego, *Printed Maps of London,* 2d ed. (London, 1978), no. 21.

16. The map was printed by October 1676 but not offered for sale until January 1677. See appendix 7 and Ralph Hyde's preface to the reproduction published in 1976 by the Guildhall Library, London, and Harry Margary, Lympne Castle, Kent, including remarks about Hollar's map of 1667.

Chapter 10. 1676–Present

1. In the 1870s, toward the end of its history, the alley was called Hebrew Place.

2. See appendix 8.

3. PROB.11/810/207; G.L.C., M.L.R.1754/III/34.

4. PROB.11/1353/61; G.L.C., M.L.R.1802/VII/551. See chapter 9, n.14.

5. PROB.11/1708/67; G.L.C., M.L.R.1813/VIII/119; 1826/V/721; 1829/V/776; 1849/VIII/544; 1863/XX/801–2; /XXII/798; 1864/XIII/442–43; 1865/III/218.

6. G.L.C., M.B.W.1810, 1840; M.L.R.1879/XI/806; 1881/X/144.

7. G.L.C., M.L.R.1740/IV/719; Guildhall, MS.6015/1–10; /32ff.

8. PROB.11/505/267.

9. G.L.C., M.L.R.1738/I/352; 1742/I/124–25. Elizabeth Oswin began paying taxes in the Boar's Head in 1742: Guildhall, MS.6015/11(Div.I, 46–49).

10. PROB.11/924/461.

11. PROB.11/1100/53; /1138/52; Guildhall, MS.6015/34(nos.52–56); /46(nos.39–42); /58(p.14); etc.

12. Guildhall, MS.6015/61(pp.15–16); /62(pp.14–15); G.L.C., M.L.R.1807/V/338–39.

13. G.L.C., M.L.R.1841/VII/944–46; 1880/XL/896.

14. G.L.C., M.B.W.1810, 1840; M.L.R.1882/IX/722; B/N.T.G./540.

15. The guides to London regularly give both addresses to 1799 and give the Boar's Head Meeting, which was on the site of the stage and tiring house, as in Boar's Head Yard, Petticoat Lane. See *A Complete Guide to All Persons who have any Trade or Concern with the City of London* (London, 1740–83) and *Boyle's View of London* (London, 1799); in the latter the Meeting is given as in Boar's Head Court, Petticoat Lane (pp. 42, 303).

16. *Middlesex County Records,* ed. J. C. Jeaffreson (London, 1887–1902), 3:364; G.L.C., M.L.R.1738/I/352; 1807/V/338; Guildhall, MS.6015/1–15; /32–47.

17. G.L.C., M.L.R.1757/IV 83–84; 1792/IV/43; Guildhall, MS.6015/12ff.;/45ff.

18. G.L.C., M.L.R.1723/V/433; Guildhall, MS.6015/1–12.

19. G.L.C., M.L.R.1738/I/352. The Oswins, their tenants, and successors paid taxes for the place until 1781, after which they paid for the rooms under it when used as warehouses, but not for the Meeting itself, which may not have been taxed after that (Guildhall, MS.6015/1ff.)

20. See *A Complete Guide to All Persons who have any Trade or Concern with the City of London,* from the first edition, 1740, to that of 1768, after which churches are no longer given; *Boyle's View of London,* p. 303; *The Perambulator* (London, 1832?), p. 252.

21. G.L.C., M.B.W.1810, 1840, 1886(p.24, 3d pagination).

22. G.L.C., M.L.R.1807/V/338; Guildhall, MS.6015/47ff.; /63ff.

23. Guildhall, MS.6015/27a/no.51–55.

24. G.L.C., J.Ste/5871.

25. G.L.C., B/N.T.G./540.

26. G.L.C., M.B.W.1810, 1840.

27. G.L.C., M.B.W.1835/5, 1877(esp. p. 72), 1886, 1810, 1840.

28. G.L.C., M.L.R.1879/XI/806; 1881/X/144; 1882/IX/722; /XVI/793.

29. One can see this and other changes from 1882 to 1894 by comparing such maps as the Ordnance Survey (1:1,056) of 1875 and those in M.B.W. 1810 and 1840 (G.L.C.) with the Ordnance Survey (1:1,056) of 1894–96.

30. G.L.C., M.L.R.1885/VII/392–93.

31. In my article "The Boar's Head Again," I supposed that Needler's alley and the one that the city built in the 1880s were the same. As a result, I misidentified the piece of land in M.L.R.1885/VII/392–93 and title 125655 (Harrow Land Registry) and so got the site of the stage and tiring house on maps after 1882 wrong by some 27'.

32. See the Ordnance Survey maps (1:1,250) of 1952 and 1971; the old Aldgate East station was closed and a new one opened two streets eastward in 1939. I am indebted to Mr. David Keller, the agent for Petticoat Lane Rentals, who in 1969 kindly remembered for me the place as it had been.

33. For the land the city acquired to widen Middlesex Street in 1964, see at the Harrow Land Registry title LN80561.

34. The registered titles confirm the maps. The southern appendage of United Standard House, hence the Carpet Supermarket, stands on the whole of one plot (in the south) and part of another (in the north), both of which have as their front on Middlesex Street an extension of the eastern line of no. 145 Whitechapel High Street. The first plot was created in the rebuilding of the 1880s and has had that western line since. The second was redrawn in 1964 so that its line along Middlesex Street would extend that of the first. See at the Harrow Land Registry titles 125655, LN186342, and at G.L.C., M.L.R.1885/VII/392–93. I am indebted to the mortgage holders, Sun Life of Canada, and to the owners of Cromlech House, City and Country Properties, Ltd., for help in identifying the titles and permission to see the abstracts of them.

35. Goulston Street began its life between 1678 and 1688, when Sir William Goulston, an insurance underwriter and merchant, created the southern part out of the alley (which Ogilby and Morgan call Boar's Head Alley) to the east of the eastern building in the Boar's Head and land he had inherited from an uncle, William Meggs, and bought from others. Goulston's mansion is no doubt the large building whose western side and garden are along that alley in Ogilby and Morgan. The northern parts of the street were later extensions of Goulston's work. See esp. Meggs's and Goulston's wills (PROB.11/356/41; 390/4); C.P.25(2)/692/Hil.33&34 Chas.II/16; and at G.L.C., M.L.R.1723/I/65. These properties of Goulston's, including Boar's Head Alley, evidently had nothing to do with the Boar's Head of Elizabethan times. In a voluminous series of lawsuits about them beginning with Goulston's death (1688) and continuing until the 1730s, and in numerous mortgages with which his son, Morris, encumbered them, no one mentioned the Boar's Head: C.7/572/46; C.9/447/153; /154; C.8/452/41; /467/63; /74; C.9/460/1; 469/69; C.11/1463/20; C.24/1247; /1252; and at G.L.C., M.L.R.1724/II/249; 1726/I/107; 1730/IV/400; 1731/II/119; 1734/III/437; etc.

Chapter 11. The Yard in Which the Playhouse Was Built

1. St.Ch.5/S.74/3, the bill and the Woodliffes' reply; Req.2/466/pt.II[/1], the bill.

2. C.24/290/3, Samwell no. 2; Browne's summary is in interrogatory 2. Woodliffe's summary is in his bill, Req.2/466/pt.II[/1], and Browne agreed with this summary in his reply to the bill. Woodliffe put the words, "on the west side of the entry of the said Inn," after those about the hall, parlor, and kitchen rather than after those about the chamber over the entry, thus getting the hall, parlor, and kitchen unequivocally on the west side of the entry, and the drinking room, etc., on the east side. Neither Browne nor Woodliffe included the back yard, because as Woodliffe pointed out in April 1600, Samwell had only the right to lay dung in it and not the yard itself; Woodliffe was trying to show that Samwell had none of the open places in the inn (St.Ch.5/S.74/3, the Woodliffes' reply).

3. For the structures around the yard, see appendix 3. Francis Langley (who wanted to diminish Samwell's part of the Boar's Head) said in April 1600 that Woodliffe had leased to Samwell only part of the place, "Certen Roomes . . . and not . . . the whole In." It seemed to the carpenter, Hoppdale, in 1601, however, that Samwell had got the whole of the Boar's Head, "or," as he added, "the greatest *part* thereof," and his master carpenter, Mago, said much the same thing in 1603. The only parts that anyone ever mentioned Samwell's not getting were the Poleys quarters (he did get the stable under them), the yard, and the "certeyne Romes." See St.Ch.5/S.13/8, Langley no. 1; C.24/290/3, Hoppdale no. 3–4; /304/27, Mago, no. 1.

4. Woodliffe and the elder Samwell called it the hostry; Browne and the younger Samwell

left off the "h"; and Willys may have alluded to it when he spoke of "the house" (C.24/278/71, no. 3). Perhaps it was the headquarters of the inn, where the Samwells lived. As Browne, the younger Samwell, and Woodliffe described it, it could hardly have been big enough to be the hostelry in the full sense of the term. See *N.E.D.*, "hostry."

5. For all the deeds, see appendix 8 and chapter 9.

6. It must have been Browne's part of the eastern building that his heirs encumbered with one of his bequests, £2 a year to the parish. At the end of the eighteenth century the money was being paid out of a property in Boar's Head Alley, at that time the passage leading north from the old entrance of the inn in Whitechapel High Street. See chapter 9; a will of 1708, (PROB.11/505/267); and a list of benefactions, 1574–1798, still inscribed on the walls of St. Mary Matfellon when it was pulled down in 1875 (G.L.C., P.93/MRY 1/92/f.25).

7. Note in chapter 9 Browne's allusions to his properties in his will and his heirs' transactions.

8. A "Pump Court" was in the northern part of the Boar's Head in 1721 (G.L.C., M.L.R.1721/V/139).

9. If this explanation is right, Browne's deed describes generally rather than exactly the southern side of his western piece of the yard. It would have lain for only a little more than half its length east to west along the northern side of his garden. Then it would have jogged about 8' south and lain east to west along the northern side of the garden west of his. According to the map, incidentally, his garden swelled east into the southern part of the yard as well as north into the central part.

Chapter 12. The Playhouse Proper

1. In the documentation about the Boar's Head, the eastern gallery and other protrusions have nothing to do with the ground under them, provided that they were high enough to allow free passage. So I do not count the width of them in my measurements of the ground. Woodliffe, Langley, and their associates argued regularly that Samwell's galleries belonged to them because the posts holding them up rested in Woodliffe's or Langley's yard. And rather than reply that the ground under the eastern gallery belonged to the eastern building and not the yard, Samwell and Robert Browne asserted merely that they had the use of the whole yard. When Woodliffe suggested that he and Samwell make their galleries 4' wider, he said that they could do so without diminishing the size of the yard. In William Browne's deed of 1621, he and Poley set aside room for an alley above which Browne had the right to build, and whatever he built was to have nothing to do with the width of the alley.

2. C.2/Jas.I/M.13/65.

3. When the builder, Mago, dismantled the gallery in 1599, as he said in February 1600, he "beganne to fall in hand wth all and to take off the roofe" (C.24/278/71, no. 4). For evidence not given in this chapter about the galleries and stage, see appendix 3, and about the playhouse otherwise, chapter 3 and appendix 2.

4. " 'Heavens,' Machinery, and Pillars in the Theatre and Other Early Playhouses," in *The First Public Playhouse*, pp. 1–15.

5. James Appleton Morgan, Introduction to *Titus Andronicus* in *The Bankside Shakespeare* Cambridge, Mass., 1888–1906), p. 27; T. S. Graves, *The Court and the London Theatres* (Menasha, Wis., 1913), p. 48.

6. The builder of 1599, Mago, listed Samwell's costs then, which came to £260. Mago, Samwell himself, and several others said that Samwell's whole cost in the playhouse was more than £300, a sum that Samwell's son (who kept his father's books) said included the building of 1598. See chapter 3 and appendix 4 (for Samwell's payments on Woodliffe's behalf).

7. Req.2/466/pt.II[/1], the reply; and C.24/304/27, esp. interrogatories 7, 9, Mago no. 3, Marsh no. 3.

8. C.24/278/71, no. 4.

9. C.24/304/27, interrogatories 3, 13, Mago no. 3, Marsh no. 3.

10. *Shakespeare's Wooden O* (London, 1959), chap. 4. In the copy of the deed at the Folger, the word is difficult to read but also seems to be "or" rather than "and." I am indebted to Laetitia Yeandle of the Folger for kindly looking at the word again.

11. Professor Brownstein, however, believes these "Galleries" were "ground stands"—scaffolds built a little above the ground to allow those who stood in them to see over the heads of persons standing on the ground—over which a second story had been built. See his dissertation, "Stake and Stage" (Iowa, 1963) and "Why Didn't Burbage Lease the Beargarden?" in *The First Public Playhouse*. See Field, *A godly exhortation* (London, 1583), sigs, B8, C2ᵛ; Raphael Holinshed, *The Third volume of Chronicles . . . continued (with occurrences and accidents of fresh memorie) to the yeare 1586* "by Iohn Stow, *and others*" (London, 1587), pp. 1,268, 1,353 (Stow included the remark unchanged in all the editions of his *Annales*—1592, 1600, 1605); Phillip Stubbes, who wrote that many people being "mounted aloft vpon their Scaffoldes, and Galleries, . . . in the middest of all their iolitie and pastime, all the whole Buildyng (not one sticke standyng) fell downe with a most wonderfull and fearfull confusion," *The Anatomie of Abuses* (London, 16 August 1583), f. 116ᵛ–17; John Dee, who noted that "the stage at Paris Garden fell down all at ones, being full of people beholding the bearbayting", *The Private Diary*, ed. J. O. Halliwell (London, 1842), p. 18; and Chambers, 2:462–63; 4:220–21, 225, 292.

12. K.B.27/1364/m.259; and chapter 4.

13. St.Ch.5/S.13/8, interrogatory 10, Langley no. 4, Roberts no. 4; /S.74/3, the bill. The same thing had happened at the Theatre nine years before. On 16 November 1590, four people who thought the owner, James Burbage, owed them money went to the Theatre on "A playe daye to stand at the doᴿ that goeth vppe to the gallaries of the said Theater to take & Receyve . . . money that shuld be gyven to come vppe into the said Gallaries at that doᴿ." See the drawing in the University Library, Utrecht, of the Curtain (as Leslie Hotson identified it in 1954) or the Theatre (as Sidney Fisher and Richard Hosley have recently identified it), and the drawings in Hollar's famous long view of the Hope and second Globe. The Theatre is discussed in my "Aspects of the Design and Use of the Theatre" and Professor Hosley's "The Theatre and the Tradition of Playhouse Design," both in *The First Public Playhouse*.

14. C.24/290/3, Samwell no. 5; /278/71, Mago no. 1.

15. St.Ch.5/S.13/8, Langley no. 2.

16. C.24/278/71; St.Ch.5/S.74/3, the bill; C.24/290/3; Req.2/466/pt.II[/1], the reply; C.24/304/27.

17. C.24/304/27, Mago nos. 14, 3.

18. *Early English Stages* 2, pt. 1:188, 196; pt. 2:99–100, 104.

19. St.Ch.5/S.74/3, the Woodliffes' reply (for Samwell's building the sinks and gutters); C.54/2471/17, and /2515/11 (the deeds of 1621). These two deeds describe the main drain in the same words, thus providing that both the owner of the part of the inn where the stage and tiring house were and the owner of the parts north of that had the use of it. But only the owner of the northern parts, Needler, had to maintain the drain and keep it "passageable" through his property; the remark about the "comon sinke & setlinge" occurs only in his deed.

20. Chambers, 2:543 and n.; R. B. Graves, "Shakespeare's Outdoor Stage Lighting," *Shakespeare Studies* 13 (1980): 235–50, esp. 247. See also appendix 4.

21. St.Ch.5/S.13/8, no. 4.

Chapter 13. The Theatrical Enterprise

1. The Admiral's men averaged about 38 playing weeks a year between 1597 and 1600, and in both 1598–99 and 1599–1600 they played exactly thirty-eight weeks between mid-August and the vacation of the next summer, twenty-seven of them between mid-August and mid-March of the first year and twenty-one of them during that period in the second. Henslowe's records do not allow one to calculate so closely how often the company played after 1600, but suggest that they played at much the same rate between mid-August 1601 and mid-March 1603. For 1597–1600, see Henslowe's lists in the *Diary*, pp. 54–60, 70–72, 94–95, 120–21; for 1600–1603, see his many notes of the day-to-day costs of playing in London, esp. pp. 136–38, 162–71, 175–87, 199–209.

2. See chapters 4 and 7 and my "Aspects" in *The First Public Playhouse*, pp. 38–42. Ignoring Roberts's remarks about which door he opened, and Samwell's remarks about where Langley's gatherer stood and whose money he took, Sisson twice declared that the £4 were the takings of

the whole house and not just of Samwell's galleries (p. 67 and n.; "The Red Bull Company and the Importunate Widow," p. 64). He also declared, without evidence, that the gatherers' share in Elizabethan playhouses was "something like a shilling in the pound," so that Langley's 5s. represented only what he had to pay his gatherer. Sisson did not take account of the note in Chambers (2:446) that gatherers at the Red Bull earned only 1s.6d. a week each in 1613.

3. See Chambers, 2:531–35.

4. John Orrell, "The Theatre at Christ Church, Oxford in 1605," *Shakespeare Survey* 35 (1982): 134–35.

5. Sisson (p. 61) guessed that the £10 was paid to the master of the revels "for licensing the theatre to" Browne and his men. Rather, it may have been paid instead of, or as a way of buying back, a bond of £100 that landlords or playhouses seem to have had to put up to guarantee that their tenants obeyed the rules of the master of the revels. If so, Samwell would have paid the money in 1598 for the first company at the Boar's Head and in 1599 for Derby's men. Browne would have paid it in 1601 for Worcester's men, and his widow in later years for, perhaps, several companies. In January 1595, Henslowe paid the master of the revels £10 "in full payement of a bonde of one hundreth powndes" and of any charges due from then until Ash Wednesday, 5 February (in the midst of a period when Henslowe paid the master of the revels no regular fees), the Admiral's men having moved into his playhouse, the Rose, during the previous summer. One of the offenses of an illegal company in 1598 was that it had not been "bound" to the master of the revels. In 1583, the license of Worcester's men was an "Indenture of Lycense" which "bound" them "to the orders of the" master of the revels. Both Mago and Marsh said that Samwell and his successor paid the £10 for "warants or [instead of 'for'] licences." See *Henslowe's Diary*, p. 44; *Henslowe's Diary*, ed. W. W. Greg (London, 1904), 2:113–18; Chambers, 1:319–20n; 2:131, 139–41, 221–22; and my appendix 3.

6. C.24/290/3, Hoppdale no. 3–4, Samwell no. 4. It was one of the agreements made in a conversation in the yard in the late spring of 1599.

7. For a revival of the play twenty-one years after the first performance, Heywood wrote a prologue (printed in 1637) in which he complained about the wretched text of 1605. So many saw the play, he wrote,

> . . . that some by Stenography drew
> The plot: put it in print: (scarce one word trew:)
> And in that lameness it hath limp't so long.

A stenographic text for our purposes, if not Heywood's, could be an advantage. See Heywood's *Pleasant Dialogues and Dramma's* (London, 1637), p. 249. The text of *Sir Thomas Wyat* is also difficult, being "clearly . . . a corrupt memorial reconstruction": T. J. King, *Shakespearean Staging, 1599–1642* (Cambridge, Mass., 1972), pp. 39–40.

8. Another play, Heywood's *The Foure Prentises of London*, may belong in this list, though it was printed in 1615 as "diuers times acted at the Red-Bull" and "newly reuised." In a preface Heywood said that he wrote it *"some fifteene or sixteene yeares agoe,"* long before the Red Bull became a playhouse. It calls for elaborate business *"vpon the walles":* many actors perform there, and two *"Enter at two seuerall dores"* and *"climbe vp the wals,"* where they fight with the actors already there *"and bring away the Ensignes, flourishing them, seuerall wayes"* (sigs. I–I2v).

9. *Henslowe's Diary*, pp. 223–25.

10. In the play Will Kempe appears as himself. If he actually played himself, the play would date from before the end of 1603, for Kempe died in that year. If the play was presented at the Curtain, as the entry in *Stationers' Register* says, Susan Browne's second husband, Thomas Greene, probably impersonated the man whom he replaced in the company. The play, of course, could have appeared before 1603 and then kept the stage after Kempe's death. The epilogue alludes to "Some that fill vp this round circumference," referring more appropriately to the Curtain than the Boar's Head.

11. D. F. Rowan, "A Neglected Jones/Webb Theatre Project," *Shakespeare Survey* 23 (1970): 128; "The English Playhouse: 1595–1630," *Renaissance Drama* 4 (1971): 44–47. W. J. Lawrence may have begun this idea in his *Physical Conditions of the Elizabethan Public Playhouse* (Cambridge, Mass., 1927), p. 83. Professor Richard Hosley developed it in "The Gallery Over the

Stage in the Public Playhouses of Shakespeare's Time," *Shakespeare Quarterly* 8 (1957): 15–31, and Sisson (p. xix) advanced it for the Boar's Head. See also Hosley's "Was there a Music Room in Shakespeare's Globe," *Shakespeare Survey* 13 (1960): 113–19.

12. See Warren Smith's suggestion: "Evidence of Scaffolding on Shakespeare's Stage," *Review of English Studies* 2 (1951): 22–29, and Dover Wilson's suggestion in his New Cambridge Edition of *Antony and Cleopatra* (London, 1950), pp. 102, 230.

13. Chambers: (for Henslowe) 1:362, 365; 2:139, 182, 249, 256, 442; (for the Burbages) 1:355–56; 2:388, 393; (for the Swan) 2:131, 412; (for Alleyn) 2:245; (for the Red Bull) 2:239. See also Bentley, 1:44; 6:180.

14. Chambers, 4:322–23, 325, 326–28, 328–29, 329–32, 332–33, 333–34, 334–35. The Privy Council may also have had an order against such playhouses as the Boar's Head "sett downe in Her Highenes Court of Starrchamber" in the winter of 1599–1600 (p. 327).

15. *Early English Stages* 2, pt. 2:9–29.

16. Chambers, 4:327.

Appendix 1. The Study of the Boar's Head

1. Sisson's articles appeared in the following journals: *Life and Letters Today* 15, no. 6 (Winter 1936): 99–107; *Modern Language Review* 37 (1942): 25–36; *Shakespeare Survey* 7 (1954): 57–68.

2. Hotson had discovered both more and less than he knew, for he wrongly thought that Sisson had used no. 6 above and not used no. 3. Both Hotson and I ignored Sisson's article of 1942, because on the face of it, it does not concern the Boar's Head. Had we looked at it with any care, either of us could have found no. 2, despite Sisson's incomplete citation, and Hotson would have seen that Sisson had used no. 3.

3. In his treatment of Francis Langley's part in the history of the Boar's Head (1978), Professor Ingram uses no additional documents: *A London Life in the Brazen Age*, pp. 234–49, 264–67. My published papers appeared in the following books: (1) *The Elizabethan Theatre I*, ed. David Galloway (Toronto, 1970), pp. 45–73; (2) *The Elizabethan Theater III*, ed. Galloway (Toronto, 1973), pp. 33–65; (3) *Shakespeare 1971*, ed. Clifford Leech and John Margeson (Toronto, 1972), pp. 12–20. I presented my other papers about the Boar's Head to meetings of the Shakespeare Association of America in 1974, 1978, 1979, and 1983.

Appendix 7. The Accuracy of Ogilby and Morgan's Map

1. Ralph Hyde, preface to the reproduction of Ogilby and Morgan's map published by the Guildhall Library and Harry Margary in 1976, p. 3; Philippa Glanville, "The topography of seventeenth-century London: a review of maps," *Urban History Yearbook 1980*, p. 81.

2. D. A. Hutchinson, "Co-ordination of Mining Surveys with the Ordnance Survey," *Transactions of the Institution of Mining Engineers* 76 (1928-29): 299–312.

3. One of the Crace copies (II, 62) is incomplete but does have the Boar's Head and scale-bar sheets. The copy at Burlington House seems to be a proof taken before the plates were fully engraved: it omits, for example, much of the lettering and the scale bar. The strong-room copy is the source of the map of the reproduction of 1894 (issued by the London and Middlesex Archaeological Society) but not of the lines of type at the top; parts of the reproduction derive from repairs to the map, some of which create inaccuracies.

4. The Ordnance Survey revised the map of 1873–75 in 1894–96 and again in 1913. The L.C.C. revised it in 1938. The Ordnance Survey resurveyed the area in 1950, issuing a new map to the scale 1:1,250 in 1952 and various revisions thereafter, the latest in 1971.

Appendix 9. Robert Browne

1. Chambers, 2:56, 127, 137–38, 224, 273–82, 285, 304, 445, etc.; *Henslowe's Diary*, p. 277; *Henslowe's Papers*, ed. W. W. Greg (London, 1907), p. 63.

2. Sisson elsewhere thought Derby's and Worcester's a joint company (p. xiii). Yet a company called Worcester's played often in the provinces from 1590 and another called Derby's from 1594. Professor Wickham, too, would have Derby's and Worcester's join, somewhat before Worcester's became the Queen's men in the winter of 1603–4 (*Early English Stages* 2, pt.2 :106–7), but a company called Derby's continued in the provinces long after 1603. See below.

3. He has, for example, Worcester's men paying extra fees to the Langleys in the winter of 1600–1601 rather than in the next one (pp. 57, 59). See also chapter 5.

4. Chambers, 2 :278–80; Willem Schrickx, "English Actors at the Courts of Wolfenbüttel, Brussels and Graz during the Lifetime of Shakespeare," *Shakespeare Survey* 33 (1980): 159–60, 162.

5. Bentley, 2 :636–37.

6. Schrickx, pp. 159–61; Elisabeth Mentzel, *Geschichte der Schauspielkunst in Frankfurt am Main* (Frankfurt, 1882), pp. 45–47; Chambers, 2 :119–20, 278–80; and chapters 4, 5, 6, and 8 above.

7. The actor was usually described on formal occasions as "gentleman," and so Browne is in legal documents when not "complainant" or "defendant." On 28 June 1602, however, an attorney described him and his opponents (Worcester's men) in a lawsuit as "players" (C.33/101/ f.735 in the A book, /102/f.798ᵛ in the B book).

8. Req.2/466/pt.II[/1], the bill and reply; and chapters 6 and 7. Browne's remark disproves a central part of Sisson's scheme. Quoting only the words "this defendant and his fellows" and ignoring their context, Sisson drew from the remark some strange conclusions about which he wrote, "there is no doubt whatever." The remark means, he declared, that Langley had abused the same company and leader two years before that Woodliffe wanted to abuse in 1603—Worcester's men and Browne. It also means, he declared, that in 1603 Browne was still a sharer in Worcester's men and still at the Boar's Head. If Sisson ignored the difficulties that Browne's words should have caused him, he also ignored those inherent in his own. Woodliffe could not have threatened Worcester's men in 1603, whether a man who lived at the Boar's Head was a sharer or not, because on other evidence they had been one of Henslowe's companies and at the Rose, hence well beyond Woodliffe's reach, since the summer of 1602. Browne's words, "two yeares past," incidentally, should have caused Sisson to realize that he had misdated the documents of the lawsuit between Worcester's men and Browne. See Sisson, pp. xx, 59, 73.

9. The records of companies in the provinces are too few and the dates too inexact to enable one to say much more about the movements of either Derby's or Worcester's men while Browne was at the Boar's Head. When the Malone Society and R.E.E.D. have finished their work among provincial records, we shall know more. We must make do now with the volumes so far published by the Malone society and R.E.E.D. and parts of some of those in progress, along with the random and apparently inaccurate lists in Murray (1 :58, 295–96) and Chambers (2 :127, 225). For the two companies from 1590 onward, see R.E.E.D., *York*, pp. 442, 455, 464, 471, 486, 488; *Coventry*, pp. 328, 332, 336, 341, 346, 350, 351, 353, 355, 358, 360, 362, 364, 371, 373, 376, 384, 397; *Norwich*, 119, 120(2); *Somerset* (forthcoming), Bath and Bridgwater; *Devon* (forthcoming), Barnstaple; and from the Malone Society, see *Records of Plays and Players in Kent*, pp. 17, 64, 110, 116, and *Records of Plays and Players in Norfolk and Suffolk 1330–1642*, ed. David Galloway and John Wasson (Oxford, 1980–1981) (Collections 11), pp. 66, 68, 156, 217, 228. See also R.E.E.D., *The Halliwell-Phillipps Scrapbooks*, pp. 105–7, 148–50. I am indebted to the staff of R.E.E.D. for consulting files.

10. C.24/500/9 and 103, nos. 1; /446/pt.I/156, Baskervile no. 1. In these depositions, four veteran actors said in 1623 that they had known her since the 1590s:

Richard Perkins (in October), "these 27. yeares or thereabouts"—since 1596
Thomas Heywood (in October), "these xxv yeares or thereabouts"—since 1598
Robert Leigh (in November), "theis 28. or 29. yeares"—since 1594–95
John King (in June), "these xxx yeares"—since 1593

and she said that she was "aged 40 yeares & above" on 17 April 1618. All the actors had been Worcester's men but only King, it seems, in the 1590s (Chambers, 2: 226, 229). He said that he had worked for the company "these 30. yeares past & vpwards" (/103, no.5). Because a person is likely to remember accurately how long he has worked for an organization, King may well have begun with Worcester's men in 1593 or a little before and met Susan at about the same time.

11. The actor King's saying in 1623 that he had worked for Worcester's men for thirty years and upward and known Susan for thirty encouraged Sisson to speculate that Browne led the company for many years and brought Susan to it as his second wife. Because the woman Sisson thought Browne's first wife died with her children in August 1593, however, he decided at first not to take King's remark as it stood. "It may be concluded that," as he wrote in 1954, King had served with Worcester's men for some time before meeting Susan. So in 1936 and 1942, he put Browne's and Susan's marriage in 1594, allowing Browne a year for mourning (ample, he thought, in Renaissance times) and in 1954 advanced it to a time we could accept "with some certainty," late 1594 or early 1595 (the child he thought their son was born in October 1595). In 1972, however, returning to King's remark, he moved the marriage back to 1593 without troubling about mourning or the bride's being fifteen or sixteen years old (pp. 7–8).

12. Registers, I, f.45ᵛ, 47ᵛ, 48ᵛ, 49ᵛ. Susan Browne appeared as almost certainly the wife of Robert Browne of the Boar's Head when she got the administration of his goods in January 1604, he having died in October 1603 (see chapter 7). Thomas Greene listed her sons and daughters by Browne according to sex and, it seems, age: Robert and William, then Susan, Elizabeth, and Anne; he noted that Susan was not yet fifteen years old on 25 July 1612 (G.L.C., DL/C/360/129). A Robert Browne's son, Robert, was baptized at All Hallows London Wall on 17 April 1601 (Guildhall, MS. 5083); but these people must not have to do with the man whose child had been baptized in Whitechapel the previous 23 December.

A List of Documents, Maps, Books, and Articles

Documents

British Museum: Additional MS 5476, f.197ᵛ

Corporation of London
  Husting Roll 248/114
  Journal 17, f.42ᵛ
  Letter Book S, f.143
  Remembrancia, II, 171, 182, 187, 188, 189, 283

Folger Shakespeare Library:
  Z.c.22(23)

Greater London Council
  B/N.T.G./540
  DL/C/360/129
  J.Ste/5871
  M.B.W. 1810, 1835/5, 1840, 1877 (p. 72), 1886 (p. 24, 3d pagination)
  M.L.R.1721/II/219
  M.L.R.1721/IV/131–32
  M.L.R.1721/V/139
  M.L.R.1723/I/65
  M.L.R.1723/V/433
  M.L.R.1724/II/249
  M.L.R.1724/IV/360
  M.L.R.1726/I/107
  M.L.R.1728/IV/263,270
  M.L.R.1728/VI/297
  M.L.R.1730/IV/33–34, 400
  M.L.R.1731/II/119
  M.L.R.1732/V/448–49
  M.L.R.1734/III/437
  M.L.R.1738/I/352
  M.L.R.1740/IV/719

M.L.R.1741/II/145
M.L.R.1742/I/124–25
M.L.R.1749/III/44–45
M.L.R.1754/III/34, 408
M.L.R.1757/IV/83–84
M.L.R.1792/IV/43
M.L.R.1802/VII/551
M.L.R.1807/V/338–39
M.L.R.1813/VIII/119
M.L.R.1826/V/721
M.L.R.1829/V/776
M.L.R.1841/VII/944–46
M.L.R.1849/VIII/544
M.L.R.1863/XX/801–2
M.L.R.1863/XXII/798
M.L.R.1864/XIII/442–43
M.L.R.1865/III/218
M.L.R.1879/XI/806
M.L.R.1880/XL/896
M.L.R.1881/X/144
M.L.R.1882/IX/722
M.L.R.1882/XVI/793
M.L.R.1885/VII/392–93
P.93/MRY 1/I, passim
P.93/MRY 1/92/f.25

Guildhall Library
MS 5083
MS 6015/1–15, 32–47, 58–63
MS 8478, f.68–68^v
MS 9050/4/f.387
MS 9051/2/f.125–26
MS 9065^k/f.167^v
MS 9168/14/f.232^v, 240^v
MS 9168/15/f.246
MS 9171/12/f.81–82, 94–96
MS 9171/15/f.224^v–25^v, 285
MS 9172/4
MS 9172/42

Haberdashers' Company
Freedoms Book, 1526–1614

Harrow Land Registry
Titles 125655, LN80561, LN186342

Hatfield House
Cecil Papers 186.24

Leicester Record Office
BR III/2/68/m.2^v
BR III/2/75/f.98–100

Middlesex Record Office
M.D.R.1726/I/107
MR/LV/1/[f.5–5^v, 17^v]

Public Record Office
  C.1/1055/17
  C.2/Jas.I/L.13/62
  C.2/Jas.I/M.13/65
  C.2/Jas.I/V.4/42
  C.2/Chas.I/L.59/54
  C.2/Chas.I/P.90/54
  C.2/Chas.I/T.48/67
  C.3/190/8
  C.3/227/19
  C.3/279/18
  C.7/250/33
  C.7/545/25
  C.7/572/46
  C.8/452/41
  C.8/467/63
  C.8/467/74
  C.9/447/153
  C.9/447/154
  C.9/460/1
  C.9/469/69
  C.11/1463/20
  C.24/55/63/pt.II
  C.24/56/35
  C.24/157/45
  C.24/157/46
  C.24/201/17
  C.24/225/38/pts. I, II
  C.24/258/pt.I/50
  C.24/258/pt.II/6
  C.24/278/71
  C.24/290/3
  C.24/304/27
  C.24/305/1
  C.24/327/61
  C.24/331(Pooley v. Beecher)
  C.24/446/pt.I/156
  C.24/500/9
  C.24/500/103
  C.24/840/pt.II/9
  C.24/1247
  C.24/1252
  C.33/99/f.127^v, 464^v, 473^v, 526, 577^v
  C.33/100/f.122^v, 452^v, 461, 518, 564^v
  C.33/101/f.207^v, 263^v, 290, 309, 324^v, 406^v, 450, 573, 611, 643–43^v, 735
  C.33/102/f.249^v, 302, 326^v, 343–43^v, 344, 433, 470^v, 577^v, 616, 648^v, 798^v
  C.33/103/f.43–43^v, 364, 700^v
  C.33/104/f.44^v, 359, 744^v
  C.33/149/f.844^v
  C.33/150/f.953^v
  C.54/2471/17

C.54/2515/11
C.54/2947/24
C.54/2964/4
C.54/3597/m.38–41
C.66/641/6/m.23
C.66/704/15/m.34
C.66/833/m.4
C.66/836/m.8, 40
C.66/1827/29
C.82/566/1
C.82/904/4
C.142/546/481/118

C.P.25(2)/173/Easter 43 Eliz./1
C.P.25(2)/173/Easter 44 Eliz./17
C.P.25(2)/173/Mich. 44&45 Eliz./13
C.P.25(2)/324/Hil. 19 Jas.I/10
C.P.25(2)/324/Trin. 22 Jas.I/17
C.P.25(2)/457/Hil. 7 Chas.I/19
C.P.25(2)/457/Easter 13 Chas.I/3, 19
C.P.25(2)/692/Hil. 33&34 Chas.II/16
C.P.40/1655/m.724^{v}
C.P.40/1693/m.1514^{v}
C.P.40/1701/m.1109

E.36/120/f.133–36
E.159/417/Trin. 41 Eliz./m.51/nos. 41, 42
E.179/141/113/m.4
E.179/141/116/m.7–8
E.179/141/122/m.2
E.179/141/131/m.5
E.179/141/136
E.179/141/138/m.2
E.179/141/140/m.5^{v}
E.179/141/160/m.11
E.179/141/154/m.19
E.179/142/167/m.10^{v}–11
E.179/142/179/m.2^{v}
E.179/142/186/m.1
E.179/142/234/m.3^{v}, 4^{v}
E.179/142/239
E.179/142/254
E.315/439/f.14v
E.315/543/m.57
E.405/92/m.10, 30
E.405/93/m.11, 13
E.405/94/m.5, 8
E.405/95/m.1^{v}, 13, 16
E.405/96/m.1, 15, 20, 20^{v}
E.405/97/m.1, 17, 19^{v}, 24, 27
E.405/98/m.1^{v}, 2, 11, 14, 14^{v}
E.405/99/m.7, 11, 14, 17
E.405/100/m.1, 5, 10, 12, 12^{v}, 20, 20^{v}

E.405/101/m.1, 5, 14v, 15, 17v
E.405/102/m.6v, 7v, 8v, 11v, 14v, 17v
E.405/103/m.1v, 5v, 14, 14v, 15, 17
E.405/104/m.1v, 6, 10, 13v, 15, 15v
E.405/105/m.1, 7, 12v, 16, 17
E.405/106/m.2v, 8, 18, 20
E.405/107/m.3v, 5v, 11
E.405/108/m.10v, 17v, 22v, 30
E.405/109/m.1, 7v, 9, 15, 27
E.405/110/m.3v, 8, 15, 24
E.405/111/m.1v, 30, 33v, 34
E.405/112/m.3v
E.405/113/m.24, 50v
E.405/114/m.16, 39v
E.405/115/m.17v, 54
E.405/116/m.10, 24
E.405/118/m.16, 35
E.405/119/m.29, 46
E.405/120/m.29v, 85
E.405/121/m.47, 99v
E.405/122/m.41, 107
E.405/123/m.33v, 96v
E.405/124/m.19v, 51v
E.405/125/m.25, 72
E.405/126/m.15v, 68

K.B.27/1280/m.48
K.B.27/1289/m.43
K.B.27/1332/m.889
K.B.27/1364/m.259
K.B.27/1367/m.199v
K.B.29/242/m.54v, 55, 55v

P.C.2/6/pp.455, 523, 550, 590, 615
P.C.2/7/pp.695, 696
P.C.2/25/p.41

PROB.6/6/f.183
PROB.11/32/31
PROB.11/34/36
PROB.11/62/5
PROB.11/75/32
PROB.11/98/47
PROB.11/122/107
PROB.11/191/35
PROB.11/356/41
PROB.11/390/4
PROB.11/505/267
PROB.11/810/207
PROB.11/924/461
PROB.11/1100/53
PROB.11/1138/52
PROB.11/1353/61
PROB.11/1708/67

Req.1/21/f.169, 172
Req.1/66/9 July [f.218]
Req.1/159/f.66ᵛ
Req.1/207/f.98ᵛ, 119ᵛ
Req.2/34/73
Req.2/199/17
Req.2/285/35
Req.2/466/pt.II[/1]

S.P.1/124/f.118, 155
S.P.12/8/15
S.P.12/15/21
S.P.14/2/100
S.P.271/34, 35
S.P.60/2/f.61
S.P.60/7/f.104–5

St.Ch.5/A.8/4
St.Ch.5/A.25/27
St.Ch.5/A.33/37
St.Ch.5/D.36/9
St.Ch.5/S.13/8
St. Ch.5/S.74/3

Maps

"Agas, Ralph" (actually anonymous). *Civitas Londinum.* London?, c.1633. (Map drawn c.1562.)

Hogenberg, Franz. "Londinum Feracissimi Angliae Regni Metropolis." In Georg Braun and Hogenberg, *Civitas Orbis Terrarum.* Vol. 1. Cologne, 1572.

Horwood, Richard. *Plan of the Cities of London and Westminster. . . .* London, 1792–99.

Leake, John, et al. *An Exact Surveigh of the Streets Lanes and Churches Contained within the Ruines of the City of London. . . .* London, 1667. (Wenceslaus Hollar engraved the map.)

Newcourt, Richard. *An Exact Delineation of the Cities of London and Westminster and the Suburbs Thereof. . . .* London, 1658. (William Faithorne engraved the map.)

Ogilby, John [and William Morgan]. *A Large and Accurate Map of the City of London.* London, 1676.

———. *A Large and Accurate Map of the City of London.* London, 1894. (A reproduction published by the London and Middlesex Archaeological Society, introduction by Charles Welch.)

———. *A Large and Accurate Map of the City of London.* London, 1976. (A reproduction published by Harry Margary, Lympne Castle, Kent, and Guildhall Library, London; preface by Ralph Hyde.)

Ordnance Survey. *London and its Environs.* Southampton, 1848–50. (Scale 1:1056.)

———. Maps of London, scale 1:1056. Southampton, 1873–75, 1894–96, 1913, 1938 (for the London County Council).

————. Maps of London, scale 1:1250. Southampton, 1952, 1971.

Rocque, John. *A Plan of the Cities of London and Westminister.* London, 1746.

Books and Articles

Acts of the Privy Council of England . . . 1542–1547. Edited by J. R. Dasent. London, 1890.

Acts of the Privy Council of England . . . 1554–1556. Edited by J. R. Dasent. London, 1892.

Acts of the Privy Council of England . . . 1556–1558. Edited by J. R. Dasent. London, 1893.

Adams, J. Q. *Shakespearean Playhouses.* Boston, 1917.

Allegations for Marriage Licences Issued by the Bishop of London, 1520–1610. London: Harleian Society, 1887.

Bentley, G. E. *The Jacobean and Caroline Stage.* 7 vols. Oxford, 1941–68.

Berry, Herbert. "Aspects of the Design and Use of the First Public Playhouse." In *The First Public Playhouse,* edited by H. Berry. Montreal, 1979.

————. "The Boar's Head Again." In *The Elizabethan Theatre III,* edited by David Galloway. Toronto, 1973.

————. "A Handlist of Documents about the Theatre in Shoreditch." In *The First Public Playhouse,* edited by H. Berry. Montreal, 1979.

————. "The Playhouse in the Boar's Head Inn, Whitechapel." In *The Elizabethan Theatre,* edited by David Galloway. Toronto, 1969.

————. "The Playhouse in the Boar's Head Inn, Whitechapel III." In *Shakespeare 1971,* edited by Clifford Leech and J. M. R. Margeson. Toronto, 1972.

Boyle's View of London. London, 1799.

[Braines, W. W.] "Holywell Priory and the Site of the Theatre, Shoreditch." In *Indications of Houses of Historical Interest in London,* Vol. 5. London, 1930.

Brathwaite, Richard. *Remains After Death.* London, 1618.

Brownstein, Oscar. "Stake and Stage." Ph.D. diss., University of Iowa, 1963.
————. "Why Didn't Burbage Lease the Beargarden?" In *The First Public Playhouse,* edited by H. Berry. Montreal, 1979.

Calendar of State Papers, Domestic Series . . . 1547–1580, Preserved in the . . . Public Record Office. Edited by Robert Lemon. London, 1856.

Calendar of State Papers, Domestic Series . . . 1581–1590, Preserved in the . . . Public Record Office. Edited by Robert Lemon. London, 1865.

Calendar of State Papers, Domestic Series . . . 1595–1597, Preserved in the . . . Public Record Office. Edited by Mary Anne Everett Green. London, 1869.

Calendar of State Papers, Domestic Series . . . 1603–1610, Preserved in the . . . Public Record Office. Edited by Mary Anne Everett Green. London, 1857.

Calendar of the Patent Rolls Preserved in the Public Record Office. Edward VI. Vol. 4 (1550–1553). London, 1926.

Carew, Thomas. *The Poems of Thomas Carew.* Edited by Rhodes Dunlap. Oxford, 1957.

Chambers, E. K. *The Elizabethan Stage*. 4 vols. Oxford, 1923.

A Complete Guide to All Persons who have any Trade or Concern with the City of London. London, 1740–83.

Cooke, John. *Greene's Tu quoque*. London, 1614.

Cotgrave, Randle. *A Dictionarie of the French and English Tongues*. London, 1611.

Darlington, Ida, and James Howgego. *Printed Maps of London*. 2d ed. London, 1978.

Day, John, William Rowley, and George Wilkins. *The Travailes Of The three English Brothers*. London, 1607.

Dee, John. *The Private Diary*. Edited by J. O. Halliwell. London, 1842.

Dekker, Thomas, and John Webster. *The Famous History of Sir Thomas Wyat*. London, 1607.

Dictionary of National Biography. 21 vols. Edited by Leslie Stephen and Sidney Lee. London, 1885–1900.

Field, John. *A godly exhortation*. London, 1583.

The First and Second partes of King Edward the Fourth. London, 1599.

Fleay, F. G. *Chronicle History of the London Stage*. [London, 1890].

The Free Customes, Benefits and Priviledges of the Copyhold Tennants, of the Mannors of Stepny and Hackny. London, 1617.

The Gentleman's Magazine. London, 1754.

Glanville, Philippa. "The topography of seventeenth century London: a review of maps." *In Urban History Yearbook 1980*.

Graves, R. B. "Shakespeare's Outdoor Stage Lighting." *Shakespeare Studies* 13 (1980).

Graves, T. S. *The Court and the London Theatres*. Menasha, Wis., 1913.

Halliwell-Phillipps, J. O. *Outlines of the Life of Shakespeare*. 2d ed. London, 1882.

The Hamilton Papers. Vol. 1. Edited by Joseph Bain. Edinburgh, 1890.

Henslowe, Philip. *Henslowe's Diary*. Edited by R. A. Foakes and R. T. Rickert. Cambridge, 1961.

———. *Henslowe's Diary*. Vol. 2. Edited by W. W. Greg. London, 1904.

Hereafter ensueth the auncient seuerall customes, of the seuerall Mannors of Stebenhuth, and Hackney. [London, c.1591].

[Heywood, Thomas?] *The Fayre Mayde of the Exchange*. London, 1607.

Heywood, Thomas. *The Foure Prentises of London*. London, 1615.

———. *If you know not me, You know no bodie*. London, 1605.

———. *Pleasant Dialogues and Dramma's*. London, 1637.

———. *The Second Part of, If you know not me, you know no bodie*. London, 1606.

———. *A Woman Kilde with Kindnesse*. London, 1607.

Historical Manuscripts Commission. *Calendar of the Manuscripts of the Most Hon. The Marquis of Salisbury, K.G., &c. Preserved at Hatfield House*. Vols. 5, 6. London, 1894, 1895.

———. *Report on the Manuscripts of Lord Middleton Preserved at Wollaton Hall, Nottinghamshire*. London, 1911.

————. *Report on the Manuscripts of the Right Honourable Lord De L'Isle and Dudley Preserved at Penshurst Place Kent.* Vol. 2. London, 1933.

The History of the tryall of Cheualry. London, 1605.

Hodges, C. Walter. *The Globe Restored.* London, 1953.

————. *Shakespeare's Second Globe: The Missing Monument.* London, 1973.

Holinshed, Raphael. *The Third volume of Chronicles . . . continued (with occurrences and accidents of fresh memorie) to the yeare 1586* "by Iohn Stow *and others.*" London, 1587.

Hosley, Richard. "The Gallery Over the Stage in the Public Playhouses of Shakespeare's Time." *Shakespeare Quarterly* 8 (Winter 1957).

————. "The Theatre and the Tradition of Playhouse Design." In *The First Public Playhouse,* edited by H. Berry. Montreal, 1979.

————. "Was there a Music Room in Shakespeare's Globe?" *Shakespeare Survey* 13 (1960).

Hotson, Leslie. *The First Night of Twelfth Night.* London, 1954.

————. *Shakespeare's Wooden O.* London, 1959.

Hutchinson, D. A. "Co-ordination of Mining Surveys with the Ordnance Survey." *Transactions of the Institution of Mining Engineers* 76 (1928–29).

Hutchinson, John. *A Catalogue of Notable Middle Templars.* London, 1902.

Ingram, William. "The Closing of the Theaters in 1597: A Dissenting View." *Modern Philology* 69 (November 1971).

————. *A London Life in the Brazen Age.* Cambridge, Mass., 1978.

————. "The Playhouse at Newington Butts: A New Proposal." *Shakespeare Quarterly* 21 (Autumn 1970).

Jones, W. J. *The Elizabethan Court of Chancery.* Oxford, 1967.

King, T. J. *Shakespearean Staging, 1599–1642.* Cambridge, Mass., 1972.

Kirkman, Francis. *The Wits.* London, 1662.

Lawrence, W. J. *Physical Conditions of the Elizabethan Public Playhouse.* Cambridge, Mass., 1927.

Letters and Papers, Foreign and Domestic, of the Reign of Henry VIII. Vol. 4, pt. 1 (1524–1526). Edited by J. S. Brewer. London, 1870.

Letters and Papers, Foreign and Domestic, of the Reign of Henry VIII. Vol. 16 (1540–1541). Edited by James Gairdner and R. H. Brodie. London, 1898.

Loengard, Janet S. "An Elizabethan Lawsuit." *Shakespeare Quarterly* 34 (Autumn 1983).

Massinger, Philip. *A New Way to Pay Old Debts.* London, 1633.

Mather, Philip E. *A Compendium of Sheriff Law.* London, 1894.

Mentzel, Elisabeth. *Geschichte der Schauspielkunst in Frankfurt am Main.* Frankfurt, 1882.

*Middlesex County Records.*Vol. 3. Edited by J. C. Jeaffreson. London, 1887–1902.

Morgan, James Appleton. Introduction to *Titus Andronicus.* In *The Bankside Shakespeare.* 21 vols. Cambridge, Mass., 1888–1906.

Murray, J. T. *English Dramatic Companies.* 2 vols. London, 1910.

A New English Dictionary on Historical Principles. 10 vols. Edited by James A. H. Murray et al. Oxford, 1888–1928.

No-body and Some-body. London, c.1606.

Nungezer, Edwin. *A Dictionary of Actors.* Ithaca, N.Y., 1929.

Orrell, John. "The Theatre at Christ Church, Oxford in 1605." *Shakespeare Survey* 35 (1982).

Partridge, Eric. *Origins.* London, 1966.

The Perambulator. London, c.1832.

A Pleasant conceited Comedie Wherein is shewed how a man may chuse a good Wife from a bad. London, 1602.

Records of Early English Drama. *Coventry.* Edited by R. W. Ingram. Toronto, 1981.

———. *The Halliwell-Phillipps Scrapbooks: an Index.* Edited by Alan Somerset. Toronto, 1980.

———. *Norwich.* Edited by David Galloway. Toronto, 1984.

———. *York.* Edited by A. F. Johnston and Margaret Rogerson. Toronto, 1979.

Records of Plays and Players in Kent 1450–1642. Edited by Giles Dawson. London, 1965. (Malone Society Collections, no. 7).

Records of Plays and Players in Norfolk and Suffolk 1330–1642. Edited by David Galloway and John Wasson. Oxford, 1980–81. (Malone Society Collections, no. 11.)

Records of the Worshipful Company of Carpenters. Edited by Bower Marsh (vols. 3, 4), Marsh and John Ainsworth (vols. 5, 6), A. M. Millard (vol. 7). Oxford, 1915, 1916; London, 1937, 1939, 1968.

Registers of St. James Clerkenwell. Vols. 1, 4. London: Harleian Society, 1884–91.

Rowan, D. F. "The English Playhouse: 1595–1630." *Renaissance Drama* 4 (1971).

———. "A Neglected Jones/Webb Theatre Project." *Shakespeare Survey* 23 (1970).

Rowley, William, and Thomas Middleton. *A Faire Quarrell.* London, 1617.

Rymer, Thomas. *Foedera.* Vol. 1. London, 1816.

Schrickx, Willem. "English Actors at the Courts of Wolfenbüttel, Brussels and Graz during the Lifetime of Shakespeare." *Shakespeare Survey* 33 (1980).

Sisson, C. J. *The Boar's Head Theatre.* Edited by Stanley Wells. London, 1972.

———. "Mr. and Mrs. Browne of the Boar's Head." *Life and Letters Today* 15, no. 6 (Winter 1936).

———. "Notes on Early Stuart Stage History." *Modern Language Review* 37 (January 1942).

———. "The Red Bull Company and the Importunate Widow." *Shakespeare Survey* 7 (1954).

Smith, Warren. "Evidence of Scaffolding on Shakespeare's Stage." *Review of English Studies* 2 (January 1951).

Somerset, Alan. "New Facts Concerning Samuel Rowley." *Review of English Studies* 17 (1966), no. 67.

Steele, Mary. *Plays & Masques at Court During the Reigns of Elizabeth, James and Charles.* New Haven, 1926.

Stow, John. *Annales.* London, 1592, 1600, 1605.

——. *Survey of London.* London, 1603.

Stubbes, Phillip. *The Anatomie of Abuses.* London, 16 August 1583.

Third Report of the Deputy Keeper of the Public Records. Appendix 2. London, 1843.

A Transcript of the Registers of the Company of Stationers of London; 1554–1640. 5 vols. Edited by Edward Arber. London, 1875–94.

Unwin, George. *The Guilds and Companies of London.* London, 1966.

Venn, John, and J. A. Venn. *Alumni Cantabrigiensis.* Part 1. Cambridge, 1922.

Victoria County Histories. *The Victoria History of the County of Middlesex.* Vol. 2. London, 1911.

Wallace, C. W. *The First London Theatre.* Lincoln, Neb., 1913.

The Weakest goeth to the Wall. London, 1600.

Webb, Sidney, and Beatrice Webb. *The Parish and the County.* London, 1963.

Webster, John. *The White Divil.* London, 1612.

Wickham, Glynne. *Early English Stages.* Vol. 2, pts. 1, 2. London, 1963, 1972.

——. " 'Heavens,' Machinery, and Pillars in the Theatre and Other Early Playhouses." In *The First Public Playhouse,* edited by H. Berry. Montreal, 1979.

Wilson, Dover. Notes for *Antony and Cleopatra.* New Cambridge ed. London, 1950.

Index

Abraham, Sara. *See* Adie, Sara
Abraham, Thomas, 81
Adams, Cranford, 128
Adams, J. Q., 220 n.27
Adie, Benjamin, 211 n.11
Adie, Sara, 211 n.11
Adie, Thomas, 211 n.11
Agas, Ralph (map of), 23, 132–33
Ager, Joseph, 87
Aldrege, John, 199 n.16
Alen, Sir John, 198 n.7
Alen, John (archbishop of Dublin), 13
Alen, Thomas, 13
Allen, Giles, 204 n.2
Alleyn, Edward, 70, 128–29, 191, 193, 195
Alleyn, Joan, 70, 195
Arches, Court of the, 50
Arras (at the back of the stage in playhouses), 109, 126, 127
Ashley, Sir Anthony, 39, 70
Assheton, John, 15
Audley of Walden, Thomas, (first baron, 199 n.9
Ayloff (lawyer), 63

Bagnall, Richard, 35, 50, 176, 202 n.2
Baskervile, James, 74
Baskervile, Susan. *See* Browne, Susan (wife of Robert Browne, actor, of the Boar's Head)
Bath's Men, Earl of (John Bourchier, second earl), 19
Beargarden, The, 112–13
Bedingfield, William, 22–23
Beeston, Christopher, 51, 75, 92

Bell, The, 30, 202 n.1
Bell Savage, The, 30, 202 n.1
Bishop, Richard, 42, 43, 45, 46, 48, 49, 70, 114, 177
Blackfriars, The Second, 107
Blue Boar, The, 107
Boar's Head Yard Meeting, 88, 212 n.15
Bodley, Sir Thomas, 211 n.14
Bond, Thomas, 209 n.18
Borne, John, Jr., 17
Borne, John, Sr., 17
Boulton, Peter, 42–43
Bowyer, William, 98, 189
Brayne, John, 30, 32
Brayne, Margaret, 50
Browker, Hugh, 53, 56, 60, 63–64, 70
Browker, Jane, 207 n.17
Browne, Anne (daughter of Robert Browne, actor, of the Boar's Head), 71, 74, 197
Browne, Anne (wife of William, son of Robert Browne, actor, of the Boar's Head). *See* Rodes, Anne
Browne, Elizabeth (baptized December, 1599), 191, 192–93
Browne, Elizabeth (daughter of Robert Browne, actor, of the Boar's Head), 71, 74, 197
Browne, Elizabeth (widow, resident in the Boar's Head), 186
Browne, Henry, 201 n.10
Browne, Humphrey, 81
Browne, John (son of William Browne, purchaser of part of the Boar's Head), 81
Browne, Robert (actor, of the Boar's Head),

33, 34, 35–36, 37–38, 40–43, 45–46, 47–71, 75, 76, 78, 88, 90, 92, 96, 110–11, 116, 122, 128–29, 164, 166, 168–69, 171–74, 177–78, 203 nn. 7 and 8, 211 nn. 10 and 13, 213 n.4, 214 n.1, 216 n.5; identification of, 191–97

Browne, Robert (actor on the continent), 191–97

Browne, Robert (baptized April, 1601), 219 n.12

Browne, Robert (baptized October 1595), 191, 192–93

Browne, Robert (son of Robert Browne, actor, of the Boar's Head), 71, 74, 193, 197

Browne, Susan (daughter of Robert Browne, actor, of the Boar's Head), 71, 74, 196

Browne, Susan (wife of Robert Browne, actor, of the Boar's Head), 36, 71, 73, 74, 76, 192, 193, 196–97, 210 n.8, 216 n.10; married Baskervile, James, 74; married Greene, Thomas, 72; owner of Boar's Head, 70, 72, 122; and Queen's Men, 72, 74, 207 n.6; and Worcester's Men, 36, 51, 196

Browne, wife of William (son of Robert, actor, of the Boar's Head), 209 n.18

Browne, William (purchaser of part of Boar's Head), 78–81, 82, 83, 84, 85, 86, 87, 89, 90, 91, 92, 133–34; his deed, 94, 97, 98–105, 108, 110, 112, 189–90, 210 n.4, 214 n.1

Browne, William (son of Robert, actor, of the Boar's Head), 71, 74, 196, 211 n.10

Brownstein, Oscar, 215 n.11

Bull, The, 30, 202 n.1

Burbage, family of, 24–25, 31, 38, 57, 73, 129, 130

Burbage, James, 24–25, 30, 32, 50, 215 n.13

Carew, George, 49–50, 52, 55, 57, 58, 60, 64

Carew, Dr. Matthew, 49–50, 52, 55, 57, 58, 60, 62, 64, 65

Carew, Richard, 50

Carew, Thomas, 50

Cecil, Robert, 34, 39, 57

Chair of state (in playhouses), 126

Chambers, E. K., 18, 156, 191, 194, 205 n.14, 216 n.2, 220 n.27

Chancery, Court of, 42, 44, 45, 48–50, 52–54, 55–56, 58–59, 60, 61–62, 63, 65, 66–69, 77, 128, 164–65, 172, 192

Chaplyn, John, 69, 70

Chaplyn, Susan, Jr. See Pound, Susan

Chaplyn, Susan, Sr. See Woodliffe, Susan

Chatwell, William, 26–27

City and Country Properties, Ltd., 213 n.34

Clench (lawyer), 206 n.15

Cockpit in Drury Lane, The, 75

Common Pleas, Court of, 16, 47–50, 53, 55–56, 58–59, 61–62, 63, 64–65, 66, 67

Cooke, John: *Greene's Tu quoque*, 209 n.1

Cordell, William, 85, 211 n.14

Cotgrave, Randle, 118

Cresset lights (in playhouses), 116, 118, 122–23, 173

Cromlech House, 92, 134

Cromwell, Thomas, 13

Cross Keys, The, 30, 202 n.1

Cuckow (carpenter), 161

Cure, Thomas, 207 n.17

Curtain, The, 19, 29, 72–73, 74, 75, 76, 124, 127, 130, 194, 196, 215 n.13

Darrell, Grace, 211 n.13

Daunte, Henry, 26–27

Day, John; Rowley, William; Wilkins, George: *The Travailes Of The three English Brothers*, 127

Day, Nicholas, 199 n.9

Dekker, Thomas and Webster, John: *The Famous History of Sir Thomas Wyat*, 125–26

Denise, Adrian, 84–85, 188–89

Denise, Jane, 85

Denise, John, 85

Denise, Mary Ann, 85

Derby, Elizabeth de Vere, countess of, 34, 43, 51

Derby's Men, Earl of (Ferdinando Stanley, fifth earl). *See* Lord Chamberlain's Men

Derby's Men, Earl of (William Stanley, sixth earl), 34, 35, 36, 41, 42, 43, 55, 60, 72, 120, 124, 126, 129, 191–97, 204 n.1, 216 n.5

Derby, William Stanley, sixth earl of, 34, 43.

Dixon, Robert, 81

Duke, John, 51, 58, 59, 72, 92

Edward the IV. See *First and Second partes of King Edward the Fourth, The*

Egerton, Thomas (lord keeper), 59

Elizabeth I (queen of England), 57, 64, 205 n.14

Essex, Robert Devereux, second earl of, 23, 176

Fayre Mayde of the Exchange, The, 125–26. See also Heywood, Thomas

Fenner, George, 34

Field, John, 112–13
First and Second partes of King Edward the Fourth, The, 126–27
Fisher, Sarah, 87, 90
Fisher, Sidney, 215 n.13
Florey, John, 186
Fortune, The, 34, 35, 57, 75, 94, 116, 122, 123; building, cost of, 35, 109; galleries, 114, 118, 120, 122; licensing, 57, 73; stage and yard, 102, 107, 110, 111–12, 120
Foxley, Alexander, 42–43, 44

Galdelli, Humfredo, 203 n.15
Galleries, Samwell's, at the Boar's Head (eastern, northern, and southern), 61, 103, 107–8, 118–19, 120–22, 123, 140–41, 214 n.1; building of, 31–33, 34–35, 51, 109–10, 112–16, 117, 159–62, 175–76; invaded by Langley, 42–43; position of, 165–69; pulled down, 78
Gallery, Woodliffe's, at the Boar's Head (western), 64, 96, 108–11, 116, 117, 120–21, 122, 123, 127, 129, 140–41, 143; building of, 31–32, 33, 35, 53; invaded by Langley, 43, 51; legal arguments about, 43, 49, 51–52, 53, 55, 56, 58, 60–61, 62, 65–70, 173–74, 178, 208 n.8; pulled down, 78
Garland, John, 74, 210 n.8
Garland, Thomas, 210 n.8
Gatherers (at playhouses), 43, 114, 115, 121–22, 215 n.2
Gawen, Thomas, 98, 189
Gaywood, George, 28
Gibbes, Anne, 16, 17, 22, 23
Gibbes, Mary, 22
Glasscock, William, 201 n.1
Globe, The, 34, 94, 116, 120; capacity, 122; cost of building, 35; galleries, 114–15, 119, 128–29; licensing, 57, 73; opening in 1599, 36, 109; stage, 112
Gonne, Richard, Sr., 26–27
Goulston, Morris, 213 n.35
Goulston, Sir William, 213 n.35
Greene, Honor, 74
Greene, Susan. *See* Browne, Susan (wife of Robert Browne, actor, of the Boar's Head)
Greene, Thomas, 72–73, 74, 92, 196, 210 n.8, 216 n.10, 219 n.12
Gregory, William, 86
Greves, Thomas. *See* Grovys, Thomas
Grove, Jane. *See* Transfield, Jane and Poley, Jane
Grove, John, 16, 17, 22

Grove, Nicholas, 198 n.8
Grove, Robert, 198 n.8
Grovys (or Greves), Thomas, 16
Gunnerships (at the Tower of London), 12, 14, 17

Halgrave, H., 13
Hallam, Nicholas, 210 n.4
Harrison, Robert, 201 n.5
Harrydaunce, John, 13–14, 18
Harryson, Jane, 50
"Heavens" (in the playhouses), 108, 109, 111, 117, 118, 124, 127, 141–43, 164, 173
Henslowe, Philip, 57, 60, 72, 73, 121, 123, 128–29, 130, 204 n.1
Heron, Giles, 199 n.18
Heywood, Thomas(?), *The Fayre Mayde of the Exchange,* 125–26
Heywood, Thomas, 51, 58, 59, 74, 92, 125–26, 216 n.8, 218 n.10; *If you know not me, you know no bodie,* 125–26; *The Second Part of, If you know not me, you know no bodie,* 125–26; *A Woman Kilde with Kindnesse,* 126–27
History of the tryall of Cheualry, The, 124–25
Hodges, C. Walter, 113–14, 128, 139–43
Hogenberg, Franz (map of), 132–33
Hollar, Wencelaus (map of 1667), 82–83, 113–14, 133, 215 n.13
Hope, The, 35, 75, 112, 114–15, 116, 128–29
Hoppdale, William, 50–51, 116, 123, 161, 168–69, 172, 176, 204 nn. 19 and 20, 213 n.3
Hosley, Richard, 215 n.13, 216 n.11
Hotson, Leslie, 112, 128, 157, 158, 215 n.13
How a man may chuse a good Wife from a bad. See Pleasant conceited Comedie . . .
Howard of Effingham, Charles, second baron, 201 n.14
Hunt, John, 49
Huntley, William, 26

Ingram, William, 189, 203 n.16, 204 n.3, 211 n.5, 217 n.3 to Appendix 1

Johnson, Cornelius, 199 n.16
Johnson, John, 42, 43, 44
Jones, Inigo, 122
Jones, Nicholas, 98, 189
Jordan, Israel, 34, 41, 45–46, 53–54, 64–66, 201 n.5
Jorden, William, 210 n.5

Keller, David, 213 n.32
Kempe, Will, 51, 72, 92, 216 n.10
King, John, 218 n.10, 219 n.11
King, Tom, 129
King's Bench, Court of, 42, 44, 45, 46, 48, 49
King's Men, 72–73

Lady Elizabeth's Men, 75, 129
Langley, Francis: at the Boar's Head, 37–62, 65–66, 68–69, 70, 78, 113, 115, 116, 119, 120–23, 128–29, 159, 164, 169, 171–72, 174, 177–78, 211 n.13, 213 n.3, 214 n.1, 217 n.3 to appendix 1, 218 n.3; at the Swan, 24, 25, 37, 130
Langley, Jane, 39, 59, 60, 63–64, 68, 70, 207 n.18, 211 n.13
Langley, Richard, 40, 37–54, 63–64, 67–68, 70
Lawrence, W. J., 216 n.11
Leake, John (map of), 82, 133
Lee, Isabel. See Poley, Isabel
Leigh, Robert, 218 n.10
Lennox's Men, Duke of (Ludovic Stuart, second duke), 74, 210 n.8
Licensing (of playhouses and players), 19, 30, 37, 57, 73, 129–30; at the Boar's Head, 16–17, 32, 41, 51, 57, 73, 116, 120, 123
Lockdale, Robert, 186
Long, Mary, 86–87, 88
Longford, William, 13–14, 18
Lord Admiral. See Howard of Effingham, Charles, second baron
Lord Admiral's Men, 57, 73, 120, 194, 216 n.5. See also Prince Henry's Men
Lord Chamberlain, 74
Lord Chamberlain's Men, 36, 57, 72–73, 194. See also King's Men
Lord Mayor (of London), 13–14, 16–17, 18–20, 29–30, 33, 57, 73, 74
Lord Strange's Men. See Lord Chamberlain's Men
Lowin, John, 51, 92
Luther, Abigail. See Poley, Lady Abigail

Machinery (stage, in playhouses), 108, 124, 142–43
Mago, Elizabeth, 203 n.16
Mago, John: attacked in the playhouse, 51; builds at the Boar's Head, 33–36, 45, 48, 50, 51, 110–11, 112, 113, 115, 116, 118; lawsuit against, 45, 46; as witness, 44, 67, 69, 129, 159–62, 164–70, 173–74, 175, 178, 205 n.7, 209 nn. 10 and 12, 213 n.3, 214 nn. 3 and 6 to chapter 12, 216 n.5

Marsh, John: attacked in the playhouse, 51; as carpenter at the Boar's Head, 110, 111; as witness, 69, 71, 161, 166–67, 173–74, 178, 203 n.8, 205 n.7, 209 n.10, 216 n.5
Marshalsea Court, 41–42, 43, 44
Marshalsea Prison, 44
Massam (widow). See Browne, wife of William
Massinger, Philip: A New Way to Pay Old Debts, 39
Master of the Revels, 122, 130, 173
Meggs, Roger, 98, 189
Meggs, Thomas, 210 n.4
Meggs, William, 23–24, 210 n.4, 213 n.35
Mercantile Carpet Company, 92
Mericke, Walter, 27
Metropolitan Board of Works, 90–91
Middleton, Thomas. See Rowley, William
Miles, Robert, 107
Miller, Elizabeth, 22
Milles, Thomas, 80, 102–3, 190
Mitchell, Elizabeth, 98, 100, 189
More, Margaret. See Roper, Margaret
More, Sir Thomas, 199 n.18
Morris, Sir Christopher, 14, 199 n.16
Moses, Levi, 88
Moxlay, Nicholas, 31, 45–46, 78, 166, 203 n.8
Music rooms (in playhouses), 124, 128, 129
Myllian, John, 22

Neale, Anne. See Rodes, Anne
Neale, Edward, 209 n.18
Needler, John, 81, 84, 102, 186, 187, 188
Needler, Samuel (son of Samuel), 81
Needler, Samuel (son of Thomas), 81
Needler, Thomas: his deeds, 83, 186–89, 210 n.3; Needler's Alley, 82, 87, 90, 100–105, 133, 134, 180, 182, 183, 185; purchase of part of Boar's Head, 78–81, 82, 84–85, 90, 97–98, 99, 100–102, 215 n.19
Newcastle, William Cavendish, first marquess of, 75, 195
Newcourt, Richard (map of), 133
Newington Butts, The (playhouse), 30, 37
No-body and Some-body, 125–26
North, Sir Roger, 76, 77
North, Ursula. See Poley, Lady Ursula

Oakley, John, 85, 90
Ogilby, John and Morgan, William (map of), 81, 82, 89, 94, 158; accuracy of, 179–85; shows Boar's Head, 82–83, 87, 90, 92, 103–5, 107, 109, 111–12, 113, 133–34, 139, 142,

211 n.14, 213 n.35
Ordnance Survey, 134, 180–85
Oswin, Amos, 86, 88
Oswin, Elizabeth, 86, 88
Oswin, John, 86, 88
Oswin, Joseph, 86, 88
Oswin, Katherine. *See* Weston, Katherine
Oxford, Edward de Vere, seventeenth earl of, 51, 57
Oxford's Men, Earl of (Edward de Vere, seventeenth earl), 51, 126. *See also* Worcester's Men

Palace Court. *See* Marshalsea Court
Palford, John. *See* Walford, John
Pallant, Robert, 51, 75, 210 n.9
Parker, Francis, 81
Parker, Nicholas, 81
Parker, Nicholas (lawyer), 211 n.13
Parker, William, 13, 14, 199 n.16
Paul's Boys, 75
Pembroke's Men, Earl of (Henry Herbert, second earl), 206 n.13
Perkins, Richard, 51, 218 n.10
Philipps, Sir Clifford William, 85
Pilgrimage of Grace, 13
Pillars, stage, 108, 141
Pleasant conceited Comedie Wherein is shewed how a man may chuse a good Wife from a bad, A, 124–25
Plevy, Humphrey, 99, 189
Pleyvie, Francis, 98, 189
Poley, Lady Abigail, 201 n.14
Poley, Anne, 15
Poley, Dorothy (daughter of Sir John Poley of the Boar's Head), 210 n.1
Poley, Edmund (died 1549), 200 n.19
Poley, Edmund (of the Boar's Head), 15, 17, 21, 22–23, 199 n.18, 202 n.6
Poley, Edmund (son of Sir John Poley of the Boar's Head), 77
Poley, Edmund (steward of Stepney), 21, 25, 199 n.18
Poley, Edward, 22
Poley, Elizabeth, 210 n.1
Poley, Elizabeth. *See* Miller, Elizabeth
Poley, Henry (of Badley), 201 n.8
Poley, Henry (of Spain), 201 n.8
Poley, Henry (of the Boar's Head), 17, 22, 23, 24, 28
Poley, Isabel (née Poley), 22
Poley, Isabel (wife of Edward Poley), 201 n.4

Poley, Jane, 17, 21, 23–24, 25–26, 28, 36, 45, 89, 96, 103, 106, 142, 165, 200 n.19, 201 n.1; leases out the Boar's Head, 24, 28, 49, 52, 75, 95, 163. *See also* Transfeild, Jane
Poley, John (of Badley), 15, 21, 22
Poley, Sir John (dead by 1607), 201 n.14
Poley, Sir John (married Abigail Luther), 201 n.14
Poley, Sir John (of the Boar's Head), 17–18, 22, 76, 77, 89, 97, 201 n.1; his deed to Thomas Needler, 186; his deed to William Browne, 190, 214 n.1; and the Earl of Essex, 23, 76; and the Poley-Woodliffe lease, 49, 76–81, 87, 88, 101, 105
Poley, John (son of Sir John Poley of the Boar's Head), 77
Poley, Raphe, 22
Poley, Reuben, 201 n.4
Poley, Richard, 15, 21
Poley, Richard (married 1601), 201 n.4
Poley, Lady Ursula, 76–77
Poley, William, 201 n.4
Polley, Isaac, 87
Polley, John, 199 n.19
Popham, Sir John, 46
Porter, John, 199 n.16
Pound, Philip, 28
Pound, Susan, 28
Price, John, 98, 189
Price, Richard, 88
Prince Charles's Men, 74–75, 124, 125, 156
Prince Henry's Men, 72, 73, 75, 191
Privy Council, 14, 39, 43, 156; and acting in inns, 77; and licensing of theatrical enterprises, 37, 57, 129–30, 205 n.14; and players, 16, 18–19, 20, 29–30, 33, 73, 74, 194–95
Props (used on stages), 108, 118, 126–27

Queen Anne's Men, 72–73, 74, 75, 124, 125, 194, 207 n.6. *See also* Worcester's Men
Queen's Revels, 191, 193
Quince, Peter, 123–24

R., W. (epigrammatist), 74
Rawson, Christopher, 19
Red Bull, The, 29, 73, 74, 75, 76, 128, 203 n.9, 208 n.4, 216 nn. 2 and 8
Red Lion, The, 30, 202 n.1
Requests, Court of, 65–67, 68, 172
Reynolds, Alice. *See* Swygar, Alice
Reynolds, James. *See* Swygar, James
Reynolds, John, 12, 13, 14

Richards, Frederick, 87
Ridley, Nicholas (bishop of London), 15
Roberts, Owen, 42–43, 44, 113, 115, 121, 169
Robinson, John, 12–14, 199 n.15
Rodes, Anne, 209 n.18
Rodes, John, 209 n.18
Rodes, Walter, 33, 44, 159–61, 165–70, 175, 203 n.17
Roper, Margaret, 199 n.18
Roper, William, 199 n.18
Rose, Mr. (actor), 191, 193
Rose, The, 30, 60, 72, 112, 123, 126, 130, 192, 195, 204 n.1, 216 n.5, 218 n.8
Rosse, Rowland, 44
Rowley, Samuel, 78, 79, 98, 100, 101, 102, 103, 187, 188, 190, 210 n.4
Rowley, William, 210 n.8; and Middleton, Thomas: A Faire Quarrell, 125. See also Day, John
Rushes (on stages), 116, 118, 122–23, 173
Rutland, Roger Manners, fifth earl of, 204 n.2

Sacke full of Newes, A, 16–17, 18
St. Paul's Playhouse, 203 n.15
Salisbury Court (playhouse), 75
Samborne, Barnaby, 26
Samwell, Rebecca, 43
Samwell, Richard, Jr., 36, 47, 51, 69, 123, 172, 202 n.6; attacked in the playhouse, 42–44; describes Samwell's part of the Boar's Head, 96, 213 n.4; and galleries in the Boar's Head, 33, 35, 109, 115–16, 161–62, 167–69, 214 n.6 to chapter 12; and leases, 40, 50, 175–76, 177–78, 203 n.8, 204 n.21
Samwell, Richard, Sr., 25, 37–38, 75, 76, 92, 163–64, 165–70; builds the Boar's Head in 1598, 32, 107, 108, 109, 159–62; conveys lease to Browne, 35–36, 177–78; describes Boar's Head, 95–96, 213 n.4; and financial arrangements at the Boar's Head, 120–23, 128–29, 171–74; leases most of the Boar's Head from Woodliffe, 31; and legal arguments over Samwell-Browne lease, 40–46, 48, 50, 51, 52, 66, 68–69; rebuilds Boar's Head in 1599, 33–35, 109–15, 117–18, 120, 159–62, 175–76. See also Galleries, Samwell's
Samwell, Susan, 69
Samwell, Winifred, 36, 43, 44
Sandford, John, 12–14, 199 n.16
Sandford, wife of John, 12
Sarraude, John, 85

Sarraude, Sara, 85
Saunders, Alice, 23
Saunders, Roger, 23
Scaliger, Joseph Justus, 50
Schrickx, Willem, 193–95
Screven, Thomas, 204 n.2
Seats (in playhouses), 33, 45, 114, 122
Shakespeare, William, 195; Twelfth Night, 47
Sheepskin and Leather Discount Centre, 92, 134
Sibdall, Henry, 209 n.10
Sibley, Frances, 86–87
Sibley, Henry, 86–87
Sibley, Joseph, 86–87
Sisson, C. J., 156–58, 175, 191–93, 196, 203 n.14, 206 nn. 10, 13 and 15, 210 n.8, 211 n.5, 215 n.2, 216 nn. 5 and 11, 218 n.8
Skeffington, Leonard, 13
Skeffington, Thomas, 15
Skeffington, Sir William, 13, 14, 15, 199 n.16
Slatier, Edward, 201 n.16
Smith, Warren, 217 n.12
Smythe, Richard, 27
Southworth, Bernard, 28
Sparks, Giles, 26–27
Spencer, T. J. B., 157
Squire, John, 15, 22
Stage, Boar's Head, 37, 77, 79, 113, 114, 116, 117, 118, 119, 121, 122–23, 124–25, 126, 127, 129, 140–43; building of, 24, 30–33, 35, 49, 70; dismantled, 78; invaded by Langley, 51–52; legal arguments about, 53, 55, 56, 58, 60–61, 62, 64, 65–69, 173–74, 178; position of, 164–67, 169–70; site of, 81, 87, 88, 89, 95, 98, 100–105, 189–90, 212 n.15 to chapter 10, 213 n.31; size, 108–12, 124
Stage doors, 109, 124, 125, 127, 141–43
Stage keepers, 173
Stamford, Robert, 186
Stansfelde, Alice (widow), 198 n.8
Stansfelde, Alice (wife of James Swygar). See Swygar, Alice
Star Chamber, Court of, 40, 44–45, 177, 205 n.4
State. See Chair of state
Staverton (lawyer), 52, 58
Stow, John, 19, 21, 113
Strayles, Anthony, 42–43, 115
Street, Peter, 34
Stukeley, Hugh, 199 n.18
Sun Life of Canada, Ltd., 213 n.34

Surrey, Henry Howard, earl of (Henry Howard, the poet), 18

Swan, The, 24, 39, 76, 122, 123, 207 n.17; drawing of, 111, 116, 127, 141; licensing of, 30, 37, 130; galleries in, 116, 119, 122, 128–29; and Pembroke's Men, 206 n.13

Swegar (alias Reynolds), James. *See* Swygar, James

Swegar (alias Reynolds), Alice. *See* Swygar, Alice

Swygar (alias Reynolds), Alice, 198 n.8

Swygar (alias Reynolds), James, 14

Theatre, The, 19, 24–25, 29, 30, 32, 35, 37, 38, 50, 107, 114–15, 121, 128

Thirtle, George, 87, 89

Thirtle, Jane. *See* White, Jane

Thirtle, William, 87, 89

Tiring house, at the Boar's Head, 65–69, 79, 81, 107–12, 116, 123, 127, 129, 141–43; the building of, 25, 30, 31–32, 49, 51, 70, 116, 121, 122; financial arrangements about, 173–74; legal arguments about, 37, 52–53, 55, 56, 58, 60–61, 62, 63, 64, 178; pulled down, 78; site of 87, 88, 89, 95, 96, 98, 100–105, 189–90, 212 n.15 to chapter 10, 213 n.31

Towse (lawyer), 63

Transfeild, Anne. *See* Gibbes, Anne

Transfeild, Frances. *See* Wybard, Frances

Transfeild, Jane, 15–16, 17, 23. *See also* Poley, Jane

Transfeild, John, 11–17, 18, 21, 23, 24, 25, 90

Transfeld, Thomas, 198 n.5

Trapdoors (on stages), 124, 125, 127

Tryall of Cheualry. *See History of the tryall of Cheualry, The*

Tusinga, Guiseppi, 203 n.15

Tutchbury, Anne, 88

Tyson, George, 22–23

United Standard House, 92, 134

Vaughan, James, 70

Vaughan, Susan. *See* Woodliffe, Susan

Walford, John, 99, 189

Walmesley, Thomas, 63

Walsingham, Sir Francis, 19, 39

Wasson, John, 207 n.1

Weakest goeth to the Wall, The, 126–27

Webbe, Simon, 199 n.16

Webster, John: *The White Devil*, 118. *See also* Dekker, Thomas

"Wedges" (in playhouse yards), 107, 111, 113

Wells, Stanley, 158

Wentworth, Anne. *See* Poley, Anne

Wentworth, Henry, third baron, 21

Wentworth, Thomas, first baron, 15, 21

Wentworth, Thomas, fourth baron, 25, 77, 78, 186, 189

Wentworth, Thomas, second baron, 21

Weston, Frances Brudenel. *See* Sibley, Frances

Weston, John, 86–87

Weston, Katherine, 86–87

Weston, Richard, 86–87

Weston, Thomas, 86–87

White, Edwin John, 87

White, Jane, 87, 89, 90

Whitefriars (playhouse), 75

Wickham, Glynne, 108, 116–17, 130, 218 n.2

Wikes, Abigail. *See* Poley, Lady Abigail

Wilkins, George. *See* Day, John

Willys, Edward, 159–61, 165, 167, 170, 203 n.17, 204 n.19, 214 n.4

Wilson, Dover, 217 n.12

Wolf, John, 130

Wolleston, Thomas, 42, 43, 48, 70, 177

Wood, Anne, 79

Wood, John, 79, 187, 188

Wood, Thomas, 26

Woodliffe, John, 27–28

Woodliffe, Oliver, Jr., 28

Woodliffe, Oliver, Sr.: at the Boar's Head, 29–36, 37–71, 75, 76, 78, 92, 95, 106–14, 116–17, 122–23, 128–29, 159–62, 163–70, 171–74, 175–76, 177–78, 195, 211 n.13; in Gloucestershire, 26–28. *See also* Gallery, Woodliffe's, at the Boar's Head

Woodliffe, Susan, 27–28, 36, 42–43, 44, 69–70, 76, 122, 166, 175–76, 206 n.10, 207 n.16

Worcester, Edward Somerset, fourth earl of, 57

Worcester's Men, Earl of (Edward Somerset, fourth earl), 36; at the Boar's Head, 51–52, 53, 55, 56–57, 58, 59–60, 61, 64, 65, 67, 69, 70, 71, 72–73, 116, 120, 124, 126, 129–30, 156, 191–97, 203 n.14, 216 n.5; at the Curtain, 72–73, 124; at the Rose, 60, 72. *See also* Queen Anne's Men

Worsley. *See* Poley, Lady Abigail

Wybard, Edmund, 22

Wybard, Fabian, 22

Wybard, Frances, 16, 17, 22, 23, 201 n.1

Wybard, Henry, 22
Wybard, Jane, 22
Wyberde, John, 201n.1

Yard, Boar's Head, 24, 31–32, 35, 51, 52, 61,
65, 66, 68, 77–78, 79, 80, 89, 94–105, 106–9,
110–12, 114–15, 116–19, 120–23, 126, 140–42,
159–62, 163–64, 165–70, 174, 175–76, 186,
189–90
Yeandle, Laetitia, 214n.10
Younge, John, 98, 189